COMBAT OVER THE TRENCHES

COMBAT OVER THE TRENCHES

Oswald Watt, Aviation Pioneer

CHRIS CLARKE

Pen & Sword
AVIATION

First published in Australia as *The High Life of Oswald Watt: Australia's First Military Pilot*, in 2016 by Big Sky Publishing Pty, Ltd
PO Box 303, Newport, NSW 2106, Australia

Reprinted in hardback format in 2017 in Great Britain by
Pen & Sword AVIATION
An imprint of
Pen & Sword Books Ltd
47 Church Street, Barnsley
South Yorkshire
S70 2AS

ISBN 978 1 52671 501 2

Printed and bound in England
by TJ International Ltd, Padstow, PL28 8RW

Pen & Sword Books Ltd incorporates the Imprints of Pen & Sword Aviation,
Pen & Sword Family History, Pen & Sword Maritime, Pen & Sword Military,
Pen & Sword Discovery, Pen & Sword Politics, Pen & Sword Atlas,
Pen & Sword Archaeology, Wharncliffe Local History, Leo Cooper,
Wharncliffe True Crime, Wharncliffe Transport, Pen & Sword Select,
Pen & Sword Military Classics, The Praetorian Press, Claymore Press,
Remember When, Seaforth Publishing and Frontline Publishing

For a complete list of Pen & Sword titles please contact
PEN & SWORD BOOKS LIMITED
47 Church Street, Barnsley, South Yorkshire, S70 2AS, England
E-mail: enquiries@pen-and-sword.co.uk
Website: www.pen-and-sword.co.uk

CONTENTS

PREFACE

According to Cambridge Dictionaries Online, the term 'wow factor' is taken to mean 'a quality or feature of something that makes people feel great excitement or admiration'. With personal initials which, by happy coincidence, contract to the acronym 'WOW', Walter Oswald Watt—usually known by his preferred name of 'Oswald', or often by his childhood nickname of 'Toby'—exhibited plenty of wow factor during his lifetime. When he died tragically in 1921, at the age of 43, there was a display of shocked disbelief and grief that was astounding for someone not holding any sort of public office in Australia at the time. That his hastily-organised and poorly-notified funeral still attracted 1,500 mourners was clear evidence that he was a well-established figure in the public eye.

Soon after Oswald Watt's death, there also appeared in print a memorial book of tributes from people who wished to place on record their personal recollections of him. Published alongside an extraordinary collection of photographs that documented Watt's life and particularly his remarkable service during the First World War, these tributes were intended as a permanent form of respect, appreciation and admiration for the man. Though four of the 'chapters' in the volume were by Oswald's brother Ernest (including one he titled simply 'W.O.W.'), the remainder of the total of 22 contributions that appeared in the book—including one which was only an eight-line poem—came from a diverse group of people that included two women: lawyers, clergy, journalists, artists and writers, military associates and some who were simply writing as friends. Even more diverse were the group who expressed their feelings about Oswald Watt in letters, extracts from which appeared over five pages in the book.

For more than 90 years since Oswald Watt's passing, the tribute book produced in his memory has formed his principal monument. Though short biographical accounts have appeared about him during that period, few have pushed the boundaries of knowledge far beyond that first publication and unfortunately they have often served to compound its shortcomings. For there were some mistakes in what people thought they knew about Watt's life in 1921; some areas where understanding was confused or incomplete, and into these gaps and failings a process has emerged which sometimes has been as much about myth-making than furthering true historical understanding. Correcting that process has been the starting-point for the account of Oswald Watt's life which follows.

Among the most commonly-encountered misconceptions of Oswald Watt is the description of him as being a 'British officer', or sometimes a 'British businessman'. Despite the undeniable fact he was indeed born in Britain, it is also true that Watt always proudly—even defiantly—regarded himself as Australian. To explain the real nature of Watt's Australian-ness, this account begins with an outline of the Watt family's origins and connections with this country, one which also helps to explain his later attachment and loyalty to the ideal behind the British Empire. Most Australians alive today probably struggle with the concept enunciated before the First World War by then Labor member of parliament (and later prime minister) William Morris Hughes, arguing that: 'A man may be a very loyal and devoted adherent to, and worshipper of, the Empire, and still he may be a very loyal and patriotic Australian all the time.' Oswald Watt was very much a product of his time, and Hughes's description fits him perfectly.

Changes that have taken place within Australia, its social structure and its lifestyle, also challenge modern understanding of other elements of Watt's story. When a largely autobiographical account of Oswald's brother, Ernest, was published in the late 1990s, this carried a foreword and introductions commenting on the personal qualities of the book's subject. There Ernest Watt was described as independently wealthy, charming, romantic, educated, a benefactor and 'a man of vision who played an imaginative part in the development of his young country… [using] his inheritance generously…[making] his mark in a way that, very probably, would not have been possible today.' It would be equally fair to say that this description also fits Ernest's younger brother.

Understanding the position in high society that Oswald Watt occupied becomes central to evaluating his place in Australian history.

Piecing together the story of Oswald Watt's life and times has involved revisiting material that has long been on the public record, in newspapers and the like, though not readily accessible before the advent of electronic finding aids in recent years. The Trove resource hosted by the National Library of Australia proved invaluable in fully discovering the hectic social world in which Watt and his wife moved in the decade after their marriage. The National Archives of Australia also holds records, particularly regarding military aviation, before and during the First World War, which were crucial to establishing a clearer picture of Watt's contribution during that period. The Australian War Memorial was also able to contribute enormously to highlighting the war years, both through its outstanding pictorial collection and a unique collection of Watt's postcards and letters sent back from the war which were donated to the Memorial by the widow of Oswald's son in the 1970s.

Knowledge of the Watt family history following Oswald's death benefited greatly from input by his grandson, Mr Robert Oswald Watt. The author was both fortunate and grateful to have had the opportunity to interview Bob at his Darwin home and to have enjoyed the company and hospitality of both Bob and his wife Alison. His contributions to a draft section of the manuscript were highly enlightening. In the same way, the author was fortunate to have made contact with Mr Ian Sumner, a prolific researcher and writer from Yorkshire, England, who has specialised in the French army and air force during the First World War. Thanks to Ian's outstanding knowledge of French official records, it was possible to connect with a range of sources about Oswald Watt's war service that do not appear to have been accessed before.

The valued assistance of other institutions and people must also be acknowledged, among them: the RAAF Museum, Point Cook, Victoria (Ms Monica Joyce); the State Library of New South Wales (for access to the photograph albums of Arthur Wigram Allen); the Library of the Australian Defence Force Academy (where the author is still a Visiting Fellow); the Air Power Development Centre (Mr Steve Allen); The Friends of Wivenhoe, Mater Dei, Camden (Sister Mary Smith); the Australian Army History Unit (Dr Roger Lee, Dr Andrew Richardson); Mr Chris Shepherd (graphic designer, Defence Publishing Service) who produced drawings of the aircraft flown by Oswald Watt in the First World War; and my partner Shawn Hazel, who did not mind a bit when my curiosity to see sites connected with Oswald Watt's life took us to some of Sydney's least visited places.

Chapter One
PRIVILEGED BACKGROUND

Mr Watt goes home

In the first months of 1876 the Honourable John Brown Watt, prominent Sydney businessman and parliamentarian, was preparing to undertake a visit to the land of his birth on the other side of the world. Although the colony of New South Wales had been the focus of his life for 33 years, he still thought of the faraway British Isles, and especially his Scottish birthplace of Edinburgh, as 'home'.

Much had changed since Watt arrived in Sydney in December 1842.[1] Then he had been a callow, sickly youth of 16, forced to give up studies when it was discovered he had contracted a severe pulmonary illness likely to develop into tuberculosis.[2] His uncle, John Gilchrist, brother of his mother Margaret (who died when her son was six), was visiting Scotland at the time and offered him a position in the Sydney mercantile and shipping firm of which Gilchrist was a principal. Young Watt embarked at Greenock in the 523-ton barque *Benares* on a four-month voyage to Australia with his uncle and new Aunt Helen, whom John Gilchrist had married in Edinburgh only seven weeks earlier.[3]

In Sydney, Watt became a junior clerk in Gilchrist & Alexander, the business which his uncle had established in Lower George Street in partnership with John Alexander in 1838. It was the start of a life of soulless drudgery on a salary which was still only £40 a year on his 21st birthday.[4] Rather than bemoan his lot, he told his father in a letter home in 1847 that he intended to make himself not merely useful to his uncle, but 'absolutely necessary'.[5] He totally immersed himself in the company's activities, and by dedication, diligence and perseverance in July 1852 he was made a partner in the business, which became known as Gilchrist, Alexander & Co.[6]

When John Alexander retired the next year, a new partnership was formed on 1 January 1854 trading as Gilchrist, Watt & Co. in which John Watt provided two-sevenths of the firm's capital. Before the new company's first month was out, John Gilchrist was selling his 'elegant household furniture' at auction, in preparation for leaving the colony to live in London.[7] By the time Watt became the firm's senior partner upon Gilchrist's death in England in November 1866, he was effectively running a business that was loading more ships on agency to London than any other Sydney firm.

Active in the Pacific islands trade, the firm also had pastoral interests and squatting agencies in Queensland as well as New South Wales.[8] It advanced finance to pastoralists and was a wool consignment agency. Watt himself had directly invested in land, and by 1859 was holding 'runs' or properties on his own; in 1866 he had six in New South Wales alone. Respect for Watt's business acumen, probity and judgment brought invitations to join the board of directors of many of the colony's public companies—mainly banking, insurance and shipping enterprises, but gas, sugar, meat and coal companies as well. In 1865 he helped to revive the Sydney Chamber of Commerce.[9]

Watt's prominence also brought him into regular contact with the leading political figures of the day, so it was not surprising that in September 1861 he was appointed to membership of the Legislative Council, the nominated upper house of the New South Wales parliament—an appointment 'for life' under the Constitution Act.[10] His steady rise into the top echelons of Sydney society, with financial means and influence to match, meant that he would be going home under very different circumstances to those under which he first arrived in the colony.

The trip on which Watt was preparing to embark was not his first visit back home. He had made the long journey across the globe twice before—the first time late in 1850, when he was aged 24.[11] His purpose on that occasion had been primarily to visit the family he left behind in Scotland: his father and step-mother, and five half-brothers and a half-sister—only half of whom had been born when he emigrated.

Although Watt then intended to be away from Sydney about a year, his plans were changed when, in the middle of 1851, news reached Britain of rich discoveries of gold in Australia. Instead of hurrying back straight away, he obtained a diploma as an expert assayer of precious metals before boarding a ship at Portsmouth in February 1852.[12] On reaching Sydney in May,[13] he induced his uncle to enter the business of buying up gold from successful miners who were keen to convert their findings into cash, unmindful of its true value on the overseas market. The fact that, less than two months later, Watt was admitted as a partner into Gilchrist, Alexander & Co. was a clear indicator that his shrewd initiative had been both welcomed and opportune.

The impetus for Watt's next trip abroad in 1866, when he was aged 40, sprang from very different causes.[14] By the end of 1865 the strain of running the Sydney operations of Gilchrist, Watt & Co. had left him suffering serious ill-effects from overwork. In need of a long holiday, he began quitting his directorships,[15] and even resigned his seat in the Legislative Council.[16]

Emphasising that this trip was restorative in purpose, and likely to be protracted, Watt took his wife and family with him. Four years had passed since he had taken the step of marrying, on 30 July 1862, at St Paul's Church, Canterbury.[17] His bride, Mary Jane Holden, was the 19-year-old Sydney-born daughter of George Kenyon Holden, then a partner in one of the city's most lucrative law firms and a voice for colonial liberalism in the parliament where he also sat in the Legislative Council.[18]

By the time the Watts embarked on their holiday, the couple already had two children—a daughter Margaret Gilchrist, born in June 1863,[19] and a son William Holden, born in May 1865[20]—and Mary Jane was expecting their third child. This turned out to be a daughter they named Eliza Florence, born on 14 August after they had arrived in Edinburgh.

Because the focus of this trip had been on helping John Watt regain his health, the family's movements for the next two years were mainly focused on resorts and holiday locations. It was this that explained the birth of another child, a little girl they named Alice Mary, on 27

March 1868 at Nice, the French resort town on the Mediterranean coast;[21] sadly, the infant died barely four months later, on 31 July, after the family had returned to Edinburgh.

It was probably at this time that the Watt family began its association with Bournemouth, the spa and resort town on the south coast of England which had been steadily establishing its name as a place for recuperation. By early October 1868 both John and Mary Watt felt sufficiently recovered that they sailed from Plymouth with their three surviving children and one servant, bound for Sydney which they reached on 19 December.[22]

The Hon. John Brown Watt, MLC. (Portrait from *Australian Men of Mark*, 1889)

Following their return, John Watt's public and business standing had continued to strengthen.

In 1870-71 he served as the Sydney Chamber of Commerce's president, and in 1872 he also became vice-president of the Marine Board of New South Wales. In November 1874 he was again appointed to the Legislative Council, which entitled him to put the title "Honourable" in front of his name.[23] The fact that Watt would not be resigning his public and political positions in anticipation of his third visit home (since he would be performing official duty of direct benefit to New South Wales) only emphasized the very different nature of this trip compared to the last.

Because he planned on being away for at least two years, he would again be taking his family with him. Three more children had been born in the years since their last return from overseas: a daughter Elinor Mary, born in January 1870,[24] followed by sons born at two-year intervals. The first of these boys, named John Gilchrist, arrived on 6 April 1872 but barely a year later, on 22 May 1873, he died from complications of teething.[25] The following year Mary Jane fell pregnant again, giving birth to Ernest Alexander Stuart on 8 December 1874.[26] After these events Mrs Watt was now the one in fragile health, both mental and physical, and her husband can have been in no doubt that his wife was in serious need of a holiday.[27]

In the week before the Hon. J. B. Watt left for Europe, he was treated to a 'complimentary dinner' to farewell him on his way, held on the evening of Monday, 1 May 1876, in the large dining hall of the Sydney Exchange on the corner of Pitt and Bridge Streets. It was a gala event, attended by about 150 of his friends and colleagues, 'representing all the principal interests of the colony'—government ministers and members of parliament, business figures, and members of the judiciary and clergy. The whole affair provided clear proof of the high public esteem in which Watt was held.[28]

While a German band played a variety of airs, the dinner got under way, and speeches and toasts then began. Following a toast proposed by Mr T. S. Mort to the "Parliament of New South Wales", the president of the Legislative Council, the Hon. John Hay, responded by deploring the fact that this was the third time in three weeks that he had farewelled a member of his chamber departing overseas. In the case of Mr Watt, he was parting with one of the most valued members of the Council and he hoped that their guest soon returned to resume his parliamentary duties.

Mrs Mary Jane Watt, from a portrait by Edinburgh painter and photographer John Horsburgh.

When the dinner's chairman, the Hon. John Campbell, MLC, rose to propose the toast of the evening, he began by commenting that the guest of honour had shown what a man could do with honesty and business-like integrity. He trusted that when Mr Watt went home he would maintain his interest in New South Wales, and would gain experience that would be for the advantage of the colony when he returned to it.

Watt, in response, said that as a boy he had entertained no thought of embarking on a business life, and if left to himself he would probably have chosen another occupation. His primary goal in taking the path he did was simply to gain a livelihood and provide for his future, but thanks to the helping hand of his employer, who was also his relative, he had been able to attain his present success.

Thanking the assembled company for the honour conferred on him, Watt declared that he had no intention of leaving the colony forever. He hoped to return before very long, for although it was the land of his adoption, he had spent far more years in it than he had spent in the land of his birth. New South Wales was where his children had been born, and where he hoped to spend his declining years. He also hoped to return less weighed down by business concerns, so that he could then devote more time to public affairs than before and provide some return to the country which had done so much for him.

The following Saturday, 6 May—ten days before John Watt celebrated his fiftieth birthday—he boarded the 3,000-ton royal mail steamer *Australia* with his wife and their five children, along with two servants, and departed Sydney. The ship was bound for Kandavu Island in the Fiji archipelago, then the main port of call on the trans-Pacific route, on its way to San Francisco.[29]

Two years abroad

The reason that John Watt took his family to Europe via North America was because the first official duty that he was to perform while away was to serve as an accredited commissioner for the New South Wales display at the world fair held at Philadelphia, Pennsylvania, on the northeast coast of the United States.[30] Formally called the

'International Exhibition of Arts, Manufactures and Products of the Soil and Mine', the event was intended to showcase a century of progress in the United States since the signing of the Declaration of Independence, but 11 nations apart from the US had their own exhibition buildings at the fair, including Britain.

While the date of the Watt family's departure from Sydney would have meant they were too late for the exhibition's opening ceremonies on 10 May, the fair ran for six months and drew an attendance of ten million visitors—a figure equal to 20 per cent of the entire population of the US. The Watts apparently reached Philadelphia just in time to experience a deadly summer heat wave that settled on the city in mid-June and lasted well into July. Once J. B. Watt's duty was done, the family was probably glad to board ship once more and leave for England.

Opening day at the U.S. Centennial Exhibition in Philadelphia, 10 May 1876. The Watt family arrived a couple of weeks later, in time for J. B. Watt to serve as commissioner on the New South Wales exhibit. (Library of Congress)

Before John Watt left America, he took the opportunity to contact the president of the New York Chamber of Commerce, in his equivalent capacity as chairman of the Sydney chamber, and to have a personal meeting with that gentleman. The interview was followed up with a formal request to the New York chamber, asking that it use its influence to encourage the American government to reduce the high trade duty imposed on wool imported from Australia and New Zealand. The letter was dated 'London, 26th October, 1876'— thereby confirming that the Watt family was gone from America by that time.[31]

Watt's presence in England by the start of 1877 proved hugely beneficial to the business interests of Gilchrist, Watt & Co., because it placed him in the box seat to take advantage of a remarkable opportunity that presented itself at this time. The shipping company trading as The Orient Line of Packets—better known as the Orient Line—had been operating a service to Australia for a decade, but now decided that the time was ripe to expand its business on this run. In February the Line approached the Pacific Steam Navigation Company about chartering four of the 11 passenger ships the PSNC had laid-up at Liverpool, as a result of over-expanding on its service to the Pacific coast of South America in previous years.

In the second half of the year, three of the ships, all iron screw steamers of more than 3,800 tons—*Lusitania*, *Chimborazo* and *Cuzco*—were seen in Australian ports after voyages around the Cape of Good Hope accomplished in record time of only 36 or 37 days. These then returned home via the Suez Canal, recently widened and deepened through dredging to handle ships of larger size. The success of these experimental runs proved that steamships could handle the direct England-to-Australia route without mechanical problems or resorting to sail. Early in 1878 the Orient Line was prompted to purchase the four ships outright and form a new line called the Orient Steam Navigation Company.[32]

The big win for Gilchrist, Watt & Co. became apparent as early as May 1877, when notices first appeared in the local press announcing that the three ships used in the Orient Line trial would be returning to London from Sydney in September, October and December, and inviting intending travellers to apply for 'plans and full particulars' to Gilchrist, Watt & Co.[33] Once the OSNC was formed next year, Watt's firm was duly appointed the new line's general agents in Australia. While Watt's personal involvement was nowhere directly evident or acknowledged, it clearly had not hurt that he was present in England at the crucial time, and able to ensure his firm's interests were not overlooked.

Not all Watt's time in England was taken up with forging or renewing personal contacts and finding new business opportunities. Midway through 1877 his wife had fallen pregnant again, and in anticipation of the birth the family went to stay at Bournemouth. The attraction of this place as a holiday destination had grown following the arrival of the railway in 1870, and in summer its permanent population of about 15,000 was swelled by large numbers of visitors from London and the English midlands. Even in winter, however, Bournemouth's southern seaside location was felt to have restorative effects on health and well-being. This probably accounts for why the family was there on 11 February 1878, when Mary Jane gave birth to her eighth child—a son they named Walter Oswald,[34] although from the first the boy was known as Oswald rather than Walter.

The choice of name was probably a nod in the direction of William Oswald Gilchrist, who was the son of the founder of Gilchrist, Watt & Co. and John Watt's partner in the firm since 1864. In any event, John Watt continued a family practice begun with the other children, and gave his new son the nickname 'Toby'. The relevance of this is now lost in time, but it at least went well with that of the baby's three-year-old brother, Ernest, which was 'Tim'.[35]

Within months of the baby's arrival, John Watt prepared to undertake what was the final official duty planned on his overseas visit. In a letter to Tim addressed from 'Meriden, Bournemouth' (possibly where they were renting a holiday villa near the beach at Canford Cliffs), he wrote on 10 May that 'Willie goes to school today, and mother and I cross over to France.'[36] In these few words were recorded the admission of the Watt's eldest son—on his thirteenth birthday—

to Harrow, the independent boarding school for boys in northwest London, and also John Watt's departure for Paris, with his wife, for the latest world fair which had been officially opened there on 1 May.

Panoramic view of the 1878 Exposition Universelle at Paris, with the Trocadero Palace at right. Oswald Watt was three months old when his parents went across from England for J. B. Watt to again act as accredited commissioner on the New South Wales display.

The Exposition Universelle of 1878 was intended to celebrate France's recovery from disastrous defeat in the 1870 Franco-Prussian War, and to that end it was attended by all major countries with the understandable exception of Germany. Nearly a third of the space set aside for exhibiting nations apart from France was taken up by Britain and its dominions and colonies, including the four largest Australian colonies by population. The Hon. J. B. Watt was again an accredited commissioner for the exhibits sent from New South Wales.[37]

Back at London in late October, John Watt and his wife, and five of their children—Willie having been left behind at school—boarded the 3,800-ton Orient steamship *Aconcagua*, accompanied by one servant. On 28 October the ship left Plymouth and, after battling strong gales and heavy seas for most of the way to the Cape of Good Hope, arrived at Sydney on 17 December.[38]

Growing up in Sydney

For members of the Watt family with memories of Sydney before they left for overseas, the homecoming after more than two-and-a-half years away was probably a happy one. Within a few months, however, the pleasure of return turned to sorrow with the death of Mrs Watt at Burwood in

April 1879, aged just 36. Her health had collapsed during the last stages of the family's time in England, and tuberculosis supervened.[39] Her remains were buried in the churchyard of St Jude's at Randwick.

The loss of his wife was a heavy blow to John Watt. Not only had he been obliged to immerse himself in business affairs and public duties immediately on return, he must now pay greater attention to providing a suitable home for his children. Caring for three daughters, aged 15, 12 and nine, and two sons aged just four and one, was a complicated business in the absence of a mother. He needed to employ a nurse and governesses, in addition to the usual household staff such as cook, coachman and gardener.

Before leaving Sydney three years earlier, the family had lived comfortably in Potts Point, at the Darlinghurst end of Macleay Street, but in the new post-return circumstances a larger house was required. To meet this need, Watt leased a property in Edgecliff called "Eynesbury" located high on the ridge overlooking Double Bay. Accessed from Albert Street, the house sat at the eastern end of the apex formed by the intersection of Edgecliff Road and Ocean Street.[40]

Panoramic view of Double Bay, Sydney, looking south-east from Darling Point towards Edgecliff Road, taken about 1870. "Eynesbury" sits at the top of the photo, slightly right of centre, behind a large retaining wall. Below Eynesbury is "Fairlight" (with tower), and to the left of Fairlight in the photograph is "Arlington"—both properties in which Oswald Watt and his wife lived before the First World War. (Caroline Simpson Library & Research Collection, Sydney Living Museums)

Originally built for Sydney solicitor John Pirie Roxburgh, Eynesbury was a well-ordered two-storey classical building with large semi-circular windows on the north-facing façade. A huge retaining wall, topped with a stone balustrade, stood in front where the land sloped down to Edgecliff Road. It was the Roxburgh family home from 1866 until 1873, when John Roxburgh died. Although his widow retained ownership, the family did not stay in the house but leased it to tenants from well-established Sydney families.

When John Watt moved his children into their new home in 1880, he found the perfect location for raising two very active boys. Son Ernest, "Tim" to his father, later wrote of the years spent at Eynesbury as 'idyllic days of absolute and complete happiness' for both him and his brother Oswald ("Toby"). The boys spent their time exploring the beautiful terraced gardens below the house, playing with the children of lawyer Frederick Darley, MLC, who lived opposite in the house called "Quambi",[41] or visiting friends in other fine houses nearby. Occasionally they were taken on excursions into the city or around the harbour, to places like Clontarf, Middle Harbour and Rose Bay, sometimes on outings to the show grounds, circus or theatre. Their summer holidays were generally spent at the Moss Vale home of their father's business partner William Oswald Gilchrist, apart from a couple of times when they travelled to Hobart in the company of Miss Elizabeth Shuffrey, the housekeeper at Eynesbury, to spend the summer in a holiday cottage by the beach.[42]

That theirs was a privileged upbringing likely to have been unknown to ordinary children at this time, in Sydney or elsewhere around Australia, can best be deduced from the fact that Oswald, even at an age of eight or nine, was able to take up an interest in photography—an activity then too expensive for most adults to pursue. In a later tribute book to his brother, Ernest pointedly included several 'snapshots' of Eynesbury that had been taken by Oswald, presumably during these childhood years.[43]

The boys themselves would have been in no doubt of their father's important standing in the community, since Eynesbury was the focus of a procession of visitors to Sunday lunch, usually up to a dozen guests—leading politicians like Henry Parkes, George Reid and Alexander Stuart, senior officers from the Royal Navy squadron based on Sydney, and often distinguished visitors from England.[44] Young Oswald's high spirits frequently made him difficult to control, especially when one of the house staff attempted to assert authority over him. Ernest Watt recounted one occasion when the housekeeper ordered Oswald out of the room during a crowded supper party. He did as he was told, but as he passed behind her seat at the table he defiantly landed a tap on the back of her lace cap. In Tim's summation, the outcome was 'disastrous!'[45]

Eynesbury's north-facing classical façade, with semi-circular windows, during the eight-year period the house was the Watt family home.

According to his older brother, Toby (Oswald) was 'always on the move, never still an instant, always doing something, generally something he was neither expected nor intended to do!' The male tutors which John Watt engaged to conduct daily home schooling lessons for his sons, and for eight or nine other boys from surrounding families with prominent surnames, found their hands more than full in controlling 'a very unruly set' in which Oswald, 'although almost the youngest, was nearly always the ringleader in wickedness.'[46]

The Watt boys, "Toby" and "Tim", pictured about 1882.

John Watt could hardly have been unaware of the challenge he faced with his growing boys, but it was simply not in John Watt's nature to think harshly of his sons, considering—as he undoubtedly did—that they missed the moderating influence of their mother as much as he missed her presence as his wife. In Ernest Watt's assessment, however, although his father's 'public life was a strenuous one, his home remained his foremost and paramount interest throughout, and no man ever worked more honestly to see that his children were afforded every chance of growing up good and useful men and women.'[47]

If John Watt hoped that his own personal example might show his children how to grow up 'good and useful' men and women, he probably hoped the same means would impart a sense of civic responsibility. For many years he had been a generous supporter of a range of community causes and charities around Sydney, such as the Hospital for Sick Children and the Prince Alfred Hospital—giving not just money, but frequently his time as a member of these institutions' boards of management.[48] He was also a benefactor of the University of Sydney, several times between 1876 and 1889 donating sums of £1000 (over $100,000 in current values) to endow scholarships which the University still offers in Watt's name to the present day.[49]

A community cause of a different—and somewhat surprising—kind was the Mercantile Rowing Club, formed in 1874 as Sydney's second amateur club. The MRC grew out of a meeting of warehousemen and merchants' clerks, and among the 250 men comprising its initial membership would very likely have been some employees of Gilchrist, Watt & Co. According to a press account written a few years after the MRC's start, the club 'immediately received liberal support both in money and members' from the mercantile community—which would probably have included Watt.[50]

From the beginning, the club needed an eminent figurehead equal to maintaining the dignity of special occasions, such as the annual balls which the club instituted soon after its formation. It was, however, not until June 1880—18 months after he returned from his third trip abroad—that Watt was recorded as being the club's president. This was clearly a prestigious position to hold, as the club then possessed over 30 boats and had also assumed a leading position, not just in Sydney but in intercolonial rowing, prompting the Mayor of Sydney to present it in 1880 with an elegant trophy called the Challenge Cup, to be competed for annually on the Parramatta River.[51]

Although Watt dutifully presented prizes at the club's regattas and stewarded at the annual balls,[52] his role as president was rarely as fulfilling as he would have liked. As he explained at a special meeting in September 1882, it was his great regret that he was not able to take part in club events more frequently because business matters so often intervened.[53] His absences were certainly not taken as evidence of lack of interest on his part, because the MRC remained happy to retain him as president for more than a decade—despite his several long absences from the colony.[54]

Public charities and causes, popular movements and even individuals all received Watt's support, sometimes just his name as patron. Often his involvement occurred at times when he was heavily preoccupied with business or political affairs, or suffering bouts of ill health. For instance, his name appears on the organizing committee for a concert in aid of the National Shipwreck Relief Society of New South Wales held on 15 May 1883,[55] which just happened to be the same day on which the colony's commissioners—including Watt—appointed to the Calcutta International Exhibition (due to run from December 1883 until March 1884) held their first meeting at the Free Public Library.[56]

Watt had already been appointed to the commission organizing the colony's display at the International Colonial and Export Exhibition held in Amsterdam, in the Netherlands, from May until October 1883. Yet through this period he was—perhaps unsurprisingly—battling ill health again, causing him to resign as chairman of the Chamber of Commerce in November 1883 and as warden of the Marine Board in February 1884.[57] At least involvement in the Amsterdam and Calcutta exhibitions apparently did not require Watt to go overseas during 1883, but other matters took him outside the colony the following year anyway.

On 4 April 1884 Watt embarked in RMS *Ballaarat* bound for England, accompanied this time by his three daughters only.[58] Tim and Toby stayed in Sydney, in the care of family friends Sir William and Lady Macleay at Elizabeth Bay House.[59] Although the boys' bachelor uncle Walter Cumming Watt lived at Eynesbury (having followed his half-brother out from Scotland and joined the Gilchrist,

Watt & Co. counting-house in about 1863), leaving them in his care was out of the question. Miss Shuffrey was entrusted with the running of Eynesbury while the rest of the family was away, and Uncle Walter reportedly 'hated the old lady'.[60]

In London Watt took part in the formation of the Imperial Federation League in July, and in November he was appointed to the League's executive committee.[61] Next month, advantage was taken of Watt's presence in the British capital to have him appointed to the New South Wales committee to act in England in respect of the Colonial and Indian Exhibition due to open in South Kensington in May 1886. This would feature displays from Britain's colonies as an 'imperial object lesson' in power and grandeur.[62]

Although this additional duty did not detain Watt until the exhibition's formal start, it was only in March 1885 that he and his daughters boarded the mail steamer *Clyde* to return to Australia. When their ship reached Adelaide on 8 May, they were met by Watt's son William who was just about to celebrate his twentieth birthday.[63] Having returned to Australia in 1882, on completion of his English education, Willie had a bad bout of typhoid in 1884, and a little later was believed to have contracted tuberculosis, which led to him being sent to England in a sailing ship.[64] After making a recovery, he had returned to Australia not long before, so now joined his father and sisters for the last legs of their journey to Melbourne, and then Sydney, which was reached on 14 May.[65]

Sometime after John Watt's return from England he was to be seen riding around Sydney in an elegant horse-drawn open carriage known as a barouche, a luxurious vehicle favoured by the rich and famous of England and Europe. Watt's barouche—burgundy in colour, its four black wheels painted with red trim—had been made in London about 1883 by Shanks & Co. of Great Queen Street.[66] It was presumably acquired by Watt during the visit he made to the British capital the following year, and either returned with him in May 1885 or arrived separately a while later. It remains remarkable that John Watt—a man not normally ostentatious in his public profile—should have allowed himself such an indulgence.

While Christian duty might be seen as one explanation for the burden of commitments which Watt shouldered in his public life, his strong Calvinist beliefs were hardly all-consuming. As his second surviving son later commented, 'his was a religion free altogether from any taint of sectarianism or bitterness', to the extent that one of his 'dearest friends in Sydney' was the first Catholic Archbishop, Bede Vaughan. Throughout the 1880s, the Watt family worshipped at All Saints' Church at Woollahra, where John Watt was a churchwarden for many years.[67]

Expectations of honours or public recognition also played no part in Watt's approach to public service. On more than one occasion he reportedly declined the offer of a knighthood, and once even a baronetcy offered by the premier, Sir Henry Parkes.[68] In 1887, when Parkes was facing bankruptcy, it was revealed that a large number of public figures had lent him money—including Watt to the extent of £470.[69] At a public meeting in October, a public subscription was opened and Watt was appointed to a committee to invest the funds raised for the benefit of Parkes and his family.[70]

In the final analysis, it seems that Watt truly meant what he had said at the farewell dinner in 1876: he took it as a solemn obligation to give something back to the country which had given so much to him. His younger sons would not have known about many of his contributions to the community until years later, because often his involvement predated their birth and early childhood. But the principle that with wealth and position went civic duty and responsibility was one which Watt's youngest son would ultimately, and fully, also embrace.

The monotremes man

On 22 September 1883 the 4,250-ton vessel *Sydney*, operated by the French shipping line Messageries Maritimes, steamed into Sydney Harbour.[71] On board was a 24-year-old Scotsman, William Hay Caldwell, described as an 'attractive young man, on the tall side of middle height and well made, with finely cut features and carefully twisted fair moustache'.[72] Bearing letters of introduction from the Colonial Office in London to the Governors of New South Wales, Victoria and Queensland, a personal salary from Cambridge university, and generous grants from the Royal Society to cover equipment expenses, he had come to Australia on an important scientific mission.[73]

For more than 80 years, scientists in Europe had been debating the reproductive biology of some of the fauna peculiar to Australia, doubting or disbelieving any knowledge provided by colonial naturalists. Caldwell's task was to attempt to establish beyond question how certain marsupials such as opossums, kangaroos and wallabies developed their young, along with the class of mammals known as monotremes (platypus and echidna), and the Ceradotus—otherwise known as the Queensland lungfish, or mudfish, because of its unique ability to breath both underwater and on land.

Despite his youth, Caldwell came well-qualified for the work expected of him. After three years at Gonville and Caius College at Cambridge, he had graduated with a first class Bachelor of Arts degree in Natural Sciences in 1880, and two years later was appointed to lecture in comparative anatomy for the university's Professor of Zoology, Alfred Newton. In 1883 a travelling scholarship was established in memory of Professor Frank Balfour, killed in a climbing accident in the Swiss Alps the year before. Who better than Caldwell, Balfour's pupil in animal morphology, to become the inaugural Balfour student in Biology—pursuing an area of research suggested to Caldwell by Balfour himself.

On arrival in Sydney, Caldwell found himself feted by the local scientific community and the government, which provided him with a suite of rooms at the Board of Health Office in Macquarie Street for temporary use as a laboratory.[74] His birthplace of Portobello, the beachside suburb of Edinburgh facing the Firth of Forth, also made him an especially welcome visitor with that part of Sydney society which still proclaimed Scottish heritage.

Making Sydney his base, Caldwell planned to 'go after' platypus first and travelled to the New England district in October—only to discover that it was the wrong season for his purposes. He accordingly decided to concentrate on koalas, wallabies and marsupial species instead, making short excursions to country areas out from Sydney for the next six months. In April 1884, he headed north to Central Queensland to begin the hunt for breeding lungfish, platypus and echidna.

Setting up camp on the Burnett River near Gayndah, inland from Bundaberg, Caldwell assembled a team of 50 aboriginal men and women to help him find the specimens he needed. This work force was actually essential to the approach he proposed to adopt towards his mission, because various accounts make clear that he had no intention of enduring personal hardship in the bush. Accompanied by a first-class cook, an excellent cellar of wines and a valet, he reportedly spent long hours smoking ultra-expensive cigars in the company of Reginald Bloxsome, the private secretary to the lieutenant-governor of New South Wales (Sir Alfred Stephen), who joined his expedition as 'guide, philosopher and friend'.[75]

In less than two months, Caldwell had the answers he was looking for. On 29 August he arranged for a message to be sent from a telegraph station at Camboon, two day's journey from his camp. The message was addressed to Professor Archibald Liversidge, dean of the faculty of science at the University of Sydney, and asked him to cable to Montreal, Canada, where the British Association for the Advancement of Science was holding its first annual conference outside Britain. His telegram in Latin, reading 'Monotremes oviparous, ovum meroblastic', succinctly declared that the platypus and echidna bred by laying yolk-filled eggs hatched outside the body. This dramatic announcement electrified the Montreal gathering, and instantly gave Caldwell an international reputation.[76]

Still needing further specimens to complete a record of platypus development, Caldwell stayed put on the Burnett for another three months—especially after suddenly coming across Ceratodus eggs he had been looking for. By December 1884 he was back in Sydney, where he gave a presentation to the Royal Society of New South Wales eight days before Christmas at which he displayed a lungfish that he had hatched and reared.[77] The first months of 1885 were spent in collecting marsupial embryos, harvested during a kangaroo drive arranged especially for his benefit by squatters in the Gwydir district of New South Wales, and in recovering from a fever contracted on the Burnett the year before.

By June Caldwell was preparing a second season in Queensland to continue his 'attack on the Monotremes'. Recognising that he would need to organize himself on a larger scale than before, to achieve complete coverage of the development stages of the target species, he engaged three times the number of Aboriginal collectors at his camp. This certainly delivered the results he wanted, and by August his expedition had 'caught' (that is, slaughtered) between 1,300 and 1,400 echidnas of both sexes.

At Brisbane on 30 July, Caldwell boarded the 600-ton coastal steamer *Currajong* as a passenger headed for Sydney.[78] According to his own account, renewed exposure in Queensland had brought on his fever again, and he left it to a colleague to pack up the expedition camp and move it south in September. The paper which Caldwell subsequently published about his time in Australia gives little clue about what he was doing after this, but it is clear that there was a considerable interval before he returned to England. Not until June 1886 was he heard of back in London, giving an account one evening to the Royal Society on the work he had been doing.[79]

But William Caldwell had not finished with Australia, nor Australia with him. During the more than two years that he spent in the colonies he had undoubtedly been pursuing interests other than purely scientific ones. One of those interests was directly addressed in the Melbourne *Argus* newspaper in September 1884, shortly after his famous telegram had drawn headlines everywhere. Describing him as 'the travelling bachelor with a commission from Cambridge', the *Argus* commented that:

> Not even an unmarried cricketer with a title has attracted more attention. As if aware of the dangers of his position, our visitor has shrunk from society. The platypus is to be picked up on the Yarra, and the echidna in the adjacent ranges, but Mr Caldwell has wisely planted himself in the Queensland bush remote from man, and from woman also.[80]

By the time Caldwell went back to England in 1886, it was with the avowed intention of returning to Australia within a short period to marry. The girl to whom he had become engaged was Margaret

Watt, the eldest daughter of the Hon. J. B. Watt. Precisely how they came to be betrothed is not known for certain, although it seems clear that there were many opportunities for their paths to cross during the times that Caldwell was in and out of Sydney—apart from the year from April 1884 when Watt and his daughters were visiting England.

Watt family and friends, pictured on the balustrade of Eynesbury c.1887. From left: Walter Watt (JBW's half-brother), Ernest, Florence, J. B. Watt (seated), Miss Shuffrey, Elinor (seated), Sir Alfred Roberts (noted surgeon), Reggie Bloxsome (lieutenant-governor's private secretary). As Oswald is not in the picture, he was probably behind the camera taking it.

Caldwell's return to Cambridge placed members of the Balfour Trust in something of a quandary, since their first Balfour Student had yet to produce any written product from his research. With the scholarship again due for filling late in 1886, the selection committee took the safest course and gave the next award to the existing holder for a further period of a year. This was a decision that angered at least one disappointed applicant for the studentship, biologist William Bateson, who declared to family contacts that the choice was 'improper and a breach of trust'. How can it be, he asked, 'that Caldwell has done other than embezzle the funds to pay his matrimonial expenses'?[81]

The committee, Bateson alleged, had favoured 'a notoriously wealthy man' (the son of a papermill owner from Inverkeithing, in Fife, Scotland), one who had practically abandoned the work he originally began, 'being too lazy to finish it':

Worst of all it was not even pretended that he should devote himself to his work, during his year of tenure. His sole business, [Professor] Newton himself says, in returning to Australia was to get married. This also, therefore, they knew. … Lastly, they knew that he had spent an integral part of the time of his previous tenure in speculating in gold—an occupation which is not one of the objects which the subscribers meant to promote.[82]

Notwithstanding such objections, to the extent that these became widely-voiced and known, William Caldwell embarked in the P&O steamer *Bengal* at London on 3 December 1886 and departed for Sydney. Travelling with him was his younger brother Herbert, to act as best man at the forthcoming nuptials.[83] The *Bengal* arrived in Sydney on 20 January 1887,[84] and a week later, 27 January, Margaret Watt and William Caldwell were married in All Saints Church at Woollahra.[85] Five weeks after that, on 4 March, the newly-weds, and Herbert Caldwell, boarded the P&O steamer *Carthage*[86] and by late April they were all back in England.

While still absent from England for his marriage, Caldwell had submitted the first account of his Australian expedition. This was received on 22 February 1887 by biologist Professor Michael Foster, the secretary of the British Association, who explained when it was read before the Royal Society on 17 March that Caldwell was 'at the present time in Australia and so unable to correct the proof of this abstract'. It was July that year before Caldwell finished a version that was edited and revised in readiness for publication.[87] This was probably the high tide mark in his record of scientific achievement.

Chapter Two
INHERITED WEALTH

Unexpected exile

Within twelve months of his eldest daughter's marriage, John Watt decided to make another visit to Britain. The educational needs of his younger sons had apparently been weighing on his mind for some time. Unimpressed by the standard of formal schooling available in Sydney, he had been reliant on the not entirely satisfactory expedient of private tutoring until then—apart from sending the boys to the Hutchins School in Hobart as day-students for three months in 1886,[1] following a summer holiday visit to Tasmania. But with Ernest due to turn 13 in December 1887, it was time he received the same opportunities as his brother Willie had derived from attending Harrow. Watt planned an extended visit that would see both his boys settled into good boarding schools, then returning to New South Wales.

On 13 March 1888, the Hon. J. B. Watt, MLC, left Sydney in the luxury Orient mail steamer *Austral* with his daughters Florence and Elinor, and sons Ernest and Oswald.[2] Travelling with the family was Miss Shuffrey, the housekeeper at Eynesbury who was going back to England where she would leave employment and retire.[3] Their ship for this voyage already held a unique place in maritime history, having capsized and sank while coaling in Sydney Harbour in November 1882 after only its second trip on the London to Sydney route. Once it was pumped out and refloated by salvage teams some months later, the ship was taken back to Glasgow where it was refitted before resuming service in November 1884.

According to the later writings of Ernest Watt, he and his brother Oswald 'had the time of our lives' during the voyage.[4] Returning in the *Austral* was the English national cricket team which had just completed a test tour of Australia. Ernest maintained that he and Oswald became great friends with several members of the team, most notably Robert ("Bobby") Abel, the diminutive batsman who was touring with his first test side after making a name for himself as a prolific run-scorer in the English county championship. The boys 'used to listen to his wonderful stories by the hour.'[5]

Ernest and Oswald Watt in 1890, photographed by their brother-in-law Gordon Caldwell.

Also on board was Herbert Caldwell, the brother of John Watt's new son-in-law, William. Since returning to England after William's wedding at the start of 1887, Herbert (or "Bertie" as he was generally known) had come back to Australia, and spent the first months of 1888 visiting the eastern colonies—partly in company with Reginald Bloxsome, who had earlier befriended his brother.[6] Again according to Ernest Watt's recollections, Bertie Caldwell proved 'excellent company', being 'full of good stories and good cheer'. He reportedly fulfilled another important function during the voyage, by becoming engaged to Ernest's 22-year-old sister Florence (called "Mimi" by her father)—chiefly to deflect the unwanted attention being paid to her by the ship's captain, J. F. Ruthven, later to become Commodore of the Orient Line.[7]

On disembarking at Plymouth in the last days of April the Watt family made their way straight away to Bournemouth, which Ernest described as 'that lovely town of pine trees' on the south coast.[8] There they went into the newly-opened Imperial Hotel for a short time, while John Watt implemented the first stage of his plan for his sons' education. Both boys were put into Cheltenham House boarding school at Boscombe, a suburb on the eastern edge of Bournemouth. The school was a very small establishment, attended by only about 15 boys. Ernest recalled Cheltenham House as situated in 'lovely grounds', but he considered it 'not at all a flourishing' school and later doubted that they learnt very much there at all.[9]

With the boys put into school, John Watt took his daughters to London, and then Cambridge where he intended to visit daughter Margaret and son-in-law William, and their infant daughter (John Watt's first grandchild) born in November 1887.[10] Since their marriage, the Caldwells had been living in a house called 'The Birnam' at 12 Harvey Road, as William was still nominally associated with the university.[11] Although he remained a Fellow of Gonville and Caius College, he had done little further anatomical work on the huge collections assembled during his field trip to Australia in 1883-86—in fact, he was conducting himself more like a "gentleman scientist". His interests had shifted back towards the field of study of his early student days, which was marine biology, and from 1887 he had become a life member (and later member of Council) of the Marine Biological Association of the United Kingdom.[12]

In an attempt to change Bournemouth's image from a health resort to attract a more general tourist trade, Invalids Walk (pictured here in the 1890s) was renamed Pine Walk in 1917.

By coincidence, William Caldwell's family were from the Edinburgh area of Scotland—the same as John Watt's family. His widowed mother still lived alone at Polton, a small village outside Edinburgh near where her husband had been engaged in paper-making at Lasswade; she subsequently moved to Portobello, a seaside town also just outside Edinburgh, where she owned a holiday cottage. Apart from William, two more of Mrs Caldwell's five sons had gone to Cambridge, both entering their brother's college of Gonville and Caius—Gordon in 1883, and Francis ("Frank") in 1884—though neither stayed to complete a degree. In 1900 Herbert, too, would gain admission to Trinity College, Cambridge, where he completed a Bachelor of Arts degree in 1903 before embarking on a late career as a schoolmaster.[13]

The Caldwells' connection with both Cambridge and Scotland fitted in ideally with John Watt's plans for his stay in Britain. While he made

Bournemouth his regular base, residing at Brunstath House in Grove Road, he began the practice of spending summer holidays in Scotland, where he would take a big house for two or three months every year to enable the family to gather around him and reconnect with their Scottish heritage. Of course, these occasions provided the only contact John Watt had with his sons once they began attending school, apart from other short vacation breaks when they could visit him at home in Bournemouth.

It was either during visits to Cambridge or the annual sojourns to Scotland that a different connection between the Watt and Caldwell families was forged. Florence Watt's shipboard engagement to Herbert Caldwell had been broken off soon after arrival in England, and it was sometime over the next eighteen months that she met Bertie's 25-year-old brother Gordon.[14] When Florence and Gordon Caldwell announced their engagement, John Watt found his planned return to Sydney facing an unexpected, though doubtless welcome, delay.

The wedding did not actually take place until February 1890, being celebrated at Cambridge in the famous Church of the Holy Sepulchre,[15] known locally as 'the Round Church' because of its medieval design. John Watt was there to give away his daughter, while his sons Ernest and Oswald were groomsmen to the younger two of four bridesmaids. After a reception held at the Birnam, the residence of William and Margaret Caldwell, the bridal couple departed for a honeymoon in Scotland.[16]

By this time, 15-year-old Ernest had left Cheltenham House at Boscombe and had just been enrolled at Clifton College at Bristol, in southwest England, a month before the wedding. The clear intention was that Oswald would follow this same path a term or two later, so the matter of the two boys' education appeared settled and John Watt could finally consider himself free to fulfill his intention of returning to Sydney. It was, however, at about this juncture that John Watt's health dramatically declined. His doctors diagnosed the onset of 'paralysis agitans', a condition better known today as Parkinson's Disease, and advised him that a sea voyage would be risky.[17] He now found himself marooned in England, but fortunately with all the immediate members of his family more or less by his side.

Toby's English education

Six months after Florence Watt's marriage to Gordon Caldwell, John Watt's hopes regarding young Oswald's education in England were dramatically, almost catastrophically, derailed. Although Toby appears to have enjoyed robust health in hometown Sydney, in the unfamiliar English climate he had already proved to be prone to, in his brother Ernest's words, 'nearly every ailment a child is heir to'.[18] But a worse misfortune was to follow.

In August 1890 John Watt followed his practice of hiring a big house in Scotland for the summer, to enable his dispersed family to gather around him. This year the place was Camusdarach Lodge near the village of Morar in Inverness-shire, on the west coast.[19] The village lies at the western end of Loch Morar, famous as the deepest stretch of freshwater in the British Isles, and one day a party headed off on a boating excursion to the head of the lake for a picnic. The steam-powered launch in which they travelled was old and had a number of holes in its boiler, including 'one big hole in the bow' that Ernest Watt recalled 'had been "mended" in a rough and ready way with a bit of wood hammered in from the outside'.[20]

Ernest later left an account of what happened:

> We were on our way home and William and Gordon Caldwell, Oswald, and I were sitting just in front of this boiler, when suddenly the wood flew out and the whole place was filled with smoke. You could not see a yard ahead of you. William, Gordon and I were sitting on the bow, but Oswald was below and he got the full force of the boiling water and steam from the hole in the boiler. Those sitting aft could not see what had happened to any of us, for we were enveloped in steam. We three lucky ones could see nothing and poor old Oswald would have been killed outright had not Gordon Caldwell heard him groan. He put his hands down in the direction of the groans and lifted Oswald up, when it was found that his legs from the knees downwards were absolutely raw, like cooked meat.[21]

What followed was a nightmare trip back to get the badly-scalded boy to medical attention. As Ernest further recounted: 'The boiler had to be patched up somehow before we could get under way, and of course we could steam but slowly and we had twelve miles to go. All we had for his poor legs was butter left over from the picnic lunch. How he must have suffered. It was nearly midnight before we got him home.'[22] Although the local doctor was immediately sent for, and the doctor undoubtedly did his best, the fearful injuries to Oswald's legs turned septic and it was many months before he could again put a foot on the ground.

Using Ernest's later account of events once more, the outcome of the accident had been a 'very near shave'. Had John Watt not removed his son from Scotland and sent him to Cambridge, where he was placed under the supervision of Dr George Wherry, consultant surgeon at Addenbrooke's Hospital (the teaching hospital associated with the university), Oswald would probably never have walked again or regained full use of his lower limbs. As it was, he walked after about a year and recovered completely within another year, 'but not until he had undergone the most appalling suffering, all of which he bore with the most heroic fortitude'.[23] He also carried scarring on both legs for the rest of his life.[24]

The long time required for Oswald to recover from his injuries inevitably interfered seriously with his education. When well enough, he was sent to Sussex to continue his interrupted studies with a private tutor named Stevens.[25] This arrangement apparently worked well enough, in that he reportedly hunted regularly and thoroughly enjoyed himself, but for a considerable period his schooling conducted away from Bournemouth and he was rarely back there except for holidays.[26]

Late in 1892 Oswald was admitted to Oakeley's boarding house of the Upper School at Clifton College, Bristol, joining his brother Ernest who was still a student at the college. Oswald spent only one term there, however, before illness again intervened; he left in December and went back to private tutoring.[27] During that same Christmas term of 1892, Ernest also contracted pneumonia. His condition was sufficiently serious that he claimed it was 'touch and go' and his family was sent for.[28] While Ernest was still recovering, it was decided that he would not go back to Clifton. He had never been happy there, considering the tone of the place to be 'lax in the extreme'. When told he did not have to return, his 'only feelings were of infinite relief' and he was 'very glad to leave it'.[29] What Oswald made of his brief experience at Clifton is not recorded.

When Ernest had thoroughly recovered from pneumonia he went to Cambridge and stayed with his sister while working for the university entrance exam with a tutor named H. N. Ferrars. The tutor did his work so well that Ernest easily passed into King's College and went into residence there in October 1893.[30] The previous August, John Watt had—as usual—rented a house in Scotland in order to have all his family around him again. This year it was Castle Stuart, a restored seventeenth century tower house on the banks of the Moray Firth, northeast of Inverness. Ferrars came up to Castle Stuart to continue Ernest's coaching, and the scene was set for an incident which Ernest took later delight in recounting in great detail.

One day during the holiday, Ferrars, Oswald and Ernest went out rabbit-shooting in company with two gamekeepers who brought with them three ferrets intended to flush the quarry from any burrows in which they took refuge. When the first rabbit appeared, both boys shot at it and both claimed the kill as theirs. 'A loud altercation followed, but it ceased when we discovered that the ferret too was dead! Of course the gamekeeper was furious...' After a discussion it was agreed to split into two parties, each with a gamekeeper and ferret, and go in different directions, with Ferrars accompanying Ernest.[31]

Ernest's group had not gone far before the next rabbit was spotted, and this time the tutor fired. Unfortunately, the shot was taken at such close quarters that the rabbit was largely shot to pieces—and there behind it lay the ferret, also dead. When they rejoined the others, it was to find Oswald looking very dejected and the gamekeeper with him even angrier than before. Toby had missed the rabbit he fired at, but also killed the ferret pursuing his target. The hunting party had been spectacularly unsuccessful, returning with a bag of only two rabbits—one largely in tatters—and with all three ferrets having been accidentally dispatched as well. Commented Ernest: 'You can imagine the feelings of the game-keepers! Poor Ferrars. Another day he came in with great glee, having shot a white rabbit. It turned out to be a pet belonging to the Head Gamekeeper's children, so his great achievement was not very popular.'[32]

Perhaps as a result of this particular episode, when Ernest and Oswald met during later holiday breaks they appear to have engaged in activities involving less blood-letting. Ernest recounted various stays that he and Oswald enjoyed with the widowed Mrs Caldwell, mother of their two brothers-in-law, both at Polton and later at Portobello. The house at the first place boasted a grass tennis court, while Portobello offered a beach—complete with pier—where fishing and swimming could be enjoyed. Mrs Caldwell herself appeared of irascible disposition, but was actually 'sweet and kind' and 'a terrific cook' to boot.[33]

The Great Court of Trinity College, Cambridge, pictured in the 1890s.

When Oswald was admitted to Trinity College, Cambridge, at the end of June 1896,[34] it was to find Ernest still in residence at King's. He had actually just completed his Bachelor of Arts degree at that time, having passed the tripos examination that marked the end of his three-year honours course in History, but had decided to stay at Cambridge for a fourth year to study Moral Science. Possibly his interest in that field of study had been sparked by thoughts he had earlier entertained of converting to the Roman Catholic faith and becoming a priest, but when that enthusiasm waned so did Ernest's desire to remain at university.[35] In April 1897 Ernest left Cambridge to proceed to Sydney, ending a nine-year absence from his homeland.

Until Ernest left for Australia he 'saw a good deal' of his younger brother, despite residing in different colleges.[36] When he left for Sydney, he was not to know that the final chapter in their father's life was about to be played out in his absence.

John Watt's will

The diagnosis that John Watt received from his doctors in 1890 completely upset the plans that had originally brought him to England two years earlier, but although in effect medically exiled from his home and business in Sydney there were some compensations to be found. As a devoted and caring father, he probably derived considerable comfort from being on hand when his eldest daughter Margaret and son-in-law William Caldwell presented him with another grand-daughter in 1890 and a grandson in 1893. Second daughter Florence and her husband Gordon Caldwell also started a family in this period, beginning with a daughter in January 1891 and followed by a son in March 1893 and another in November 1895.[37]

The extension of the family's stay became the occasion for John Watt's youngest daughter to also find an English husband. On 27 April 1892 Elinor married Christian de Falbe, a Lieutenant in the Worcestershire Regiment, at St. Peter's Church in Bournemouth, where her father was on hand to give the bride away.[38] Despite the groom's surname (he was the elder son of a former Danish naval captain), Nellie's new husband actually had an Australian connection, because his mother Emmeline was the daughter of Hannibal Macarthur of New South Wales and maternal granddaughter of Philip Gidley King (the colony's third Governor in 1800-1806).[39]

Whatever hopes that John Watt might have held for Elinor's union were disappointed, because de Falbe was universally disliked by his Caldwell in-laws and members of the Watt family who suspected that he had married with an eye to his father-in-law's wealth. The grasping aspect of de Falbe's nature was apparent even to 14-year-old Oswald, who reportedly wrote an account of his sister's wedding which noted that 'Many handsome presents were received and many more expected.'[40] The couple went to live in Worcester, but there enjoyed much less contact with other members of the extended family than they would have if Nellie's husband been better accepted. The marriage was, unsurprisingly, not a success, and there were no children before it ended in divorce under a decade later.[41]

If John Watt's last son-in-law brought a less than illustrious reputation to the family, the patriarch was also confronted by growing evidence that the former glow of William Caldwell's standing at Cambridge had begun to lose its lustre. In mid-1893 a prestigious science journal reported that a meeting of the Zoological Society of London on 6 June had been made the occasion 'for some indignant remarks on the action of a member of the University [at Cambridge], in suppressing and rendering useless for the purposes of science, materials collected at the public expense…in Australia':

> If Mr. W. H. Caldwell is unable to make use of the specimens he was deputed to collect, it is high time that he reported to that effect to the public institutions that endowed his research; and it would be well if in future the Royal Society added some clause to the conditions on which the Government grant is awarded, preventing any repetition of such circumstances.[42]

It was probably this pungent and very direct challenge to William Caldwell's position at the university which finally decided him on abandoning academia for some other occupation. According to Ernest Watt, it was in 'about 1892' that his father advanced his son-in-law 'sufficient capital'—£40,000 is the amount mentioned (about $4-5 million at today's values)—with which 'to buy a large paper mill, at Inverkeithing, on the other side of the Forth Bridge' in Scotland. Ernest went on to state that William left Cambridge—which he certainly did do, late in 1893—and found a house near the mill.[43] Joining him as partners in this enterprise was Gordon Caldwell and their younger brother Francis ("Frank"). Situated alongside Harbour Place at Inverkeithing, where it had access to good water, along with cheap coal and freight, the business traded as 'Messrs. Caldwell & Company' and quickly established a name making 'printings, writings, and grease-proof parchments from esparto [grass], rags, and wood-pulp'.[44]

William Hay Caldwell, erstwhile scientist and later papermaker.

As it happened, these three were not the only Caldwell brothers to follow in their father's footsteps as paper-makers at this time. In 1894 Bertie Caldwell also, along with his 28-year-old brother Alfred, inherited a paper mill at Kevock, Lasswade, from their uncle, W. Alfred Sommerville. With the mill came Sommerville's two-storey residence, Greenfield Lodge in Lasswade, which is where the nephews lived. Unfortunately for the two brothers, the business they received was already unviable, being heavily burdened with debt. In July the company estates of W. Alfred Sommerville & Co. were sequestrated by the Court of Session in Edinburgh, and with it the individual estates of the brothers as owners.[45] A lengthy legal process followed, and it was not until six or seven years later that they were finally discharged of creditors.[46]

Matters did not go any more smoothly for Caldwell and Company, although the unravelling was slightly longer in coming. According to Ernest Watt, the brothers gradually fell out amid quarrels over the failure of the mill to pay its way.[47] In July 1896, Gordon Caldwell retired as a subscriber of the firm, leaving William and Frank to carry on the business without him.[48] Two years later Frank Caldwell did the same thing, with William continuing the business under the same name but on his sole account.[49] So bitter did Gordon Caldwell feel about the falling-out that he would not speak to his older brother again, despite the best efforts of Willie Watt to patch things up.[50]

Family disputes and discord were not John Watt's only worries during his enforced stay in England. During his absence, his business interests back in Australia were being ravaged by a range of adverse economic events, including maritime union strikes, a banking crisis, and the onset of a severe drought. Cut off and powerless to help Gilchrist Watt & Co. cope with its difficulties, John Watt struggled to keep abreast of these distant events. He was grateful that his son William was still periodically in and out of England, even after purchasing a property at Howlong in the Riverina district of southern New South Wales in 1888. This helped allay his sense of isolation to some extent, but otherwise the visits he received from old friends from Australia during their short stays in England became his principal pleasure.[51]

After fire destroyed William Caldwell's papermill at Inverkeithing, Scotland, in 1914, his rebuilt factory dominated the local skyline for nearly a century before it was demolished in 2012.

For the first few years of his time in England John Watt still planned on getting back to Sydney, his real home after 50 years spent mostly living away from Britain. When the family left for England in 1888, their furniture and household effects had been removed from Eynesbury and placed in storage, in expectation of an eventual return; only in December 1890—once it had become clear that a long sea voyage must be deferred indefinitely—was the furniture and goods sold off by auction.[52] In the meantime Watt followed an annual routine which saw him spend the colder months from October to May at Bournemouth, before venturing on visits to London and his daughters' homes at the start of the warmer weather, followed by a summer holiday in Scotland.[53]

After maintaining his preferred routine for five years, by 1896 John Watt had become so ill that he was effectively an invalid and remained confined to his house at Bournemouth. After Nellie moved away following her marriage, Brunstath was managed by a housekeeper, Mrs Andrew, even during the winter months when each of his daughters came to spend a month or two with him in turn. Whenever Ernest and Oswald came home to Bournemouth during school breaks Mrs Andrew was 'a perfect mother' to both boys, to whom she became known as "Aunt Fanny".[54]

At the start of autumn in 1897 John Watt's condition suddenly worsened and he died on 28 September.[55] Although he had been seldom out of pain during the preceding five or six years, his family had reportedly been expecting him to live on for many years. In the end it was a bout of pneumonia to which he succumbed.[56] The patriarch's remains were eventually returned to Sydney and interred in the churchyard of St Jude's at Randwick.

The news of his passing came as an 'overwhelming blow' to Ernest, who had just returned to Australia to begin working in Gilchrist Watt & Co.'s Sydney office and was on a familiarization tour of the firm's Queensland stations with brother Willie at the time. The two returned straight away to Sydney, and William was shortly afterwards on his way to England to attend to his father's affairs.[57]

The extent of John Watt's considerable wealth finally became known when details of the will were published nearly a year after his death. His estate in New South Wales was valued for probate at £196,386, and his property in England a further £33,125.[58] All up, this combined amount of a little under £230,000 would be worth—in purchasing power—somewhere between $25-30 million today.

In addition to various legacies to brothers and cousins, and bequests totalling £2000 to public charities in Sydney (with smaller amounts to some English charities), the bulk of Watt's wealth was left to his six children. His daughters each received an annuity of £500 plus the income from a legacy of £15,000 for each, which his trustees were to invest for their benefit. His half-share in the sheep station known as Goonal, in the Gwydir district of New South Wales, and his 9/20th share in two cattle stations in Queensland—Glenprairie adjoining the coast at Marlborough, and Stoodleigh north of Rockhampton—were bequeathed to his sons, in trust, in equal shares as tenants in common. The will also directed that the residuary trust estate be held in trust for the children, and gave instructions regarding the mode of investment and ultimate distribution of the property.[59]

After John Watt's death in England, Eynesbury was sold and finally demolished in 1934. Only the gate posts that graced the entrance to the property were retained and now frame the entrance to the house called "Carmel", built in 1940 for Sydney stockbroker Stanley Utz.

As a result of these provisions, both Ernest and Oswald both suddenly became independently wealthy young men while still aged in their early 20s. Neither would have any real need to work for a living, although both now faced the challenge of finding something worthwhile to which they could apply themselves.

After Cambridge

Eleven weeks after John Watt's death, his son Ernest packed his bags in Sydney and on 15 December 1887 departed for England by a roundabout route through Hong Kong, Japan, Hawaii and America.[60] On arrival in London he made visits to his married sisters, before finding rooms in a house at Cambridge where a colleague boarded, and where he stayed until the end of the term. Ernest later wrote that, during this visit he saw quite a lot of his brother, Oswald, who was evidently enjoying his time at the university and experiencing none of the ill health of previous years. 'We had some great times together…,' recalled Ernest, 'I met a great many of his Cambridge friends, and a very interesting lot they were.'[61]

Subsequently Ernest went to London and took rooms in Jermyn Street, close to Piccadilly. He later complained of having an intensely lonely time, until joined there by Oswald while on his summer vacation.[62] This arrangement, too, did not last long before Ernest was on his way back to Sydney, where he arrived in early September 1898.[63]

After less than a year away, Ernest Watt was back in England once more, arriving in August 1899. Initially he made his way to Morar, to spend time with his eldest sister Margaret who was then living there, but then he headed to London. By that stage Oswald had faced the examiners at Cambridge for the last time, sitting the Natural Sciences Tripos which earned him a Bachelor of Arts degree with Third Class Honours.[64] Ordinarily this would have seemed a quite modest achievement, but Ernest was moved to declare that he considered his brother's performance 'an exceptionally brilliant one, for his education had been decidedly spasmodic'. More tellingly he added, 'I am perfectly certain he never worked very hard at Cambridge. Of course he made lots of friends and enjoyed his time there immensely.'[65]

With his university days finally behind him, Oswald joined Ernest in rented rooms at No. 15 Jermyn Street. Ernest complained that it was lonely when his brother was away, 'and he was away for some time, too.'[66] With his study commitments finished, Oswald had celebrated his new-found freedom by heading to Germany in July for the famous music festival at Bayreuth that featured the operas of the nineteenth century German composer Richard Wagner. His travelling companion on this adventure was William Otter-Barry, a fellow student at Trinity. After Bayreuth the pair went touring Upper Bavaria, staying for a couple of days as guests at Schloss Neubeuern about 50 kilometres south-east of Munich in early August.[67]

Although Ernest did not accompany Oswald, he solemnly declared a certainty that 'Wagner's music has seldom impressed anyone more powerfully'. Oswald was, he said, 'always fond of music, and could play the piano quite well, though too modest to admit it. He also played quite well on the banjo.'[68] With this depth of musical knowledge, it is not known whether Oswald might have actually shared the reservations of celebrated Italian conductor Arturo Toscanini (1867-1957) who—after noticing the lack of ensemble between orchestra, chorus and singers at the 1899 festival—told a friend, 'These Bayreuth performances are a real hoax for people like me who are hoping to hear perfection.'[69]

Schloss Neubeuern in Bavaria, Germany, the former hotel (now school) where Oswald Watt's name appears in the guestbook for August 1899.

No sooner was Oswald back from Germany, he departed for the United States to watch the yacht races being sailed off New York for the tenth America's Cup competition in October. In 1899 former Glasgow grocer and wealthy tea magnate Thomas Lipton (knighted in 1901 and created a baronet the next year) was making his first challenge for the Cup on behalf of the Royal Ulster Yacht Club. According to Ernest Watt, it was his understanding that Lipton had invited his English financier and philanthropist friend Sir Henry Burdett to bring a party to New York as his guests, and Oswald went by virtue of being at Cambridge with one of Burdett's four sons. 'Curiously,' wrote Ernest, 'I don't think Oswald ever actually met his host', but he had 'a wonderful time' and 'thoroughly enjoyed himself.'[70] Lipton lost the three-race series, but went on to challenge four more times by 1930— earning him a special award as "the best of all losers".

When Oswald returned, he and Ernest became (in his own words) 'very interested' in an American musical comedy playing in London called The Belle of New York. The show had not lasted long after opening on Broadway in 1897, but when transferred to the West End with its entire 63-person original cast in April the following year it

46

became a major success—despite its flimsy storyline about a Salvation Army girl who reformed a spendthrift, made a great sacrifice and found true love. London's leading theatrical paper labelled the show 'bizarre', but still described it as 'the brightest, smartest and cleverest entertainment of its kind that has been seen in London for a long time.'[71] This was just as well, as the Watt brothers went to see the production multiple times—the two of them always going, as Ernest explained, alone.[72]

In these few episodes from the latter part of 1899 might be seen a foretaste of the lifestyle which would be Oswald's for much of the next decade, and Ernest Watt's for a lot longer. The only other highlight recalled from the brothers' stay in London involved a night-time burglary of their Jermyn Street rooms, in which a new suitcase that Ernest had given to Oswald was taken, and a stack of letters opened evidently in the hope of finding negotiable postal orders. Recalled Ernest, 'I heard him [the burglar] come into my room, which was on the first floor, and I remember shouting out, thinking it was Toby. I soon fell asleep again, but fortunately he took nothing of mine, thinking I was still awake.'[73]

As the end of the year approached, the brothers prepared to return together to Australia—this time in company with their elder brother, Willie, who had also been in England since their father's death. On 14 December the 6,600-ton P&O mail steamer *Himalaya* left London bound for Australia.[74] Ernest recalled that, 'It was such a crowded ship that we had a cabin between the three of us.'[75] Aden was reached on 1 January 1900, and the ship pressed on—taking the 22-year-old Oswald Watt to the homeland he had not seen in nearly 12 years.

Chapter Three
LIFE IN AUSTRALIA

Return to Sydney

The *Himalaya*, with the three Watt brothers on board, entered Sydney Harbour at 8 a.m. on 26 January 1900, the 112th anniversary of the founding of the colony of New South Wales. Since federation of the Australian colonies was still a year away, the date did not then bear the national significance later attached to it. Nonetheless, Anniversary Day celebrations were planned in Sydney—the main event being the annual regatta on the Harbour, for which the *Himalaya* was to serve as flagship from moorings in Neutral Bay. To enable the steamer to play its special role by 10 a.m., arrangements were made to land passengers as quickly as possible using a steam tender from Watson's Bay, and the brothers probably felt like they were rushed ashore with unseemly haste.[1]

Soon after landing the Watts would have made their way to Etham Cottage in Darling Point, which Willie and Ernest had first made their home late in 1898 (after moving out of Knellerpore, their Uncle Walter's house at Double Bay) and furnished to suit their personal comfort.[2] Ernest later described them living there as 'a very happy family',[3] but it was an arrangement that did not last for long. While in England Ernest had proposed by mail to a girl in Sydney, and she had accepted him, so he had returned to Australia with the express purpose of marrying as soon as possible. The wedding took place on 3 April at St Mark's Church, Darling Point—with Oswald as best man—and shortly after the honeymoon, Ernest took his bride to live in London.[4]

With Ernest having removed himself from Sydney once more, it devolved on William to help Oswald settle back into his former hometown, and to fill him in on the full extent of the business interests he had inherited from their father. The station properties mentioned

48

in John Watt's will were not the full extent of the patriarch's pastoral pursuits, as there were a number of others which were not held under freehold title but by occupational licence. Under these arrangements, the Watt brothers were also part-holders of Llanillo, near Walgett, and Gunningrah, near Bombala, New South Wales; and Strathmore, near Bowen in Queensland.

Willie very likely also introduced his brother to "Howlong", his own station of 45,000 acres of freehold land situated near Carrathool, about 50 kilometres east of Hay, in the Riverina district. The property had a frontage of six miles along the Murrumbidgee River, and William had only recently built himself a palatial country residence which he called "Malalue". Although making only periodical visits to the property, he reportedly took great delight in its rooms which were described as 'handsome and unique, and most prettily furnished'.[5] A photograph showing a party of guests that William Watt brought to Malalue, circa 1900, includes someone who looks very much like a 22-year-old Oswald.[6] If this was Oswald, he must have visited Howlong before mid-November 1900—because it was then that Malalue was accidentally destroyed by fire, along with all its contents.[7]

Visitors to William Watt's "Malalue" residence at Howlong in 1900. The young man seated on the ground appears to be Oswald Watt (compare the hairline with his wedding portrait).

The process of helping Oswald to find his footing in his new surroundings was greatly assisted by his entry into some of Sydney's most important social groups. By November, for instance, he was already a member of the Royal Sydney Yacht Squadron, having acquired ownership of a 5-ton cutter called *Freda*.[8] He had also gained membership of the Union Club, which then occupied premises in Bligh Street. Founded in 1857, it was one of Sydney's oldest gentlemen's clubs and provided access to New South Wales' social and business elite. This was an important network of influence, reflecting a world of private incomes and interlocking families where participation in the life of the club frequently passed from generation to generation. Such was certainly true in Oswald's case, since he was following his father, his uncle Walter Cumming Watt, and brothers Willie and Ernest.[9] Over the next 20 years the club would come to fill a special place in Oswald's life, at times serving virtually as his second home.

The Union Club's original premises in Bligh Street prior to construction of a new clubhouse in Bent Street in the late 1950s.

From the moment that the Watt brothers stepped off the boat in Sydney, they were left in no doubt that New South Wales was in a distinctly martial mood. In October 1899, while they were still finalising their travel arrangements in England, a war had started in South Africa between Britain and the twin republics founded along the Vaal River by Dutch farmers known as 'boers'. The local papers were full of news of the opening engagements of the conflict, and about the contingents of troops that all the Australian colonies were raising to fight alongside British regulars to help subdue the improvised Boer armies intent on defending their sovereignty.

In a rush of imperial patriotism, it may have occurred to the brothers to offer their services, too, but in those early days the preference of recruitment authorities was for men with prior military training, or "bushmen" who combined horsemanship with familiarity of the rigours likely to be encountered on the veldt (the African equivalent of the Australian outback). For the time being, the brothers were content with each contributing £50 in February to the public subscription being collected for the 1st Bushmen Regiment, the first contingent raised through general enlistment which was preparing to leave the colony.[10]

While William and Ernest soon had other considerations to take into account, the idea of donning army uniform in some capacity stayed with Oswald. After sitting an examination at Sydney's Victoria Barracks to first qualify for commissioned rank, he was appointed to the military forces of New South Wales on 30 April 1900 as a Second Lieutenant, on probation, in the Fifth (Volunteer) Infantry Regiment (Scottish Rifles).[11] This was—as its "volunteer" status implied—an unpaid, part-time component of the colony's forces, which contained few full-time troops and a much larger number of partially-paid militia. The 650-strong Scottish Rifles was one of three "national" corps that existed (the others being the English Rifles and Irish Rifles), its members drawn from men who were Scottish-born or Australian-born of Scottish descent or extraction.[12]

The Scottish Rifles was a socially-exclusive entity in other ways too, since its members were men who could afford time away from employment to undertake military training, even though commitments of this sort were less than for the militia—usually comprising an encampment over the Easter holidays. Although the equipment, arms and ammunition of volunteer regiments were sponsored by the government, the officers had to possess sufficient means to buy their own uniforms and kit, which in the case of the Scottish Rifles entailed kilts and other expensive regalia. This meant, in effect, that the corps Oswald Watt was joining was as much a social organisation as the Union Club, its ranks filled with some of the best and influential names of Sydney society.

Oswald's accession to the officer list of the Scottish Rifles may not have been as uncontrived as might first appear, as its timing could not have been more fortunate. Even as the Watt brothers reached Sydney in January, rumours had been circulating that the Governor of New South Wales, the 27-year-old Earl Beauchamp, wished to retire at the end of the year—despite having taken up the vice-regal post only in May 1899. In August the premier confirmed the rumour, announcing that Lord Beauchamp would leave early in December, and the government would take its time before giving consideration to a successor.

In the event, the Earl brought forward his departure by more than a month, taking extended leave immediately after a farewell levee was held at Government House on 1 November.[13] In accordance with accepted practice, a brief ceremony was arranged the following day to swear-in the colony's lieutenant-governor, Chief Justice Sir Frederick Darley, to exercise the powers of governor during the absence of the formal holder of that office. Newspaper accounts of Darley's swearing-in also reported the first appointments to his staff. These included his son Harry, a probationary Second Lieutenant in the NSW Lancers, and Second Lieutenant Oswald Watt. Both became 'extra' (meaning unpaid) aides-de-camp and were granted honorary rank of Captain.[14]

It clearly had not hurt Oswald's chances of preferment for this post that he had grown up next to the Darleys while living at Eynesbury, a period in which the Darley children had been his playmates. He was wearing the rank of Captain exactly six months after receiving his first army commission, although it would be another five years before he was promoted Lieutenant (on 21 March 1905) and finally substantively to Captain (20 September 1905).[15] Captain's rank would be the height of Oswald's advancement through the officer grades before he ceased to have an active connection to the military forces in January 1908,[16] but it was a title that he carried with pride for many years beyond that.

It so happened that Oswald was not in Sydney for the announcement of his appointment as ADC, having sailed the previous day for Melbourne with his brother William—most likely to attend the annual Victorian Spring Racing Carnival.[17] He was back in Sydney later that month, however, to take up his new duties at Government House. When Lady Darley held a garden party on 27 November, the newspapers reported that Captain Darley and Oswald were on hand and 'assiduous in their courteous attentions to all comers'.[18] Watt would have looked resplendent in his kilted uniform, although his was not the only splash of tartan on display that day, as the band of the Scottish Rifles provided part of the afternoon's musical entertainment.

Four days later, when Lady Darley and her youngest daughter Sylvia departed in the mail steamer *India* for a trip to England, Watt was also on board the ship—but booked to travel only as far as Adelaide.[19] Presumably his presence was meant to smooth the passage of the two women as they began their voyage, but it is not known who bore the expense of this gesture. If it was a cost from Watt's own pocket, this suggests that his possession of a private income was an important additional qualification for the role he now filled at Government House.

There were a number of calls on Watt's time to perform duties for the Lieutenant-Governor during 1901, but these were never so frequent or onerous as to become a burden. The chief benefit to Watt would have been the exposure he gained in circles concerned with running the now State of New South Wales in the newly-federated Commonwealth of Australia. Attending Sir Frederick Darley during formal occasions, such as the opening of the Royal Agricultural Society's show or the first day of the Australian Jockey Club's spring racing meeting, would have provided little opportunity to actually meet the dignitaries who were present—but the eyes of the public were certainly upon him at such occasions. There was more opportunity to mix and be noticed when Darley entertained a large group of members of parliament to dinner at his private residence, Quambi, in July, at which Captain Watt was recorded as being present too.[20]

Sir Frederick Darley, lieutenant-governor of New South Wales, watches the arrival of new Governor-General Lord Hopetoun in Farm Cove from the front gate of Government House, 15 December 1900. He is flanked by his aides-de-camp, son Captain Harry Darley (left) and Oswald Watt (right). (State Library of NSW, a2879020u)

Exposure of a different kind came on several occasions when one of the Darley daughters represented their father (or mother) at official functions before largely female gatherings, and Watt went along in tow. While Miss Darley made a presentation to the wife of the departing Lord Mayor in March,[21] or next month opened the Home for Working Gentlewomen,[22] it can be imagined that many of the matrons present were assessing the young, handsome and wealthy ADC as potential husband material for their unwed daughters. Equally, when Senator Albert Gould and his wife gave an "at home" in July to welcome back their son Clarence from the war in South Africa, it was likely that Oswald owed his presence as a guest as much to his new-found military status as to the fact that Eynesbury had been his childhood home.[23]

Probably more to Watt's liking was the duty he was tasked to perform in November, when Sydney received a visit from Major General Sir Hector ("Fighting Mac") Macdonald—one of Britain's most celebrated soldiers who had risen through the ranks during more than 20 years of military campaigns, most recently in South Africa. From the moment this hero of the empire stepped ashore at the Sussex Street wharf on 7 November, Watt acted as the general's aide—accompanying him to a reception organised in the visitor's honour at the Town Hall, then to Quambi to call on Sir Frederick Darley. Watt would almost certainly have been involved in the parade of the Scottish Rifles mounted at Bellevue Hill two days later, and also the citizens' dinner on 11 November at the Town Hall when the general was escorted into the hall by a regimental band of pipers and received a further guard of honour from the Scottish Rifles.[24]

As the year 1901 came to a conclusion, it had become obvious that the name of 'Captain Oswald Watt' was now well-recognised in the social columns of Sydney's newspapers. In late November about 60 young people enjoyed a small dance given by the widow of Sydney Burdekin, at her residence in Macquarie Street. It was reported that: 'During the evening Miss Burdekin and Captain Oswald Watt danced a cake-walk, which created great amusement.'[25] A few nights later, when a new musical comedy called "Floradora" opened at the Theatre Royal, it was thought noteworthy that Captain Oswald Watt was among the audience.[26]

The Judge's daughter

In the last days of December 1901 Sir Frederick Darley became seriously ill.[27] He had already indicated that he was contemplating retirement from the judiciary the previous September,[28] but now that it became questionable whether he could continue as Lieutenant-Governor moves were quickly put in train to formally appoint a successor to Lord Beauchamp. On 29 January 1902 it was announced that Vice-Admiral Sir Harry Rawson would become the 21st Governor of New South Wales, although it was nearly another four months before the admiral and his wife arrived in Sydney to take up the post.

Until Admiral Rawson's swearing-in on 27 May, Sir Frederick Darley struggled on with performing his vice-regal duties. In March, for example, when the Lieutenant-Governor made a special trip into the city from "Lilianfels" (his summer residence at Katoomba in the Blue Mountains) expressly to open the Easter show, this was his first public appearance since his illness began. Both Oswald Watt and Harry Darley were in attendance as ADCs when Sir Frederick was driven into the grounds and taken to the grandstand enclosure for a formal reception.[29]

Exactly a month after Sir Harry Rawson became Governor, it was announced that Honorary Captains W. O. Watt and H. S. Darley were appointed as extra ADCs on his staff—that is, to continue in the same capacity as they had served under Sir Frederick Darley.[30] To all outward appearances, Oswald's life seemed set to remain unchanged from the previous 18 months, except that in the meantime there had been a major development in his personal life: two weeks before the Rawson swearing-in, Oswald had become engaged to be married.[31]

The young lady upon whom Watt had set his sights was Muriel Maud Williams, aged two years younger than him, who was apparently visiting from Melbourne and staying with friends while enjoying the social season following the Australian Jockey Club's autumn racing festival. The first known occasion when their paths may have crossed was the opening day at Randwick on Saturday, 29 March,[32] followed by the second day's racing (on Easter Monday)—at both of which 'Miss Muriel Williams (Melbourne)' was reported as attending, while Captain O. Watt was present in the vice-regal box with members of the Darley family (though not the Governor).[33]

Other opportunities soon followed. On 3 April, Mr G. Skelton Yuill gave a dance in the Paddington Town Hall for about 200 people, with the names of Captain Watt and Miss Muriel Williams both appearing separately on the guest list.[34] What is clear is that this was no protracted romance. If their first meeting was about the end of March/start of April, then the engagement followed barely six weeks later.

The announcement of their intention to marry was viewed with surprise in many quarters. The social columnist for the *Bendigo Advertiser* put this down to the fact that 'the young lady has had many admirers' in the past, but apparently without being tempted by any of her suitors. Considered 'the most prominent' of Victoria's 'beauties', it was said that 'she has a certain dashing style, at times approaching the outré', and was 'tall and generously proportioned, too.' The 'bridegroom-elect' was approvingly described as 'rich', 'of the upper crust', and 'an old Cambridge man'.[35]

Watt's suitability as a partner for Miss Williams would have been—for many observers—the more significant factor in the equation, for the future bride held no lack of certainty about her own standing in the social stakes. She was the second daughter of Sir Hartley Williams, the senior puisne judge of the Victorian Supreme Court, who equally had full confidence in the moral superiority of his position within Australian society. Melbourne-born but educated in England, including at Oxford, he had practised at the colonial Bar for 14 years until appointed to the Supreme Court bench in 1881, at age 38. Then the youngest judge in the colony, he had been prominent in legal circles ever since, and was knighted in 1894.[36]

Frustrated in his attempts to enter politics in 1874, Williams had nonetheless become equally prominent as a public speaker on a range of issues concerning religion and morality, and often drew criticism for his unorthodox views. A pamphlet he published in 1885 called *Religion Without Superstition* provoked a strong reply from Melbourne's Anglican bishop. Undeterred, he continued to lecture in Melbourne and country towns—some of these addresses being published as articles in the major newspapers and later in collected book form. One such collection titled *Addresses* appeared in 1902, but it was apparently articles on the subject of "Death and beyond", appearing in the *Argus* and *Age* in May and June that year, that caused another pamphleteer to rebut his views as 'antagonistic to Christian truth'.

Convinced of his own moral rectitude, Sir Hartley would accept an invitation to deliver a lecture for the Australian Natives' Association at Hamilton, in western Victoria, on 17 October 1902—not even a month after his daughter's wedding—on the subject of men, women and marriage. Still controversial, the judge argued that woman's character had been moulded by 'centuries of serfdom' and tended to develop 'qualities of deceit and guile'. Man, on the other hand, 'as the dominant power', had no occasion to resort to deceit and hence was more brutally straightforward. Sir Hartley hailed the enfranchisement of woman, saying that when she received the privilege of voting, her efforts would benefit the community by helping to suppress the great evils of drinking, gambling, and swearing:

He also dwelt upon the care and judgment which should be exercised in the selection of a partner for life, because upon the suitability of the union depended the happiness, not only of the parents, but also of their children.[37]

Sir Hartley Williams. (From *The Leader*, 14 Feb 1903)

Chapter 3

The truth of this prognosis, in the case of his own daughter, had yet to play out over ensuing years.

Until the day of the wedding, Oswald continued with his duties on the state Governor's staff. On 10 September he was at Sydney's central railway station for the arrival of Lord and Lady Tennyson, who were making an official visit from Melbourne. Previously Governor of South Australia, Lord Tennyson's visit was in his capacity as Acting Governor-General since July, and protocol required that the vice-regal couple be welcomed accordingly by a range of local dignitaries such the Premier, the principal under-secretary, and the state commandant. As Sir Harry Rawson was not present, Watt was there to represent the Governor of New South Wales.[38] Later that same day Lord Tennyson attended the races at Randwick, and again on 13 September for the final day of the Australian Jockey Club's spring meeting. Present on the latter occasion was Admiral Rawson and his daughter, attended by Captain Watt as ADC.[39]

A fortnight later Watt was preparing for his wedding. The ceremony took place on Saturday, 27 September, in the highly-fashionable St John's Anglican Church in Toorak Road, Melbourne, performed by the Reverend C. E. Drought (the incumbent) assisted by the Reverend Saumarez Smith from Sydney, in the presence of a large number of guests and spectators. Predictably, it was a memorable society event which attracted huge public interest, as evidenced by the amount of column inches of newsprint expended in describing it to readers.[40]

Not just every detail of the bride's 'exquisite gown' was reported, but those of the two little girls holding the brocade court train, the seven other bridesmaids 'daintily gowned to represent the morning and evening primroses', and the floral decorations arranged inside the church by the bride's female friends. As the social columnist for the *Bendigo Advertiser* observed, Muriel Williams was 'as much noted for her originality and chic as her beauty', with the result that 'it was as original as a wedding could be'.[41]

Wedding portraits of Muriel and Oswald Watt. (From *The Australasian*, 27 Sep 1902)

With so much attention focused on the bride, it was only incidentally noted that Oswald's brother William was best man, and Tom Gilchrist from Sydney one of the groomsmen. Because of the large number of bridesmaids, it was commented that Oswald had obviously felt the need to establish some balance to the wedding party by naming additional groomsmen—although 'someone remarked that the bridegroom showed a little nervous anxiety in having so many friends to attend him'.[42]

After the ceremony a reception was held at "Flete", the Italianate-style mansion of Sir Hartley and Lady Williams in Boundary Road, Malvern, for a large party of guests which included the Chief Justice Sir John Madden and Lady Madden, the state commandant Brigadier General and Mrs Gordon, and Oswald's uncle Walter Watt from

Sydney. A wedding tea was served in a large marquee erected on the lawn. No speeches were made during the tea, but there was a slight departure from tradition when Sir Hartley Williams asked the guests to drink the health of the bride and bridegroom.[43]

Newspaper accounts of the occasion noted that the wedding gifts received were 'numerous and valuable', including several from important figures unable to be present in person. Among these were a handsome cut glass and silver tantulus from Sir Harry and Lady Rawson, a silver pencil from Miss Rawson, an opal pin from Lord and Lady Tennyson, and a travelling clock from the Governor of Victoria, Sir George Clarke, and Lady Clarke.[44] One of the most beautiful presents was reportedly a diamond and ruby pendant from the bride's grandmother in England.[45]

Later in the afternoon Watt and his bride left for a honeymoon at Flinders, a seaside holiday village on the western side of the entrance to Western Port Bay. Muriel's travelling gown was described as a 'dainty confection' of tussore silk trimmed with applique point de gaze lace, worn with a large picture hat of biscuit-coloured Tuscan straw that was draped with a lace scarf and defined at the brim by a band of black velvet. While waiting for bride and bridegroom to depart, Mr. Walter King sang "The World of Praise" in the drawing room.[46]

The arrival of Oswald and Muriel Watt in Sydney after their honeymoon coincided with the triumphal first return to Australia of the famous lyric soprano formerly known as Mrs Helen ("Nellie") Armstrong, who now used the stage name 'Madame Melba'. (Another 16 years were to pass before she became better-known to her countrymen as 'Dame Nellie Melba'.) For her first Sydney concert, held in the Town Hall on 11 October, 'Captain and Mrs. Oswald Watt' were noticed as sitting amid the vast audience which attended, rather than with the vice-regal party, which occupied specially reserved seats on the orchestral platform.[47] But when Admiral Rawson entertained the singer at a dinner at Government House two nights later, the Watts were among the guests who were specially invited to meet her.[48]

A few days later—on Friday, 17 October—the mayor and mayoress hosted a reception at the Town Hall in honour of Melba, and again the

Watts were among the 'brilliant assemblage' reported as present.[49] Two weeks later, on 23 October, the 'famous diva' herself entertained guests at supper at the Hotel Australia, following her last Sydney concert, and once more the Watt couple were on the select guest list.[50]

On 25 October the Watts boarded the London-bound mail steamer *Omrah*, but were booked only as far as Melbourne.[51] They were heading south to enjoy the festivities associated with 'Cup Week'. These kicked off on the Monday before the running of the Melbourne Cup, with a dance for more than 500 guests given by Lord and Lady Tennyson at State Government House (then "Stonnington" mansion in Malvern), at which Muriel garnered much attention by again wearing her wedding gown.[52] The gowns she wore the next day at the races, and at a garden party on the afternoon of 5 November (at Stonnington), and also a reception the next day (Stonnington again), were all faithfully reported in the social pages.[53] 'Mrs. Oswald Watt' had undoubtedly arrived on the Australian social scene.

Oswald and Muriel returned to Sydney, but barely a week later were again on board a mail steamer departing Australia. When the P&O ship *Oceana* sailed on 15 November, this carried both 'Captain and Mrs. Oswald Watt', and maid, bound for 'Colombo and Indian ports'.[54] As foreshadowed at the time of his marriage, Oswald was beginning 18 months' leave of absence from Sir Harry Rawson and taking his new wife to India, Cairo, England and Europe, then home to Sydney via America.[55] Even as their ship left Australian waters on 24 November 1902, his brother Ernest and wife Annie were expected back in Sydney in another P&O vessel, the *Oroya*.

Among the social elite

Practically nothing is known about the eighteen months that Oswald and Muriel Watt were away from Australia after their marriage, apart from the statements they made about their intended plans before they left. Almost certainly they would have spent part of their time in England with members of Muriel's family, including her parents who had retired to London to live after Sir Hartley Williams resigned from the Victorian Bench in May 1903.

Not just Muriel's father, but her stepmother also, had family members already living in England, and presumably some time would have been devoted to introducing Oswald to these newly-acquired relatives—many of whom Muriel would have last met in 1900, while her father was on an 11-month holiday for medical rest. Oswald's three sisters were also still living in England and Scotland, including Elinor (who had remarried in September 1902, after her divorce the previous year, and was now the wife of Major Henry Bethune of Cupar, Fifeshire), so he was probably keen to introduce Muriel to them as well.

Some commentators, noting that Oswald received a Master of Arts degree from his old university in 1904, have assumed he must have also undertaken further study at Cambridge during this period. But university rules allowed the Cambridge MA to be automatically conferred on graduates who applied, providing that at least two years had elapsed since they received their Bachelor degree, so the likelihood is that he would have only briefly visited Cambridge—if he went there at all.

One further reminder of their time in England is known to have existed in the form of a portrait of Muriel painted by a London artist named Frank S. Eastman (1878-1964). Although still at the start of a long painting career, Eastman had already been exhibiting at the Royal Academy of Arts for two years, and when the Academy's 1904 exhibition opened in May his portrait of "Mrs W. Oswald Watt" was among two works that he had on display.[56] The present whereabouts of that portrait is unknown.

When the Watts returned from London in the *Himalaya* on 14 April 1904,[57] they initially took the lease on a property in Sydney to begin their first period of settled married life together. The house was "Arlington" in Edgecliff Road, Woollahra, vacated earlier that same month by Oswald's brother Ernest when he went off to England again with his wife and three-year-old daughter.[58]

Dating from 1870, Arlington was a large house with three reception rooms and four bedrooms on a block of land 'tastefully laid out in lawns, gardens and glasshouse'.[59] The property was ideal for a young couple keen to join Sydney's fashionable moneyed set, which was where Muriel aspired and felt herself entitled to be. At the time of their marriage in 1902, Oswald had made a generous transfer of property into Muriel's name as a trust intended to provide for her personal needs for the rest of her life.[60] The income she received was sufficient to enable her to employ a maid and keep up with the latest fashion styles in clothes, and maintain a conspicuous position within high society in both Sydney and Melbourne.

Three weeks after their return, the Watts were at State Government House (Cranbrook, at Rose Bay) dining in distinguished company which included a visitor to Sydney, Lord Monk Bretton.[61] The Governor, Sir Harry Rawson, was attended by Captain Leslie Wilson (wearing a Distinguished Service Order won in South Africa), his aide-de-camp since mid-1903, which probably signified to Oswald that his services as an extra equerry were no longer required and he was not expected to resume a role on the governor's staff immediately.

A fortnight later Muriel was recorded as attending a ball in the Melbourne Town Hall on 25 May, in aid of the Homeopathic Hospital, while visiting the southern capital.[62] She was back in Sydney at the end of the month, however, in time to accompany Oswald to another ball at Paddington Town Hall attended by both the Governor-General and State Governor.[63] From these beginnings, the pace of the Watts' participation—as a couple—in the social life of Sydney began to build at giddying speed within a short time. Their attendance at grand and glittering occasions was increasingly reported by the press, with the result that their names seemed rarely out of the news during the months that followed.

Balls (official, charity and private), garden fetes and parties, "at homes" and dances in the houses of the rich and famous—all clamoured for position in the Watts' crowded social calendar. These occasions invariably gave Muriel scope to show off her fashion sense and expensive tastes, for satins, plisse chiffon, and 'glorious lace'.[64] The spring race meeting of the Australian Jockey Club at Randwick provided another unparalleled platform to shine in public, which Muriel duly seized by turning up in a black velvet dress with a black picture hat trimmed with white feathers and a white feather boa.[65]

By November it was reported in the press that the Watts were preparing to escape the anticipated summer heat of Sydney by repairing to the southern highlands, where they had taken the lease on the "The Grange" at Sutton Forest, 'the pretty home which belonged to the late Mr. William Laidley'.[66] This choice of holiday spot perfectly positioned Oswald and Muriel to join in the gaiety of the annual Bong Bong picnic races (outside Moss Vale) late in January 1905. Again, Muriel stole the limelight by attending the racing in 'soft pale green floral taffeta voile…worn with a green mushroom hat', and the ball that marked the end of the meeting wearing 'pale blue satin, trimmed with cream lace, and a large bouquet of red roses on the bodice'.[67]

Following the couple's return to Sydney, Oswald and Muriel went separate ways for several weeks. While Oswald headed north to Queensland in March, making a tour of the Strathmore and Woodhouse properties in the Bowen River District of which he was part-owner or stakeholder,[68] Muriel went south to her home town where she made her presence felt in Toorak and claimed some more space in the social pages.[69]

Sometime before mid-1905 a signal was received that the Oswald Watts' participation in the Sydney social scene was about to change, when it was learnt that Muriel was expecting their first child. They continued on as before for several months, even attending a performance of the "Mikado" at the Theatre Royal in July, but by September Oswald was attending functions on his own. The baby, a boy they named James Oswald, was born at Arlington on 11 October, and thereafter the couple's lifestyle became very different.[70]

Perhaps it was the impending birth which prompted Oswald to want to make a home for his family outside Sydney, deciding that he had had enough of the city's mad social whirl. Perhaps he was simply inspired by ideas about the idyllic quality of country life such as he would have encountered in Britain. What is certain is that in late May 1905 reports appeared in the press that he had bought the Wivenhoe Estate (just past Narellan travelling west from Campbelltown, on Sydney's south-western outskirts) for £10,000, and that he intended to make this his permanent residence.[71]

The estate covered over 900 acres and included a two-storey Georgian stone villa dating from the late 1830s, sitting in park-like landscaped grounds on a ridge overlooking the Camden Valley and the village of Cobbitty. Believed to be the work of colonial architect John Verge, the house was originally built for Charles Cowper, five times premier of New South Wales between 1856 and 1870, and which served as his country seat. In 1875 Wivenhoe passed into the ownership of Henry Arding Thomas, and after his death in 1884 the house remained the home of his widow Caroline, until her death at Neutral Bay, Sydney, in January 1903 when the property came up for sale.[72]

Because so little change had occurred at Wivenhoe over the previous three decades, Oswald decided that a rebuilding program was necessary to modernise the house before it would be suitable for his wife and the child they were then expecting. He engaged Sydney architect J. W. Manson to draw up plans, not just for alterations to the interior of the house (including a replacement staircase, internal bathrooms and built-in wardrobes), but for major additions in the form of a new west wing, a conservatory, and enlarged servant quarters.[73]

Until construction at Wivenhoe was finished, around the middle of 1906, Oswald and Muriel maintained Arlington as their home. Five weeks after the birth of baby James, Muriel was back on the social circuit once more and the Watts resumed the high lifestyle they had previously enjoyed. On 18 November it was reported in the press that Mrs Oswald Watt was among the women 'noticed' at a review held in Centennial Park earlier that day, induced by the 'fine, cool and bright weather … to wear their smartest gowns'.[74]

A week later the Oswald Watts were at Randwick for a 'complimentary meeting' arranged by the AJC in honour of the Earl of Jersey, a former Governor of New South Wales (1890-93) who was visiting Australia. Muriel must have been thrilled to be noticed in the vice-regal box—in company with Lord and Lady Chelmsford (newly-appointed to Government House in Brisbane), and several members of the Darley family—in a gown of soft rose pink tussore silk, worn with a honey-coloured straw hat with pink roses and a pale blue ribbon.[75]

Once more the invitations and social engagements began to mount, for dinner parties and luncheons at State Government House and Quambi, first nights at the theatre, and functions on board warships of the locally-based British squadron and visiting navies. At the year's end Oswald and Muriel again headed to the relative coolness of the highlands at Sutton Forest, and in January 1906 enjoyed the fun of the Bong Bong races.[76]

By April it was reported that the Watts had left The Grange at Sutton Forest 'and are in town for the Easter gaieties'.[77] This placed them at the epicentre of the virtual storm of activities that were unleashed in Sydney that month, beginning with the opening of the AJC autumn carnival at Randwick on the 14th when Muriel blitzed the fashion field wearing an oyster white cloth coat and skirt, a white panne hat trimmed with long feathers, and a white fox fur stole.[78]

Oswald was also at the racing on this and subsequent days—on the 16th in company with brother Willie (who had just returned from London in the *Orotava* ten days earlier)[79]—but seemed lucky to be even mentioned in the newspaper columns under 'attendance'. Muriel garnered the bulk of the attention, on the third day of the meeting (18 April) turning out in 'pale blue crepe-de-chine, with a black picture hat.'[80] On the concluding day her outfit consisted of 'white cloth with a wine-coloured hat trimmed with shaded roses, and a set of beautiful white furs.'[81]

It was at this juncture that Oswald and Muriel gave an entertainment of their own, hosting a small dance at Arlington on the evening of 26 April. According to newspaper accounts of the occasion, the host and hostess received their guests in the drawing-room, which was beautifully decorated with pink and white chrysanthemums. 'Mrs. Watt looked remarkably well in a dress of black chiffon velvet, with deep lace bertha and diamond ornaments.' Perhaps reflecting the space limitations of Arlington, dancing took place in the large school hall next door at "Shirley" (which was lent by the two ladies who ran the school)—the passage-way between the two houses being carpeted and illuminated with Chinese lanterns. The guest list included names such as Fairfax, Allen, Knox, Dangar, Suttor, along with several British and American naval officers.[82]

Over the course of the next three months, things continued much as before. When the Watts made a noteworthy appearance on Empire Day (24 May) at a full dress reception at Federal Government House (the former State Governor's residence), one admiring social columnist reported that Mrs Oswald Watt 'looked as beautiful as she always does, in rose pink taffeta, her pretty dark hair having quaint becoming twists of rose pink chiffon velours.'[83]

On the last evening of May, the couple attended 'another pleasant little dance' on board HMS *Powerful* for about 100 guests. Once again Muriel 'challenged admiration' when she turned up in a handsome sunray-pleated gown of blue crepe de chine, 'the skirt edged with a deep band of chiffon velours, the entire bodice being of blue chiffon finished with a deep bunch of brown roses'. Not only was this described as 'one of the handsomest dresses seen', Muriel must have been thrilled to see it reported as 'worn by one of our beauties, Mrs. Oswald Watt.'[84]

Next month began with a dance given by Oswald's older brother Willie on 4 June. This event was held at "Larissa"—a house in Nelson Street, Woollahra, that belonged to the Watt Estate and had been recently done up—and was intended as a 'farewell to friends' before Willie left on a holiday to Africa two days later. Both Oswald and Muriel attended, with Muriel assisting Willie in receiving his guests.[85] The day after Willie's departure, Oswald attended a dinner of the New South Wales Masonic Club as ADC to the Governor, Sir Harry Rawson, and afterwards also at a ball in Paddington Town Hall in aid of the Homeopathic Hospital; these appear to be the first occasions on which he had returned to duty on the governor's staff.[86]

After further balls and shipboard dances, by late July Oswald and Muriel were 'among others' reported to be in Melbourne 'enjoying a round of social festivities'.[87] This visit south almost seems to have been a "last hurrah" before beginning their new lifestyle in the recently-renovated house at Wivenhoe, it being reported in mid-August that Arlington had just been let to Mr. and Mrs. James Marks now that the Watts' new home at Camden was completed.[88]

Squire of Wivenhoe

When Oswald and Muriel moved into the house at Wivenhoe about the middle of 1906, it must have seemed that they were embarking on a very different if not entirely new lifestyle. In his biography of Charles Cowper, historian Alan Powell remarked that—when not engaged in the hurly-burly of colonial politics in Sydney in the mid-nineteenth century—Cowper liked to play the country squire on the estate.[89] As Oswald reputedly spent £10,000 over and above the original purchase price in remodelling the house,[90] it might have seemed that he had something more in mind than simply using the property as an occasional rural retreat from a hectic social calendar.

The house at Wivenhoe following completion of Oswald Watt's renovations—conservatory on left, new west wing visible at right.

Within a short interval after taking up residence, however, it became apparent that very little about the Watts' lifestyle had really changed, since they were frequently away from Wivenhoe for sometimes weeks at a stretch. For example, once the week-long AJC spring racing carnival began at the end of September, Oswald and Muriel departed for Sydney to take part in the range of associated festivities that lasted well into October—not just the racing at Randwick, but balls, vice-regal garden parties, and other sundry entertainments.

At the end of October, the Watts boarded the steamer *Orontes* and joined 'quite an exodus of Sydney people' heading south for the Melbourne Cup.[91] Again, it was not just the racing that brought them to the Victorian capital, but the variety of other events held in conjunction with Cup Week, such as the 'great annual ball' given by the Governor-General. As always, these were occasions for Muriel to show off her expensive fashion tastes which invariably earned her special mention in social columns back in Sydney. Even after they had returned late in November, the Watts stayed in Sydney rather than went back to Wivenhoe since they were noted among the crowds attending the first performances of a new stage play at the Criterion Theatre.[92]

The pattern of absences from Camden begun in 1906 soon re-asserted itself in the new year. In late February 1907 Oswald and Muriel sailed from Sydney on a visit to Melbourne. Their ship, again *Orontes*, was making a round trip to Hobart, taking pleasure-seekers on a cruise timed for the start of Tasmania's apple harvest.[93] In the event it appears that the Watts—Muriel, at least—were in no rush to head back home; it was reported that on 1 March Muriel attended a dance at "Homeden", the Toorak mansion belonging to Justice Henry Hodges, a former colleague of her father's on the Victorian Supreme Court bench.[94]

A month later, both Oswald and Muriel were back in Sydney to join in the usual 'festivities' associated with Easter; the mere fact that the Watts were staying in the city rated mention in the social pages.[95] During the first ten days of April, the couple attended the AJC races at Randwick, the usual Government House ball, and the opening night of a new play at the Theatre Royal. On 9 April they were among the invited guests at the jubilee ball given by the Union Club at the Sydney Town Hall.[96] Amid everything else that was happening over Easter, Oswald somehow managed to find time to attend the annual training camp of his volunteer regiment, the Scottish Rifles.

Officers of the NSW Scottish Rifles Regiment at the 1907 Easter camp. Captain Watt is sitting first left; seated second from right is Captain Henry MacLaurin.

During the last weeks of May, the Watts were again in Sydney attending the opera season at the Theatre Royal.[97] There then followed a period of nearly two months when they dropped from public view, presumably spent for the most part quietly at Wivenhoe. By late July, however, they were again in the public spotlight in Sydney, attending a dinner party at Cranbrook on the 21st,[98] and on the 26th the annual ball of the 1st Regiment of the Scottish Rifles at Paddington Town Hall. As there was a record attendance of over 400, with many of the men present in Highland dress, the scene was described as 'colourful' and 'most brilliant'. For once, Muriel found herself facing tough competition, despite wearing black glace silk with 'overdress of silk net and jet', and touches of black chiffon velvet.[99]

Still the Watts stayed in Sydney, apparently uninterested in returning home to Wivenhoe. On 25 July the city had acquired a new entertainment attraction in the form of an ice skating rink called the Glaciarium. Sydney's rink was actually Australia's third, after similar ones opened in Adelaide and Melbourne, but the new centre was the biggest and grandest, operating in a huge shed-like structure set behind buildings fronting onto George Street West. The novelty of skating quickly established the Glaciarium as a favourite resort of the society set, with the Governor's daughter becoming a frequent visitor during its first week. Oswald and Muriel were among others noticed in attendance soon after the opening.[100]

On 1 August the Watts were participants in one of the most memorable charity events which Sydney had seen in a long time. The Palace Theatre was the scene for a 'packed-out' amateur theatrical entertainment in aid of the District Nursing Association, 'undertaken by well-known society people, who have generously given their time and services',[101] and for which almost every 'society beauty girl' had been roped in. The program consisted of a "duologue" and a short original farce—both directed by Captain Leslie Wilson, the aide-de-camp to the Governor (who was in the audience and 'laughed as heartily as anyone')—and a set of "tableaux vivants" in which well-known artworks were brought to life within large golden frames set up on the stage.[102]

The final item on the program was a skit that served as an advertisement for Schweppes fizzy soda water, presented by Oswald and Muriel. Their performance, according to accounts, 'received almost an ovation; it was so clever'.[103] More importantly, it added five guineas (donated by Schweppes, presumably) to the more than £250 raised for the designated charity through the evening's effort.[104] The precise form of the item is, unfortunately, nowhere further described. Sydney had become the site of Schweppes' first overseas factory when the company expanded outside England in 1877, and by the early 1900s Schweppes waters and fruit juice cordials were to be found in all the leading hotels throughout Australia, so the audience at the Palace would have readily appreciated the humour of the gag presented to them—but where the inspiration for the skit had come from remains unknown. Perhaps it was based on something the Watts had seen performed onstage during their visit to England.

Only after their minor stage triumph were the Watts seemingly interested in returning to Wivenhoe—if simply because Muriel's sister Edith, the wife of William Pomeroy ("Roy") Greene (owner of the "Greystones" pastoral estate near Bacchus Marsh, west of Melbourne), was coming to stay with them.[105] By early September the couple were back in their Sydney playground once more, on the 3rd attending a dance given by the captain of the flagship HMS *Powerful*,[106] and next day attending a garden party for 200 people given at Admiralty House, Kirribilli, by Vice-Admiral Sir Wilmot and Lady Fawkes.[107]

By 6 September Oswald and Muriel were home again at Wivenhoe, in time to receive a party of visitors who travelled out from Sydney in a chauffeur-driven motor car belonging to wealthy lawyer Arthur Allen.[108] A fortnight later, however, they were back in Sydney for a skating party at the Glaciarium hosted by Mrs J. O. Fairfax for over 200 of her nearest and dearest friends, including Sir Frederick and Lady Darley.[109] The next day, 18 September, the couple attended the Darlinghurst wedding of Helen Gilchrist, the eldest daughter of a former business partner of Oswald's father.[110]

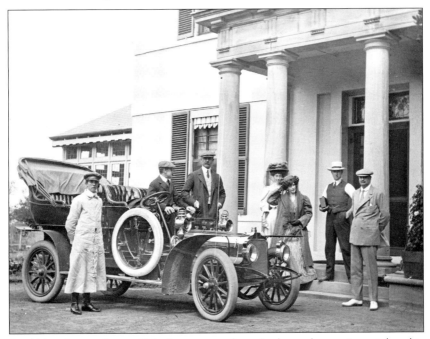

Oswald (standing top of steps, with book or camera under arm) welcomes the motoring party brought to Wivenhoe by Arthur Allen on 8 September 1907. In the group were Harry Darley (far right) and Oswald's brother Willie (sitting in front passenger's seat). (State Library of NSW, a2883025u)

The arrival of October brought a crush of social engagements in Sydney that, while in some respects was quite usual for the Watts at this time of year, was even heavier than previously. The fun began with the AJC spring meeting that commenced on the 5th. Late on the afternoon of 9 October, following the third day's races at Randwick, Oswald was one of ten gentlemen who hosted a party at the Glaciarium for 200 guests.[111] After the skating, Oswald and Muriel took 'a large and fashionable gathering' of friends to dinner at the Australia Hotel, and later on to the Tivoli Theatre.[112] On the 10th they attended a garden party at State Government House for nearly 2000 people; the size of this gathering was probably behind Oswald being asked to assist—once more, it seems, as an extra ADC—with the reception of guests.[113] On the 11th Oswald and Muriel attended the race week ball hosted by the Australian Club in the Town Hall.[114]

The scale and pace of commitments in the couple's social calendar may well have been what prompted Oswald to make the momentous decision about this time to become the owner of a motor car. That he did so there is no doubting, because pictorial evidence exists showing that on 13 October he drove what appears to be a De Dion-Bouton to Sunday luncheon at Arthur Allen's beachside holiday mansion "Moombara" at Lilli Pilli, overlooking the Port Hacking estuary, 26 kilometres south of Sydney. Captioned photos of the occasion record that eight to ten cars brought most of the revellers to Port Hacking, and 38 people sat down to eat at 1 p.m. The host noted that Oswald's car was 'the only one that came to grief, delaying his party for about two hours'.[115] Whether Oswald and Muriel drove from Wivenhoe or Sydney is unknown.

Ten days later, Oswald's skills as a driver were employed in support of a charity event in Sydney, a "children's bazaar" aimed at raising funds for the Royal Alexandra Hospital. The afternoon fete was held in the grounds of the Darlinghurst home of Dr and Mrs Arthur Cox, and among the amusements offered the many children who attended (and their paying parents) was a choice of pony rides or the chance to take a ride around Potts Point in Oswald's motor car, for which he charged a small fee.[116]

There is, therefore, no question that during the second half of 1907 Oswald had joined the small but growing band of motorists in New South Wales. According to motoring journalist Pedr Davis, Oswald purchased his 8-horsepower De Dion-Bouton from a Sydney import agency known as the General Motor Company, which newspaper advertisements from the period show was trading from 16 Queen's Place (next to 57 Pitt Street). He clearly rejoiced in his purchase, and—unlike many of Australia's elite who bought cars but employed chauffeurs to do the driving—learnt to drive himself. This supposedly set the scene for a notable motoring feat claimed for him at this stage, but about which there remains considerable uncertainty.

Again according to Pedr Davis, it had actually been in early September 1907 that Oswald attempted a high speed dash by car from Sydney to Melbourne, having declared his intention to make the journey non-stop and in record time. Reportedly setting off from the GPO at 6 a.m. on the 2nd, carrying on board his entire fuel requirements for the trip in cans, and accompanied by an 18-year-old mechanic named Gerald de Lissa, Oswald supposedly arrived in Melbourne half an hour before midnight on 4 September—having covered the route in two days, 17 hours and 26 minutes. (It was not much of a record, in reality, because in January 1908 it was easily beaten by two Victorian drivers who planned on completing their run in under a day but ended up logging 25 hours and 40 minutes.[117]) Nonetheless, claimed Davis, it was Oswald Watt who had begun a 'craze' to create speed records for road travel within Australia.[118]

Unfortunately, the credibility of this tale suffers from the fact that—as recorded earlier—Oswald was otherwise occupied in Sydney on the crucial dates of 2-4 September, attending (with his wife) a dance on board HMS *Powerful* on the evening of 3 September, and a garden party at Admiralty House of the afternoon of 4 September. The chance discovery of a subsequent claim in a newspaper, that Muriel was among passengers booked to make the sea voyage from Sydney to Melbourne for Cup Week in November 1907, on her own[119] (a claim seemingly confounded by a subsequent report that Oswald apparently travelled with his wife),[120] at least opened the possibility that Davis' informant might have simply confused the month. But Oswald's confirmed presence at Flemington racecourse for VRC Derby Day on 2 November 1907[121] suggests that the dates of Oswald's alleged speed feat must be wrong apart from both day and month. As will be shown, later evidence suggests the story may actually be out by two years.

While enjoying the festivities of Cup Week that year, Oswald and Muriel did the usual thing of attending the Governor-General's Ball on 6 November.[122] Even after the running of the famous race on 9 November, however, they appeared in no rush to get back home. Instead, they seemed to be part of a group noticeably inclined to prolong their stay. As the correspondent for the *Town and Country Journal* observed more than a week later, Menzies Hotel was still thronged with people:

> Looking round the…scene at luncheon or dinner time…one saw various small parties at tables, and scattered here and there such well-known society people as Captain and Mrs. Oswald Watt…A good many of the Cup visitors seem unwilling to leave this gay city.[123]

Eventually, they did return home. In December Oswald was spotted among an enormous audience attending a concert in the Sydney Town Hall by the famous diva Madame Melba, then making another of her periodic return visits to Australia.[124] The Watts appeared to have their focus elsewhere than on their country estate outside Camden, and it almost seemed like Muriel was seizing any opportunity not to spend time there. In the lead-up to Christmas, *Town and Country Journal* even reported that the couple was planning to 'leave for Victoria this month, to spend the summer at Flinders, where they have taken a house.'[125]

The fizz fades

The significance of holidaying where Oswald and Muriel spent their honeymoon five years earlier is lost more than a century later, but it seems that the decision for what came next was taken about the beginning of 1908. Perhaps it was at Flinders that Muriel finally told her husband she was not happy at Wivenhoe and wanted to live in Sydney, thereby bringing into the open what had become patently obvious anyway. Possibly already knowing this, Oswald had initiated action to address what had become a serious rift between them.

On 8 January Captain Watt was placed onto the army's Unattached List of officers,[126] which might be seen as one indication that he was not planning to have active involvement with the Scottish Rifles for the foreseeable future. Two months later newspapers reported that the Watt family had booked passage to England with the intention of being away 'about a year'.[127] Leaving Sydney by train on 9 March, Oswald and Muriel, with Mrs Watt's maids and infant Jimmy, travelled to Melbourne and boarded S.S. *Geelong*; the steamer departed on 14 March, bound for London via Natal and Cape Town.[128]

Whatever beneficial effects that time away from Australia might have had within the Watt household were quickly cut short by news received soon after arrival in London, to the effect that Oswald's elder brother had died on 2 May, while himself en route to Britain.[129] According to Ernest Watt, Willie had contracted tropical fever while big-game hunting in Africa in 1906, and it was to a recurrence of this same malady while at sea in the *Himalaya* one day after leaving Colombo that he succumbed.[130] The problem created by Willie's death was that Oswald was an executor of his brother's will, and his presence was now urgently required back in Australia. Travelling by the *Moldavia*, the family arrived in Sydney on 2 July[131]—having been away less than four months.

When probate was granted on Willie's will, it was found that he had left a large estate finally valued at £131,032 (worth $13-15 million at today's values).[132] After making numerous bequests to relatives and employees, the will gave the ultimate residue of Willie's property to his brothers in equal shares.[133] No less importantly, however, a codicil enacted at Cape Town on 12 July 1906 had bequeathed Willie's share and interest in two New South Wales stations (Gunningrah and Dry Plains) to Ernest, but to Oswald had given Howlong Station in its entirety.[134] Oswald was now the owner of a large and valuable pastoral property, and in future years would describe his own occupation as 'grazier of Howlong, Carrathool'.

Under the terms of the will Ernest and Oswald were also to receive Willie's shares in the company Gilchrist, Watt & Sanderson Ltd, which had taken over the lucrative shipping business of Gilchrist Watt & Co soon after their father's death. Unfortunately, this bequest did not take account of an article in the company's partnership agreement that these shares had to be first offered to the other existing partners, William Gilchrist and their uncle Walter Watt. According to Ernest Watt, these two gentlemen 'insisted on their rights', with the result that J. B. Watt's two youngest sons were kept out of a business which their father had built up and which owed everything to him.[135]

At least the two brothers received the compensation of being made partners in Gilchrist Watt & Co at this time, officially from 1 July 1908,[136] as this ensured that when a similar situation arose a decade later they could not be again excluded in the same fashion. For Oswald, his newfound position in Gilchrist Watt & Co. also brought an invitation in September 1908 to join the Sydney board of directors of an insurance company, the Ocean Accident and Guarantee Corporation Ltd.[137] At last he had his feet on the first rungs of a business career.

The false-start created by Willie's death had, of course, done nothing to resolve what to do about Wivenhoe. What Oswald did next was to seek to build a grand new home for his family in Sydney. According to Ernest Watt, later during 1908 Oswald purchased an old mansion in Point Piper, overlooking Seven Shilling Beach off New South Head Road, and had it pulled down to make way for a new house.[138] The property involved was 'Buckhurst', built in the 1850s by Frederick Tooth (of the well-known family of Sydney brewers) and lastly the home of the widow of George Want (1820-1895) until her death in 1901.

The demolition of Buckhurst had no sooner been completed than Oswald and Muriel decided to resume their plan to go overseas. Whether this was inspired or influenced by the departure of the Darleys for London in January 1909 is another unknown—the Watts were present at Circular Quay on the 30th to witness the farewell presentation to the Chief Justice and his wife[139]—but what is definite is that by late February the first advertisements appeared advising 'Pastoralists, Professional Gentlemen, Stud Masters, Racehorse Owners, and those in search of a country estate', that Wivenhoe was for sale.[140]

Making one final fling on the Sydney social scene, on 6 March the Watts attended a performance of a revived musical farce called "The Dairymaids" that was enjoying a two-week season at Her Majesty's Theatre. Symbolising the gulf that now appeared to be separating the couple, it was noted in press reports that Muriel 'graced' one box in the company of a male friend, while another box 'claimed' her husband and another colleague.[141] Within days it was further reported that the couple, with Jimmy and a nurse, had boarded the P&O liner *Moldavia* at Circular Quay, ahead of its departure at noon on 10 March for London, via Hobart, Melbourne and usual ports of call.[142]

In fact, the newspaper reports were not strictly accurate, according to Ernest Watt. He later wrote that it was *him* who accompanied Muriel and little Jimmy in the *Moldavia* to Melbourne; Oswald, he said, 'went overland'[143]—presumably driving himself in a motor car, since it is not stated that he went by rail. Perhaps in these arrangements lies the true explanation for the story of Captain Watt's speed record for inter-city travel between Sydney and Melbourne supposedly accomplished in 1907. Oswald's overland dash may have had nothing to do with setting a record at all, but was determined solely by the need to reach Melbourne in time to board the *Moldavia* before it ended its stop-over at that port and resumed its voyage to London on 16 March.[144] It can only be guessed why Oswald needed to drive to Melbourne, but one possibility is that he was delivering his De Dion-Bouton to a new owner before departing the country.

Ernest Watt's account is of interest for several other reasons. First, he mentions that when he arrived back in Sydney from London early in March 1909 it was to discover that Oswald was on the point of leaving in the other direction. This he found 'most depressing', not simply because the brothers had seen little of each other in the previous ten years, but because he was dismayed to find that Oswald's marriage was in much the same state of discord as his own—Oswald and Muriel had, he declared, 'already decided that divorce was the only possible solution' to their situation.[145]

Again according to Ernest, the purchase of Wivenhoe seemed to be the focus of dissension in his brother's marriage, especially after Muriel decided that she preferred to live in Sydney rather than at Camden. But Oswald's attempt to assuage her with his plans for Buckhurst had proved no solution, because she evidently further decided she did not want to live in Sydney either. Even as Oswald made his final arrangements for departure overseas, he was trying to sub-divide the Buckhurst site to recover the money he had outlaid on purchasing that property's freehold title. 'By great good luck,' wrote Ernest later, 'he just got his money back in the end, but he had to wait some time before doing so.'[146]

As it happened, the date that Ernest boarded the *Moldavia* in Sydney, with Muriel and Jimmy, was the day that Wivenhoe was due to go to public auction.[147] Press reports that the Watts had already sold Wivenhoe, along with 'all their decorative bits of furniture', were quite wrong.[148] The auction on 10 March actually did not achieve a purchaser for the property, while the sale—also by auction—of surplus furniture and effects from Wivenhoe (all reportedly removed from "Fairlight", the house in Edgecliff Road, Woollahra, which the Watts had apparently rented while Oswald hatched his plans to redevelop Buckhurst) was not scheduled to take place until two days later.[149]

After arriving in England on 22 April, little is known about what the Watts got up to. They were certainly in London on 10 June, when Oswald and Muriel attended the Mayfair wedding of Captain Leslie Wilson (the former ADC to Sir Harry Rawson, during his recently-completed term as Governor of New South Wales).[150] Oswald, however, could still not forget the unfinished business remaining at Sydney. In September Wivenhoe was re-advertised, it now being reported that the owner was 'determined to realise' a sale and had instructed his agents 'to receive offers for the property, regardless of the cost to him.'[151] It was very likely anxiety over the state of his affairs in Australia which decided Oswald in November to return. He would travel on his own, however—Muriel was determined to stay in England.

Precisely when Oswald reached Sydney seems to have escaped the usual notice in the shipping columns, suggesting that he was happy to have slipped back in without attention. He was definitely in Sydney on 27 December, however, when press reports noted that he attended a dinner party at Paris House given by his brother Ernest to farewell a visiting British female novelist.[152] During January 1910 he was back in his usual haunts of days gone by, attending the Bong Bong picnic races and the AJC races at Randwick, again in company with Ernest.[153] The brothers were also seen together at Sydney theatre shows, living the life—as one columnist wrote—of 'young men with money to burn'.[154] Ernest would also later record that every Sunday he and Oswald took big parties (in 'three or four cars, and very often even more') to Cronulla, 'for the surf-bathing', and in the same period enjoyed small parties with friends including the *Bulletin* journalist John Dalley.[155]

After six months, Oswald was apparently ready to rejoin his wife in England. According to later statements by Muriel, her husband arrived back in London in May.[156] The month of his return was, however, more likely to have been June, because on 12 May Oswald and Ernest were both guests at the wedding in Sydney of Arthur Cunningham, who managed Strathmore Station in Queensland for Gilchrist, Watt & Co.[157]

Probably Oswald would have been happy to leave Sydney after this, because it seems that he had finally found a buyer to take Wivenhoe off his hands—although the sale was not finalised until 23 August.[158] The new owners were the Trustees of the Sisters of the Good Samaritan in Australia, who paid just £7000 (barely a third of the amount that Oswald had spent on the place) to turn the property into a new Mater Dei Orphanage. A century later Wivenhoe is still owned by the Catholic Church, maintained as an historic home with occasional use as a function venue.

Chapter Four
LEARNING TO FLY

Australia's first military pilot

Oswald and Muriel Watt were much smaller figures in the lofty and glittering social scene of the British capital than they were in Sydney and Melbourne, and they quickly disappeared from public view. Nothing appeared in newsprint about them or their activities until December 1910, when it was reported back in Australia that Oswald had attended the funeral of Sir Harry Rawson the previous month. The old admiral died in London on 3 November after an operation for appendicitis, barely 18 months after leaving office as Governor of New South Wales. When laid to rest five days later in Bracknell parish churchyard in Berkshire, both Oswald and Sir Harry's other ADC in Sydney, Captain Leslie Wilson, were among the mourners.[1] Since returning home Wilson had made two attempts to enter Parliament, both unsuccessful, but he would eventually forge a prominent political career before himself becoming a state governor in Australia (of Queensland) in 1932, for a record 14-year term.[2]

Next month Oswald took himself off to Egypt, returning to London shortly before Christmas. In February 1911 he took Muriel with him on a trip back to Cairo.[3] If this was a holiday intended to smooth over differences that had developed between them, it was apparently not successful. According to Muriel, she returned alone to London not long after they arrived and Oswald came back some time afterwards. Clearly, the strains in the Watt marriage were ongoing. When Ernest Watt arrived in London in March, he discovered that his brother had 'bought a very nice little house in Berkeley Square, No. 51, but this was not their home for long, either. As a matter of fact, Oswald returned to Australia before the end of the year.'[4] Ernest appears to have been mistaken about the house number (the British census taken on 2 April listed Oswald and Muriel at 53 Berkeley Square), but he had correctly picked up on the undercurrent of feeling at that West End address.

It might be guessed that Ernest was not entirely unhappy to discover that Oswald and Muriel were leading largely separate social lives, because Ernest's domestic affairs were in an identical state and this meant that his younger brother was free to join him in many of his own activities—much as they had done while Oswald was in Sydney on his own in the first half of 1910. Ernest took rooms in Jermyn Street, and proceeded to have 'a wonderful time' with other Australians who were visiting London for the June coronation of King George V. Two of his particular friends were women who were seeing London for the first time, and with Oswald added to their number Ernest later recalled that 'the four of us had some very cheery parties'.[5]

Of great assistance in the Watt brothers' pursuit of good times would have been the fact that Oswald had acquired his own motor car in London. This was a Daimler Silent Knight,[6] so named because its American designer, Charles Yale Knight (1868-1940), had developed an engine using the sliding sleeve principle (instead of the more common poppet valve construction) to produce much quieter running—an achievement the Daimler company in England had taken up for some of its car models from 1909. Oswald still had a passionate interest in motor cars and engines, to such an extent it was later claimed that he went to the trouble at this time of obtaining an owners' driving certificate from the Royal Automobile Club.[7]

Oswald Watt's fascination with cars might very well have been what drew him to Brooklands, on the southwestern outskirts of London, where the world's first purpose-built motor racing circuit had been opened in 1907. Although it cannot be known for certain, it could have been at Brooklands that an interest in aviation was also suddenly sparked in Oswald. While visiting there for one of the regular motoring events, he could easily have had his first encounter with aircraft, as from 1908 Brooklands was also one of Britain's first aerodromes. In October 1909 Brooklands had even hosted its first public flying display for 20,000 spectators, so that from 1910 it rapidly became a major centre of flying in the United Kingdom. On any day when weather conditions were suitable it was commonplace, reported the London Standard in May 1911, to see 'as many as five machines ... in the air at the same time'—an occurrence that would have been visible for miles around, including to visitors at the adjoining racing circuit.

Driving certificate issued to Oswald Watt by the Royal Automobile Club in June 1911, showing his address as 53 Berkeley Square, London.

Sometime in May 1911 Watt applied to join the Royal Aero Club of the United Kingdom, an application approved on 30 May when he was declared an elected member.[8] It appears to have been entirely coincidental that exactly a week before this date, on 21 May, the Australian minister for defence (Senator George Pearce, who was in London for the 1911 Imperial Conference) also visited Brooklands to see the latest developments in flying for himself.[9] So far as is known, the paths of the visiting politician and Oswald never crossed at this time. Though Pearce would later maintain that it was his visit to Brooklands that convinced him of 'the wisdom of having a flying school in the Defence Department' in Australia, he did nothing to act on this discovery for more than six months.[10]

Chapter 4

Oswald, too, did not immediately act on his aero club membership. Instead, he took himself off to the Epsom races—leaving Muriel to amuse herself with having her portrait taken on 6 June by the 'Royal Photographers', Bassano Ltd, at their studios in Old Bond Street. The trip to Epsom Downs, undertaken on 7 June with Ernest and his two lady friends, proved memorable for reasons entirely unrelated to the annual running of the Derby. That year happened to see the worst weather event in the history of the race—then already 130 years old—with 62 millimetres of rain falling in just 30 minutes. Recalled Ernest, it was 'the worst storm I have ever experienced. The two girls were terrified.'[11]

A month later Oswald was ready to further his new-found interest in aviation. On 5 July he fronted up at the flying school operated on the Salisbury Plain in Wiltshire by the British and Colonial Aeroplane Company Ltd. (already more commonly known as the Bristol Aeroplane Company) to be taught how to fly. According to *Flight* magazine, he was given his first lesson that night (clearly limited to ground instruction) and early the next morning made his first flight as a passenger with Henri Jullerot, the French manager of the school who was in charge of tuition during the absence on a promotional tour of Collyns Pizey, the chief flying instructor, and his assistant Harry Fleming. On the evening of the 6th, Watt and another pupil were given long lessons and allowed to take full control of the levers. Next morning, both trainees were sent up to each make two straight-line solo flights, despite the presence of 'a good deal of mist'.[12]

By the third week of July Watt had clearly made considerable progress, working under the combined tuition of Jullerot and the chief pilot, another Frenchman named Maurice Tétard. On the 21st he made 'a very fine cross-country flight', performing two figures of eight round Stonehenge and 'finishing with a beautiful vol plané [a controlled dive, with engine shut off] from 60 ft.' He was by then described as a pupil 'in the solo flight stage of his course', and was performing admirably. Judged on his work up till then, it was confidently predicted that 'the date of his qualifying for his brevet is not far distant.'[13]

Bassano portrait of Muriel Watt, 6 June 1911 (National Portrait Gallery (UK) x103873)

That confidence proved justified when, on the evening of 27 July, Oswald began the first tests for his certificate. These reportedly required the trainee to pilot his machine through ten figures of eight, and demonstrate the ability to fly at a sustained level height of 150 feet. When he completed the last of the tests by 8 a.m. the following morning, it had taken him exactly three weeks to qualify. This was an impressive achievement, made all the sweeter by the fact that at the school, at the same time as him, there were a number of officers from the British and Indian armies; and he had gained a certificate in a shorter time than any of them, though aged 33.[14]

Although he had successfully completed his tests, Oswald kept up his flying practice for more than a month. Even after he knew that the committee of the Royal Aero Club had formally awarded his aviator's certificate (No.112) on 1 August,[15] he was airborne most days honing his skills in solo flights around the Salisbury Plain. It was only in mid-September, however, that *Flight* magazine carried the headline "A Colonial Officer takes his brevet", declaring:

> Captain Watt is the keenest of patriots and is the first Australian military officer to obtain a certificate and probably the first overseas Colonial officer to fly, including Canada and South Africa. Captain Watt proved himself an extremely apt pupil at the Salisbury Plain Bristol School ... After he had only three passenger flights he made a solo trip at the first attempt.[16]

Flight was probably safe in its claim that Oswald Watt had become Australia's first military pilot, although as a volunteer officer on the unattached list from the Scottish Rifles his actual army status was becoming fairly tenuous. It was not the case—as some later commentators assumed—that he was the first Australian to have attained the RAeC certificate. The real first was a 23-year-old Victorian named H. R. ("Harry") Busteed, who had received certificate No.94 on 13 June 1911 after also qualifying at the Bristol School. He was then employed as Bristol's chief test pilot, and even while Watt was undergoing training was recognised as a very popular instructor at the school. Busteed was actually one of four men from Victoria who had proceeded to England in 1911 in pursuit of careers in aviation, and it happened that another of this group, 25-year-old Eric Harrison, was also in training on Salisbury Plain while Oswald was finishing his course. Harrison received his certificate (No.131) in September, just a month after Oswald.[17]

By early September Oswald felt free to leave the Salisbury Plain behind him for the moment. This was just as well, as Muriel had decided to claim some of her husband's time by making him take her on a holiday to Russia.[18] The details of this trip are not known now, but most likely it involved a sea voyage up the Baltic Sea to the then imperial capital at St Petersburg, at the head of the Gulf of Finland. Whether this was intended as some sort of gesture of reconciliation is unknown, too, but if it was, the outcome was almost exactly opposite. According to a later account by Muriel, when the couple returned to England Oswald informed her that he wanted separation or divorce. She allegedly responded that she did not want either, at which point they agreed to each go their own way for a while. While Muriel decided she would go to Delhi,[19] to attend the Durbar (the mass spectacle to mark the succession of George V as Emperor of India, scheduled to take place in December), Oswald opted to return to Australia.[20]

Embarking in the mail steamer *Moldavia* in October, Oswald reached Fremantle on 7 November.[21] There he found a journalist eagerly waiting to talk to him about what he planned to do with his newly-gained pilot's certificate. Declaring that 'the time is rapidly approaching when an aero corps will have to be inaugurated in connection with the Australia military defence scheme', he told his interviewer that he intended 'to offer his services in that connection'. Although he did not have an aircraft of his own, he believed that there was one at Sydney which would be 'at his disposal.' When asked about a rumour that he planned to attempt to fly across Australia from Sydney to Fremantle, he reportedly replied emphatically that he had 'never dreamt of it'. He was not, he assured his listener, 'so mad as all that.'[22]

On 12 November, a Sunday, the *Moldavia* moored in Hobson's Bay (the port area of Melbourne off Williamstown) for a scheduled two-day stopover before proceeding on to its way to Sydney.[23] Oswald used that time to seek a meeting with the minister for defence, Senator Pearce, in his Melbourne office. That such a meeting did take place was confirmed by Pearce himself on 18 November. He informed the press that he had had 'a conversation' with Captain Watt, who 'had offered his services in connection with the aviation work to be done by the Defence department', whereupon the minister had referred his visitor to the acting Chief of the General Staff. Perhaps not wanting to get anybody's hopes up—least of all Watt's—Pearce was careful to emphasise that only 'a small sum' had been provided on the current Estimates for the development of military aviation.[24]

By that stage, Oswald had already re-embarked in *Moldavia* and on Tuesday afternoon departed for Sydney. When the ship reached its destination on 16 November,[25] Oswald Watt could only rejoice at being back in familiar surroundings, and await whatever response might be forthcoming to his offer to help the army make a start in aviation.

Aviation adviser to Defence

While waiting to hear from the Department of Defence, Oswald Watt slipped back into the rhythm of life in Sydney at the start of an Australian summer. In the first days of December he was seen at a match at the Sydney Cricket Ground between New South Wales and a visiting English side.[26] When he first arrived he most probably stayed at the Union Club, but in December he moved into "Cromer" in Phillip Street—serviced flats where Ernest had lived before leaving for London earlier in the year.[27]

Oswald also reconnected with the circle of friends with whom he and Ernest had mixed during his last stay. Among this group were some the two brothers knew from the Union Club—such as solicitor John Sydney ("Syd") Richardson, and W. H. ("Harrington") Palmer who was receiver in the Bankruptcy Court, associate of Arthur Allen, and auditor for the Bank of New South Wales. A bachelor, Palmer divided his time between the Union Club and the family mansion in North Sydney which he shared with his widowed mother. Dr Sydney Jamieson, a pathologist at Sydney Hospital who Oswald had first met while he was Sir Harry Rawson's ADC, was another who became a great friend at this time, along with Jamieson's wife Roslyn. Others were from the theatre crowd which Ernest in particular so loved.[28]

It was probably one of these friends, the deaf *Bulletin* journalist John Bede Dalley, who reintroduced Oswald to the enjoyment of Sydney's seaside, especially the northern beaches with which Dalley's family had long been associated.[29] John was the son of William Bede

Dalley, the Manly lawyer and politician who—as acting premier in 1885—sent the first Australian military contingent to an overseas war (Britain's campaign in Sudan). Just a year after Dalley senior made his grand gesture to London he had acquired land at Bilgola, a beach on the Barrenjoey peninsula about 30 kilometres from the city, on which he built a holiday residence and a separate caretaker's cottage. The family did not have long to enjoy the property, as William Dalley sold it five months before he died in October 1888. Since May 1909 the house at Bilgola had been in the ownership of Henry Zeddon Jones, a Manly salesman, who installed his brother Stephen as caretaker and let it out to visitors who came to picnic, or enjoy the fishing and surfing on offer. Oswald had instantly fallen for the peace and serenity of the sparsely-settled area, and became a regular visitor at Bilgola.[30]

In March Oswald was finally contacted by the Department of Defence, which asked him to visit the site of the future national capital to look at areas that might be suitable for a military flying school. By this time Watt would have known that advertisements had already appeared in the *Commonwealth Gazette*, and in Britain, for two competent 'mechanists and aviators' to staff such a school, and the government appeared committed to its establishment. In accordance with his instructions he visited the Federal Capital Territory on 7 March, and after inspecting five sites he returned to Sydney to prepare a report. Writing from the Union Club on 9 March, he declared that he considered the plain below the Royal Military College at Duntroon 'absolutely ideal for flying and superior to any aerodrome or area I saw in England, not even excepting Salisbury Plain, which … it very much resembles.'[31] Watt's judgement might appear to be confirmed by the fact that the site is these days covered by Canberra Airport.

While Watt appeared uninterested in seeking a paid position for himself at the proposed school—an attitude he could afford to take with his private wealth—he was eager to be of further use in shaping the development of the army's aviation scheme. He accordingly sat down to write an article he titled "Australia and the Fourth Arm", in which he presented his thoughts on the direction in which progress lay.[32] Believing that his visit to Canberra had settled the question of the flying school's location, he confidently declared:

> Our military aviators will probably be trained on the plains
> at Duntroon, where an aviation ground offers itself as good as, if
> not better than, anything in Europe. The school course, in my
> opinion, should be two months per year for the first two years at
> least; and after that one month's "refresher" course should be ample
> unless the weather proved extra villainous and prohibited flying.

In these remarks he appeared to be anticipating some of the objections
that might be mounted against his recommendations.

In the same vein, Watt also recounted a story from his own
experience on Salisbury Plain which seemed to have the purpose
of pre-empting objections of Canberra residents regarding aircraft
noise. To show how horses had got used to aircraft passing overhead,
he recalled:

> On one occasion Collyns Pizey … started off for a flight
> to a camp some 10 miles distant, and as he did not return by
> dusk we got anxious about him, and I started off across country
> in my car to find him. In the dusk I ran across the horse-lines
> of a Territorial regiment, and the little grey car, a quiet Silent-
> Knight Daimler, nearly caused a stampede. Just then Pizey, who
> had been repairing a broken skid, passed overhead flying only
> some 300 feet high and making a terrible noise, but no horse
> paid any attention to him at all.

Oswald neglected to mention that what frightened the horses might
not have been the sounds of his car, but the trail of smoke habitually
emitted by the Silent Knight engine.

Also noteworthy were Watt's observations on the aspect of local
manufacture of aircraft. Here he opined that 'We should certainly later
on build our own machines in Australia, and the most satisfactory way
would be to build under "license".' All that was needed to do this,
he said, was a designer's measurements and notes, and these would
be supplied on payment of a license fee. 'In this way we could build
in our Government workshops, under license, any type of English or
foreign machine identical with the manufacturer's models.' If Watt
seemed to be hewing to a very orthodox and "safe" line of argument

in such matters, the explanation for this probably lay in his belief that aviation was 'not going to "revolutionize" warfare, or do many of the things the ultra-enthusiasts claim for it.' Nonetheless, he was adamant that 'the warplane well deserves its place in the modern army, … [and] no efficient army can afford to be without an aerial fleet.'

It seems that even before writing this article, duly submitted to the *Commonwealth Military Journal*, Watt had already determined another course that he planned to follow. On 4 March the acting Chief of the General Staff, Lieutenant Colonel F. A. Wilson, wrote to advise the secretary of the Defence Department that "Captain O. Watt, Reserve of Officers", would be proceeding to England on 27 March and 'intends spending some considerable time on Salisbury Plain and at other flying centres', with the idea of reporting back to Australia on the progress that was taking place in aeronautics, including the types of machines available and their military value. Watt did not seek any remuneration for this work, 'but would be glad if he could receive official recognition from the Government, so as to assist him in his enquiries.' Wilson said that he had spoken to Senator Pearce, who had agreed to Watt's request, so he now asked the secretary, Samuel Pethebridge, to make the necessary arrangements with the War Office in London.[33]

Pethebridge duly did as he was asked, writing to the Department of External Affairs on 13 March to advise of Watt's impending visit and explain his mission:

> The Minister would therefore be glad if the High Commissioner [in London] would be so good as to make arrangements with the War Office for Captain Watt to see as much as possible of what is being done in the United Kingdom in the way of military aviation, and for his attachment, if necessary, to the Air Battalion or to any military school of aviation that may be in progress during his visit – it being understood that no expense will be incurred by the Commonwealth.

Oswald may have planned to leave Sydney late in March, but other events now transpired that caused him to delay his departure. Strangely, published accounts of his adventure only appeared in early

June[34]—more than two months after he was gone from Australia—and so late March is the only period in which the episode can have taken place. What it entailed was a 2,000-kilometre road trip from Adelaide to Melbourne and thence to Sydney, carried out with Oswald behind the steering wheel and a colleague from the Union Club, stockbroker John McKeown (1882-1936), keeping his eye on the map and the driver fed at regular intervals. Although the purpose of the trip—along with many other details—is maddeningly absent from the published accounts, it can be inferred that the undertaking was somehow related to, or at least inspired by, the Military Dispatch Relay Ride that was scheduled to take place over the Easter weekend in April 1912.[35]

Sponsored and organized by the Dunlop Rubber Company for the Defence Department, the 1912 ride was devised as a test of the relative utility of motor cars, motor cycles and bicycles for rapid military communications, and followed a similar event—again sponsored by Dunlop—held in April 1909, but for cyclists alone. Although it is known that a French-made Vinot car with company representatives had been sent along the route in the first week of March to finalise arrangements for the ride,[36] the trip made by Watt and McKeown was perhaps an additional reconnaissance or survey on behalf of the organisers to ensure that all was in readiness—unless it was an unrelated effort undertaken purely for private amusement.

On 2 April, a week later than the departure date originally proposed, Watt left Sydney in the new P&O ship RMS *Maloja* bound for London.[37] After the liner had completed its stop-over in Adelaide on 11 April and was headed west across the Bight, it passed the RMS *Malwa* steaming in the opposite direction, bringing passengers from London. On board the east-bound vessel was Muriel Watt and their son, coming back to Australia at last.[38] Muriel's later complaint that she had received a "Marconi-gram" (a radio message) from her husband in the Bight, advising that he was in the other ship and enquiring only after the well-being of Jimmy, strongly suggests that Oswald had knowledge of his wife's travel plans and was sending her a powerful message.[39]

In April 1912 Oswald Watt purchased the beachside holiday property called Bilgola.

In the days before he boarded ship to England, Oswald had also taken another step with important meaning for the future. Although the process was apparently not settled until later in April, he had decided to buy the holiday bungalow at Bilgola as his own personal haven.

Bilgola retreat

In May 1912, shortly after Oswald Watt stepped off the ship in England, his article on 'the Fourth Arm' appeared in the *Commonwealth Military Journal* back in Australia. Its impact on discussion and thinking about aviation for local defence was all that he could have hoped for, with the article's contents being reported and quoted in some of the leading daily newspapers across the country.[40] Upon learning in August that his article had also been awarded a prize of one guinea (21 shillings—$80-$100 at today's values) as the best original contribution to the CMJ in the three months ending on 30 June, he told the director of military training in Melbourne that he wanted to decline it. Returning the form that he had been sent to claim his prize money, Oswald said that he 'would very much prefer not to avail myself of it, as I wrote the article in question purely to give any help I could towards the founding of our aviation corps.'[41]

Chapter 4

Writing from the Royal Aero Club premises in Piccadilly on 22 May, Watt reported to the secretary of the Military Board that he had already called on Major P. N. Buckley, the military representative at the Australian High Commission, and that arrangements were being made for him 'to see everything the home government is doing in aviation'. Buckley had showed him the papers regarding the Defence Department's plans for engaging two aviators and four aeroplanes for Australia's flying school. Buckley also said that he had advised Melbourne to delay making a selection on the types of aircraft for the school until after an upcoming design competition the British war office had arranged with manufacturers was over. Watt thought this advice was 'very wise', because he had seen 'several of these "competition" machines & they are all a distinct advance on previous models'. He himself planned to go down to Salisbury Plain 'in about a fortnight', to learn to fly the Bristol monoplane (a new two-seat trainer designed for the Bristol company by Henri Marie Coandă, a Romanian).[42]

Oswald's communication in May appears to have been the last that authorities in Melbourne heard from him for several months, and by the time he got in touch again at the end of August nearly all the major decisions required to bring Australia's flying school into being had been taken. During July, the selection of the two aviators required to initiate the school had been made and publicly announced; they were Harry Busteed and a 28-year-old English pilot named Henry Petre.[43] These men were expected to arrive from England at the start of October, along with the four aircraft—two monoplanes and two biplanes—which had been purchased on the recommendation of the War Office, to begin establishing the school on an aerodrome to be built near Duntroon in the Federal Capital Territory[44] Under the plan formally approved by the Military Board on 12 July, a year after the school was established it was to be expanded to a full squadron of 12 aircraft, manned by 19 officers and 131 other ranks, and Australia's flying corps would have become a reality.[45]

Of all these arrangements, only the matter of the school's site bore the imprint of any input from Oswald Watt—and, in the event, no aspect of the plan so far decided would survive without modification, even the school's location. Before what became known as the Central Flying School finally opened, in March 1914, at Point Cook on Port Phillip Bay in Victoria, both its staffing and aircraft had also undergone important adjustments. After Busteed decided that he would prefer to stay in England and withdrew from his appointment in September 1912,[46] his place was taken next month by Eric Harrison. And in December 1912 the Department of Defence was prompted to place an order in England for a fifth aircraft for the school, after Colonel J. G. Legge (Australia's representative on the Imperial General Staff) visited the Bristol company's operation on the Salisbury Plain the previous month and reported back to Melbourne that the four machines already acquired were actually unsuitable for training pilots. It was on Legge's recommendation that a slower type, a single Bristol Boxkite pusher biplane, was purchased.[47]

Throughout the crucial period in which the plans for Australia's aviation branch were being decided, Oswald Watt had remained silent—absent even from the sidelines of discussion. When he finally bobbed up into view again and got in touch with the authorities in Melbourne, all he could do was offer his opinion that the 'arrangements made here on behalf of the corps are … excellent'. Writing to the director of military training on 30 August, he said that the two aircraft types selected, both the Deperdussin [Monocoque] monoplane and the B.E.2a tractor biplane, were types 'un-surpassed by any', and he could only heap praise on Busteed and Petre as skilled and respected pilots. Busteed, he said, he knew well and had 'watched his progress ever since I saw him flying on Salisbury Plain 15 months ago. He is an extremely nice fellow with iron nerves and a beautiful touch on a control—and *never* takes unnecessary risks, a fine thing for a school instructor. Petre I do not know personally but his record is a good one.'[48]

The factor that had taken Watt out of the picture was—as his letter explained—personal illness; it was this, he wrote, that 'has prevented me from seeing and doing all I should have liked in aviation matters'. In adding that 'I have opportunities of talking things over with active aviators and hearing their unbiased opinions', Oswald may have meant to indicate that he hoped to make up for having offered so little so far. It appears that he did manage to attend the annual manoeuvres of the British army the following month, held this year in and around the familiar surrounds of Cambridge, and during which aircraft performed work that was regarded as 'a complete vindication' of the Royal Flying Corps—then in existence less than six months. But Oswald's opportunities to explore the British aviation scene in depth on behalf of the Australian government were about to be curtailed by other matters, things calculated to only add to the poor state of his health.

Oswald Watt was not normally prone to ill health. Indeed, his brother Ernest later made the point that from the time Oswald went to Cambridge university 'his health was perfectly sound and he was never ill again until 1912-13'.[49] Whatever his illness was, it does not appear to have required surgery or hospitalization, and taken with other evidence there are strong grounds for concluding that he was sick more in spirit than in body. From later statements by his wife, it might be adduced that he was actually suffering from acute anxiety and stress over the unhappy state of their marriage. In early July he appears to have finally decided on a course of action calculated to bring the issue to a head; he wrote to Muriel providing her with ammunition to institute divorce proceedings—a letter that could only severely damage his name, reputation and standing.[50]

Having fired off this deadly missive, he sat back to await its effect. This would have come while he was attending the army manoeuvres in September, when he no doubt received news that Muriel was on her way to England from Melbourne. When her ship (*Malwa*) passed through Fremantle on 21 September, Muriel told the local journalists little about the purpose of her trip. She spent much of her time travelling, she merely said, and was now 'returning to take up her life in England'.[51] Knowing—or at least guessing—that his wife was on her way, Oswald decided it was time to reverse the traffic flow and booked passage back to Australia. This was likely to have been sometime in October or November, but no mention of his return appeared in passenger information routinely published in the shipping news. He had apparently decided to keep his name out of the newspapers.

It seems certain that Watt was in Sydney before December 1912, because of two seemingly unconnected events that occurred during that month. The first concerned Oswald's formal status in the military forces. For more than a year, both he and the Defence Department had been under the impression that he was already on the Reserve of Officers, an inactive category just one step short of the Retired List, rather than the Unattached List on which he had been placed in 1908. Perhaps this misunderstanding stemmed from the fact that, after the introduction of universal training at the start of 1912, there had been a reorganisation which saw volunteer units like the Scottish Rifles absorbed into the Militia. For some reason not readily apparent, the mistake was only discovered about the time that Oswald arrived back in Australia, and a Military Order was published which formally notified that Captain W. O. Watt was transferred from the Unattached List to the Reserve of Officers, 'Dated 2 December 1912.'[52] It was most likely, though not necessarily, the case that Watt's presence back in Australia had caused this.

The second event more clearly demonstrates that Oswald must have duly let his old friends in Sydney know that he had returned. John Dalley would later recount a motoring trip that he undertook with Oswald to fish for trout in the Duckmaloi River near Oberon, about 180 kilometres west of Sydney. Although Dalley did not specify when the expedition took place, apart from describing their departure as occurring 'on a burning December day', he finished his account by mentioning that on their return they called into Springwood to visit the well-known artist Norman Lindsay.[53] As Lindsay only took up residence at Springwood late in 1912[54] and Oswald did not spend another December in Australia for the next eight years, the Duckmaloi trip can be effectively dated.

In addition to confirming Oswald's presence in Australia at this time, Dalley's account is memorable for giving a glimpse at a little-seen side of Oswald. According to Dalley, he and Oswald had intended only a short break in their journey at Springwood but ended up staying the night at Lindsay's house. Norman and Oswald 'took to one another at once, and sat talking into the early hours of the morning while a summer storm raged and the rain teemed down outside.' It was Lindsay who did most of the talking 'in his quick, feverish way', while Watt listened, or gravely acquiesced, or gave a light laugh in appreciation of their host. Toby was 'a brilliant listener, which is so much rarer than a brilliant talker.'

Others in Watt's circle have left accounts that confirm that he returned home from England at this time in a bad way, with his doctor friend Syd Jamieson recording that Oswald's health had 'threatened to break down' not long before the start of the First World War. It was then that Oswald's purchase of Bilgola came into its own, providing a restful retreat not just for himself but his 'friends and intimates'. According to Jamieson, Oswald made 'many stays of longer and shorter duration at his delightful seaside home' at this time, and Jamieson was himself invited to spend a weekend there with him, 'the prelude to many happy visits'.[55]

While Oswald may have sought to keep a low profile, he remained eager to wield whatever influence he could in furthering his passionate belief in aviation. To this end he wrote another article for the *Commonwealth Military Journal* entitled "Recent Aviation Developments and Australian Aerial Organisation". Published in January 1913, the article began by describing the aircraft trials held by the War Office shortly before the 1912 army manoeuvres in Britain, aiming to find 'practical results … for [future] guidance'. Attention then turned to arrangements for Australia's flying school, with Oswald particularly noting that it seemed 'doubtful policy' to make the scheme dependent on just two 'aviator-mechanics'; 'even a slight mishap' threatened the viability of the entire show, he warned, so there was a need for more non-flying mechanical staff to take charge of the 'planes and motors'.[56]

Inevitably, Watt then returned to a pet theme in emphasising that local manufacture of aircraft was essential if Australia was to become self-reliant in its own defence. Noting that even Britain was building foreign types in its factories, he argued that this supported the wisdom of avoiding the need to import 'such cumbersome goods from such a distance', since Australia would then be in a better position to repair and rebuild damaged engines 'as well as to construct later on such experimental aircraft as were deemed advisable'. Moreover, the excessive amount of engine trouble experienced at the recent British trials 'pointed obviously to the weak spot generally in present-day aviation.'

Finally, Watt's article then referred to the French review held at Versailles in early October (which, his wording made clear, he had not attended personally) by reflecting on the spectacle of having over 70 machines present for the War Minister's inspection. As these aircraft took off to return to their bases, 'the spectators must have realized how firmly the aeroplane has taken its place amongst the deadly paraphernalia of war; as well as the fact that mankind can, at least, with some truth, boast to have conquered the air'

If Watt was hoping that this article might have a similar impact to his previous effort for the Journal, he must have been disappointed. It was apparent that the Defence Department was no longer interested in what he had to say on aviation, nor attached much weight to his views. In December 1912 the Chief of the General Staff, Brigadier-General J. M. Gordon, received a letter from the Administrator of the Federal Capital Territory asking for a 'technical examination' to be made of the various sites around Canberra that Watt had considered for the flying school aerodrome. This request had been inspired by a letter dated 15 November from the Director of Commonwealth Lands and Surveys, Charles Scrivenor, who objected to Watt's recommended site on the grounds that the 'average aeroplane is extremely noisy even at a distance of a mile'; opined Scrivenor, 'I regard the proposed site as quite unsuitable for the purpose intended,' and he also felt that people using the Queanbeyan-Uriarra Road would be endangered.[57]

Oswald might have thought he had adequately answered the concern expressed by Scrivenor in comments he made in his journal article the previous May, but General Gordon lacked sufficient confidence in Watt's recommendation to simply ignore the Administrator's request. The CGS consequently assigned the task of making a review to Henry

Petre, after he reached Australia in January 1913. Although Petre visited the FCT in February and confirmed that Watt's recommended site was 'a very good' one, he went in search of others and in March solved the CGS's dilemma by giving preference to Point Cook—based on his personal wish not to be posted in rural isolation at what was regarded as a 'bush capital'.[58]

Watt probably had an inkling of how he was now regarded in army headquarters, based on what he saw as liberties taken with the editing of his January article in the *Commonwealth Military Journal*. On 5 March he sat down in the Union Club to write a six-page letter to the editor in which he made 'a few notes on points where my meaning has been altered and the article commented on'. After a long and combative defence of his analysis of the British aviation scene and its main features and figures, Oswald turned his attention to safety in the air, mentioning that he had sent 'to the authorities two safety belts and a sample "Warren" helmet which I hope will be used'.[59]

He also took aim at criticism that had recently been aired publicly by one local aviator, Sydney dentist W. E. ("Bill") Hart, to the effect that the altitude of the Duntroon site (situated 200 kilometres north of Mt Kosciusko in the Australian alps) was too high for the low-powered aircraft acquired for the flying school, giving several reasons why he did not think Hart's views needed to be taken seriously. In what was a somewhat disorganized and rambling letter, it was not as a conclusion that he repeated the sentiment he had expressed before: 'I trust the General Staff, if they see this letter, will take it in the spirit in which it is written as my only wish is for the success of our corps.'

Although the letter received a polite reply from headquarters dated 10 March, there was nothing in this that indicated Watt's views commanded respect with the CGS and his staff. The captain who replied took issue with him on several points and ended with a slightly curt assurance that, 'The Department much appreciates your present of safety Helmet and belts.'

Perhaps the most interesting aspect of this correspondence is that Watt appeared to have recovered from whatever malady he had been suffering from during 1912 and by the first months of 1913 was reengaging with the world more generally. This impression is confirmed by other steps he took to advance the cause of public safety, by writing to the Automobile Club of Australia (of which he was a member) offering to donate £25 to a fund to be used for repairing roads and removing other dangers. He particularly suggested cutting down scrub which created a visual hazard to motorists travelling from Manly to Sydney by concealing the presence of trams at the point where the tramline joined the road. It can probably be assumed that Watt had personally received a nasty experience at that particular juncture.[60]

In response to Watt's proposal, the Auto Club forwarded the letter to the Good Roads Association of NSW, which at its June meeting decided to ask if he would be willing to give to the Association's general campaign. Whether Oswald agreed is unknown, but by June he was no longer in Australia anyway so the likelihood is that the Association missed out on his donation.

Oswald's departure overseas actually came in late March, shortly after his contact with the Defence Department ended. That he had booked passage in the *Moldavia* when this mail steamer next left for London was something which—very unusually—was foreshadowed several times in Sydney newspapers in the weeks leading up to the ship's departure date of 22 March.[61] There was, in all this, a hint that Watt had learnt that Muriel was on her way back to Australia, and what he had been doing was clearing the decks before ensuring that the two of them were not in the same space at the same time.

Society divorce scandal

In mid-1913 the storm that had been brewing for the previous three years over the failing Watt marriage finally burst amid a blaze of publicity, as Muriel sued her husband for a divorce on the grounds of alleged adultery. Just as Oswald had anticipated, the press eagerly seized upon the lurid details of the action brought in the Sydney divorce court, and for four months (off and on) from June to early October, newspapers big and small across Australia (and New Zealand, too) were full of headlines about the 'Society Divorce Suit' and 'Watt Divorce Scandal'.

The petition lodged by Muriel claimed that her husband had been guilty of misconduct with several women, unknown to her, at Sydney and Melbourne between November 1909 and June 1910, and again between October 1911 and July 1912, and also with a woman named Ivy Schilling between 18 December 1911 and 4 July 1912. Muriel sought not only dissolution of the marriage but custody of the couple's seven-year-old son. She had returned from England expressly for the hearing of her suit, and engaged Lewis Whitfield, one of Sydney's foremost barristers in the matrimonial causes jurisdiction, to represent her.[62]

Oswald had no intention of contesting these charges—indeed, it quickly emerged in court that he had invited them by sending his wife a letter containing admissions of alleged infidelities. Since he felt no need to defend or explain his transgressions, he did not even bother returning to Australia so soon after departing for overseas in March. He did, however, engage the equally prominent barrister E. Milne Stephen, to watch his interests in the matter of custody and the settlement that would follow the expected granting of a divorce.[63]

On Monday, 16 June, the case received its first hearing before Justice Alexander Gordon, a judge notable for his dignified manner, domed forehead and walrus moustache. Muriel began proceedings by taking the witness stand to recount her suspicions about her husband's supposed extra-marital affairs dating back to May 1910. Matters had come to a head following her return to Australia in April 1912, when she had passed Oswald in a ship going the other way, and began hearing 'such extraordinary rumours' about him. The following August she received a letter from him dated 5 July which caused her to go away to London to consult her solicitors, and it was on their advice that she had put divorce proceedings in train.[64]

What His Honour made of Mrs Watt's evidence is not recorded. Later described as one of the most able and popular judges on the Supreme Court bench, and well-known for his humanity, Justice Gordon might have wondered if her account accorded with the Oswald Watt he probably knew from the Union Club, where they were both members. The reporter for the *Truth*, a populist newspaper equally well-known for its saucy accounts of divorce cases, mockingly described Muriel as 'looking ye high-born ladye…a tall, stylishly-arrayed, well-spoken, and superior-looking woman' who, despite being born in Victoria, 'spoke with that haw-haw enunciation peculiar to the middle-class English and their butlers and waiting-maids.'[65]

Worse was to follow with the next witnesses that Whitfield had to offer—two housemaids and a lift operator at the Cromer Flats in Phillip Street, where Oswald had moved into shortly before Christmas 1911. All three could attest to Ivy Schilling, then a 19-year-old up and coming dancer and actress in musical theatre, being a frequent visitor to Captain Watt's rooms, which were on the first floor and away from the other flats. At various times she had visited every day, sometimes arriving alone and at other times with other people including Watt, who she called "Oz" while he called her "Bob" (then the slang name for a shilling in Australia's pre-decimal currency). On a Saturday afternoon, Ivy had even been known to go out driving with Watt in his motor-car.[66]

But when the former house staff were questioned about whether they had ever found anything to indicate the presence of women in Watt's bedroom, the best they had to offer was one afternoon when Ivy was seen walking about the flat after removing her hat, which was left sitting on the Captain's three-quarter bed; another occasion when, perhaps unsurprisingly, a hairpin was found on the floor; and yet another when two items described as 'pearls' were discovered in Watt's bed while it was being made up one morning. One of these items was produced in court and promptly made an exhibit. It was left to the *Truth* reporter to later make the telling observation that it was actually a pearl *button*, such as 'might have adorned any man's singlet'.[67]

Announcing that he had one more witness who was unable to attend court that day because of ill health, Muriel's counsel declared that the evidence for his client was concluded. Justice Gordon only then made it plain that he was far from impressed by what he had so far heard. On the evidence presented, His Honour considered that no misconduct had been proved. So far as Ivy Schilling was concerned, it was possible to conclude nothing more than that she had been 'seen on certain occasions', and he was not prepared to say that she was guilty 'on mere suspicion'. Had she appeared in court he would have discharged her from the suit, since not a scintilla of evidence had been produced against her.[68]

Regarding the husband's letter making a general admission of guilt, the judge said that he viewed this with the greatest suspicion since it showed nothing more than that it had been written for the express purpose of ending the marriage. He did not doubt that Watt desired to be rid of his wife, for reasons which did him no credit, but the law required there to be substantial corroboration of claims made in cases of this kind.[69] When Whitfield attempted to argue that the failure of both Watt and Ivy Schilling to appear to defend the suit should be regarded as evidence of guilt, His Honor said that their absence did not help the court at all, and did not remove the suspicion attached to the letter. With that, he ordered the case be adjourned to allow for the presentation of further evidence.

Ten days later—on Thursday, 26 June—the court heard what was confidently expected to be the real 'conclusion of evidence' in the Watt case. On hand was the witness who had been unable to attend the first day's hearing. This was Henry Zeddon Jones (his middle name spelt incorrectly as 'Leddon' in all subsequent newspaper accounts), the man who had sold Bilgola (called 'Balgowlah' throughout) to Watt in April 1912. Jones had formerly lived on the property, and used to let the bungalow's rooms—all furnished with single beds—to fishing parties. He could recall that Watt and a lady he heard called 'Ivy' were among parties that several times arrived in motor-cars at weekends, usually after the theatre entertainment in town was over.[70]

When asked by Whitfield, Jones could remember only one occasion when the pair in question were alone at the house, having arrived very late on a Friday night while the rest of their party did not get there until the following day. The next morning, when Jones went for his usual "dip" in the ocean at 5.30, he had passed Watt's room and observed him through the open door apparently asleep on his own, while Miss Schilling occupied another room opposite.

Directly questioned by the judge, Jones admitted that he had never witnessed any impropriety between the two.[71]

At the conclusion of Jones' evidence, Justice Gordon stated that he would probably give his judgment the following afternoon.[72] Owing to other cases being heard on the Friday the judge did not deliver a ruling as foreshadowed, which was probably just as well, given the unfavourable outcome that had been indicated as likely by his remarks the previous week. Then another unexpected event intervened to add further delay and buy more time for the two hopeful parties to the suit. On Saturday, 28 June, Muriel's counsel (Lewis Whitfield) was playing golf at the Royal Sydney Golf Club's links at Rose Bay when he dropped dead, terminating the afternoon's play.[73]

Mrs Watt had already booked her return passage to England, and undeterred by this added set-back sailed from Melbourne in the mail steamer *Medina* on 1 July, bound for London.[74] No doubt she was keen to get back to her country house in Framewood Road, Stoke Poges, Slough, in Buckinghamshire, close to Windsor, where she had already engaged Gertrude Jekyll—then the most fashionable garden designer in England—to prepare drawings that would transform her grounds at Fulmer Court.[75] Whether she had time to hire a replacement barrister before she left is unknown, but it was another two months before the divorce suit was again ready to proceed.

On Monday, 15 September, the case resumed before Justice Gordon to hear additional evidence from a fresh witness. This was a man named John Gregory, who had been night porter at the Oxford Hotel in King Street during the period when Ivy Schilling had been a guest at that establishment. He also recounted that Watt was a frequent caller on her, at times coming by in his motor-car 'every night about seven o'clock' to collect her. If he did not enter the building and take himself up to her room on the top floor—he was so well-known to staff that he had 'the run of the hotel'—he would instead sound the car-horn, and she would recognize the signal and come down to join him at the front door.[76]

Gregory, too, described a pattern of weekend carousels, with the pair disappearing on Saturday evening and not returning until 'unconventional' hours on Monday morning—on several occasions at 3 and even 4 a.m. But again, when the judge asked whether familiarities had ever been observed, the reply was 'never at the hotel'; nothing more salacious than a handshake had passed between them. In concluding the petitioner's case, her new counsel (Alexander Ralston, KC), nonetheless argued that Gregory's testimony had placed a different complexion on previous evidence about the goings on at Cromer Flats, and was 'sufficient to bear down the balance against Watt'.[77]

Still the wily old judge was unconvinced, remarking: 'It is curious that none of the witnesses have seen them together, or seen any act of familiarity between them.' When Ralston argued that Watt was such a well-known figure he 'would never make an exhibition of himself by hugging and kissing the girl in a hotel corridor' when going to her room, or 'make a fool of himself before witnesses' while there were ample other opportunities, His Honor said that he had no doubt about Gregory's evidence but still felt the need to exercise considerable care in weighing the value of Watt's admissions, since the circumstances of these were open to grave suspicion. Eventually, however, when delivering judgment two days later, Justice Gordon said that he had decided—on the basis of the evidence now before him—that he should pronounce in favour of the petitioner on the third count of misconduct with Ivy Schilling. Accordingly, he made a decree nisi, returnable in six months, gave the wife custody of the son (unopposed by Oswald's counsel), and ordered the husband to pay costs.[78]

Watt had achieved what he set out to do, for both himself and Muriel, but this had come at a huge cost—both financial and in terms of his personal reputation. The financial pain came immediately, but he probably considered it bearable, and value for money. During October 1913 an indenture of settlement was executed which said Watt had agreed that, in return for his ex-wife refraining from applying for alimony, he would make further provision for his son in addition to that made at the time of his marriage. As well as surrendering all reversionary rights to money settled on Muriel in 1902, he placed a further £45,000 ($4-5 million at today's values) in trust for Muriel and Jimmy.[79]

Bassano portrait of Ivy Schilling, 28 Feb 1916. (National Portrait Gallery, UK, x34263)

On 23 April 1914 the decree nisi granted by Justice Gordon six months earlier was made absolute in the Sydney divorce court.[80] The next month, on 20 May, the former Mrs Oswald Watt was married in London to Colonel Sydney Lawford, a 48-year-old widower commanding the Essex Territorial Infantry Brigade.[81] Muriel was wasting no time in moving on—indeed, given the brief time interval, it appeared that she had found her new partner before even lodging her petition for divorce. Colonel Lawford was, in fact, the brother of Jessie Lawford, who in 1887 became the second wife of her cousin Hartley Williams, Muriel's father.

In mid-1914, too, Ivy Schilling embarked from Sydney with her dance partner Fred Leslie, intending to try her theatrical fortunes in London.[82] It would be seven years before she returned, having shed the letter 'c' from her surname during the First World War to make it appear less German in origin. She, too, had lost nothing from allowing her name to be dragged through the divorce court in connection with the Watt case. It was only with the publication of Ernest Watt's memoirs 85 years later that most people would have noticed Ivy Schilling had been the special friend of Oswald Watt's elder brother, before he left Sydney for England at the start of 1911, or how much the brothers had been addicted to weekend beach parties at Cronulla—despite the difficulties in getting back to Sydney, involving long waits for the Tom Ugly's ferry which often resulted in them getting home after midnight.[83]

Marking time in Egypt

Where Watt went, after leaving Sydney in the *Moldavia* in March 1913, is not known until the end of that year—when he surfaced in Cairo. Most likely he had simply left the *Moldavia* as it passed through the Suez Canal on its way to England, but there is no certainty of this. The heat of the approaching summer would not normally have made the Egyptian capital the most congenial place to be, but because the city generally emptied of its European population during the middle months of the year this may well have suited Watt's presumed intention of riding out the publicity associated with his divorce.

With the return of cooler weather to Egypt come foreign visitors, and the winter of 1913-14 was later regarded as a 'great' tourist season. Among those flocking to Cairo this year was the 50-year-old English novelist and playwright William Locke, who arrived accompanied by his wife Aimee and eight-year-old adopted daughter Sheila Baines. Locke was a refugee from the winter cold of England, regularly seeking more moderate climes around the Mediterranean (particularly the Riviera) since contracting tuberculosis in 1890.

It was in Cairo, Locke later wrote, that he first met Oswald Watt, describing him as a young man 'at unrest with himself and the world' and recounting that, 'Almost his first words to us, when the men who had introduced him had gone, were: "I am an Australian and I haven't got any manners".' The Lockes, both husband and wife, quickly came to realise, however, that Watt's characterisation of himself was 'prompted by defiance of a world against which his young soul was then at strife'. He was actually 'one of the greatest gentlemen'—to the extent that Mrs Locke, though horrified by the furious speed with which Watt usually drove his two-seater car, had no qualms when he took their daughter and her 10-year-old friend on excursions around Cairo, so circumspect was his driving when he had the two children under his care.[84]

British novelist and playwright William Locke, pictured with his daughter Sheila at Cairo, Egypt, in 1914.

The last days of 1913 also brought to Cairo a reminder of another of Watt's passions, in the form of a sudden influx of aviators. Earlier in the year, when he would first have arrived, there was not a single aircraft in the skies of Egypt, but from the last weeks of December a large assortment of flying machines began arriving. As the Royal Aero Club's only set of eyes and ears on the ground, Watt eagerly took up a role as local correspondent and began contributing regular reports—and frequently his own photographs[85]—to the main aviation publications of London, the weeklies *Aeroplane* and *Flight*.

As it happened, Cairo already had an established aerodrome—courtesy of a one-off aviation gathering three years earlier which was the first such event staged on the African continent. For a week in February 1910 a dozen pilots and 18 aircraft from all over Europe had competed for prize money in races held on a landing and take-off area, measuring five kilometres by three, staked out in the desert east of Heliopolis, the luxury suburb on Cairo's north-east outskirts that housed most of the capital's wealthy foreigners.[86] The aerodrome still remained, though turned to more recent use as a polo field.

First to re-occupy the aerodrome were two Frenchmen, Marc Pourpe and Louis Olivier. Watt advised that the former had arrived in a Morane-Saulnier single-seater aircraft in mid-December and had already undertaken a magnificent flight around the Pyramids in a gale. Watt probably did not know that the youthful Pourpe's 60 h.p. monoplane was actually the identical machine that fellow-countryman Roland Garros had used in September when becoming the first man to fly non-stop across the Mediterranean, from the south of France to Tunisia. He plainly did know, however, that behind Pourpe's presence was an intention of setting another record by flying up the Nile to the Sudanese capital, Khartoum. A first attempt to put this plan into effect had been upset when Pourpe encountered fog over Cairo that forced him to turn back, and he up-ended his aircraft in soft sand upon landing. Fortunately, the resulting damage was minor and Pourpe considered he needed only a few days to put his machine right again.[87]

Olivier arrived in Cairo claiming to have flown earlier in 1913 for the Bulgarian army at the siege of Adrianople (Edirne in modern

Turkey), during the First Balkan War. He brought with him an 80 h.p. Henri Farman biplane in which he reportedly flew at Adrianople, although Watt somewhat pointedly informed the editor of *Aeroplane* on 23 December that 'when I was at Heliopolis on Sunday it was still in its case'.[88] Olivier soon had the Farman unpacked and assembled, ready to start flying tourists around the Pyramids.

Hard on the heels of Olivier and Pourpe came a further five French aviators, in three separate aircraft. On 29 December Jules Védrines arrived at Heliopolis in an 80 h.p. Bleriot XI monoplane. Three days later, on the first day of 1914, a Nieuport also touched down carrying Marc Bonnier and a mechanic, followed on 7 January by Pierre Daucourt and his mechanic Henri Roux in a Morane-Borel-Saulnier. All three aircraft had just flown from Paris—following a route across Europe and around the eastern end of the Mediterranean, through Turkey and Palestine—in response to a challenge issued by the French *Ligue Nationale Aérienne* (National Air League) to test the viability of long distance air travel.

Although the presence of this French contingent of flyers soon lost much of its public appeal, after an undignified row between Védrines and Roux that assumed almost farcical proportions, the initial arrival of Védrines in his Bleriot seems to have triggered a response from Watt which looks very much like pure impulse. At some stage about the end of December, or shortly after, Watt contacted the Bleriot Company in France to order his own aircraft—a two-seater Model XI, just like Védrines' machine, only powered by a 60 h.p. Gnome engine. Oswald had finally been inspired to enter the small and exclusive ranks of private aircraft owner-operators.

By late January *Aeroplane* newspaper was reporting that the Bleriot that Watt had purchased was passed through its tests at the company's aerodrome at Buc (21 kilometres south-west of Paris and a couple of kilometres south of Versailles) on the 18th of that month, 'in the presence of M. Pierre Prier, formerly of the Bleriot Company, and of Mr. Samuel S. Pierce.'[89] The speed with which Watt's order had been filled was explained by a later report in *Aeroplane*, to the effect that his Bleriot was a machine that had been shown at the French Aero Show in December,[90] so it seems his willingness to take a display model had eliminated waiting-time for manufacture.

Just a few weeks later, Watt's aircraft was delivered to him in Egypt, accompanied by a Bleriot employee who was to assist and instruct him with his new purchase. The man sent by the company was Samuel Pierce, the same as had been involved in testing the machine at the Bleriot works.[91] He was an American, who in 1909 reportedly built at Colorado Springs one of the first monoplanes in the U.S., before joining Bleriot the following year. It was reported that during the recent Balkan War he had worked with the Serbian Army, where he had charge of some Bleriot machines.[92]

Oswald Watt with newly-purchased Bleriot XI in front of his hangar at Heliopolis, Egypt. (Australian War Memorial C02799)

On 14 February Watt took to the air for the first time in his Bleriot XI, which he had named "Malleleu".[93] According to some press reports, this made him the first British subject to fly in Egypt.[94] Photographs were also published which trumpeted that the hangar he had specially constructed at Heliopolis to house the machine was the 'first in the land of the Pharaohs to fly the Union Jack.'[95] While the latter claim may very well be true, the belief that he was the first British subject to take to the Egyptian skies was definitely mistaken.

In fact, during the last week of December 1913 a four-man British aviation team led by wealthy Irish aviator Frank McClean had arrived at Alexandria, in preparation for also making an attempt to become the first to fly up the Nile to Khartoum. To achieve this object, they had brought with them a machine known as a 'hydro-aeroplane' (essentially a floatplane able to take off and land on water) that had been specially designed by the English engineering firm Short Brothers. By 3 January this team had begun making test flights over Alexandria, before heading to Cairo on the first leg of their adventure, so it was undoubtedly McClean and his colleagues who could claim to be the first Britons to fly in Egypt, not Watt.[96]

Unfortunately for McClean's aspirations of achieving a major aviation landmark, Pourpe was not only clearly bent on upstaging the British goal but more advanced in his preparations. On 4 January he set off from Heliopolis in his Morane-Saulnier with the aim of being the first to travel the 2,000 kilometers to Khartoum, which he did in little more than a week.[97] After resting for another week, he then flew back down the Nile in leisurely stages before arriving back in Cairo on 23 February. Meanwhile McClean's machine, being plagued by repeated breakdowns which caused long delays while awaiting delivery of spare parts, took nearly three months to reach Khartoum, whereupon McClean decided to dismantle the aircraft and ship it back to England. By then the Frenchman was long gone from Egypt. After Pourpe returned to Cairo, Oswald Watt had allowed him to house the Morane-Saulnier in his hangar at Heliopolis (where it was photographed), before Pourpe flew out to Suez about the end of February.[98]

By that time there were other French aviators visiting Egypt, including Maurice Chevillard (with a Henri Farman) and Maurice Guillaux (Bleriot XI). Presumably Watt would have made the acquaintance of both, especially since both were major participants in a flying 'meeting' held at Heliopolis on 19-22 February. The first day's flying involved mainly displays of 'looping the loop' by both

Chevillard and Guillaux, while Olivier gave joy flights to passengers. On the 20th, Guillaux reportedly looped nine times in succession during a single flight.[99]

There was no mention of Watt in connection with the Heliopolis meeting, though he was most likely present. He was certainly still in Cairo in late February, a fact attested to by two photos he took of a special occasion when French industrialist Jacques Schneider trialed a propeller-driven 'glisseur' (skimming-boat) on the Nile. An aviation enthusiast with a special interest in hydroplanes, Schneider carried with him as passenger Field Marshal Lord Kitchener, the de facto British ruler of Egypt during the last three years of Abbas II Hilmi Bey's formal reign as Khedive. The *Aeroplane* captioned one of its photos (both of which *Flight* credited to 'Mr W. Oswald Watt'[100]) as having been 'taken by a friend of this paper, to whom Lord Kitchener kindly gave special permission for it to be reproduced'[101]—which could be taken to mean that Watt had personally met the Field Marshal.

Jacques Schneider (centre, behind wheel) about to take Lord Kitchener (second from right) on a trip across the Nile in his 'glisseur' craft, February 1914; photo by Oswald Watt. (*Flight*, 7 Mar 1914)

While Chevillard appears to have mostly concerned himself, like Olivier, with flying passengers around the Sphinx and Pyramids, Guillaux was on a different mission entirely. His time in Egypt was merely an interlude on his way to Australia and New Zealand, where he planned to undertake a series of demonstration flights in his Bleriot. Before he embarked in *Orontes* in late March, bound for Sydney, Guillaux spent some time in Watt's company—a fact clearly demonstrated by a photograph that has survived showing Guillaux in the cockpit of his aircraft, inscribed (in French): 'To Mr Watt, very cordially. M. Guillaux. Heliopolis, 9 March 1914'.[102]

Photograph inscribed to Oswald Watt by Australia-bound Frenchman Maurice Guillaux in March 1914. (Australian War Memorial A05282)

Although we have no way of knowing for sure, it seems likely that Guillaux's ability to fly aerobatic manoeuvres in his Bleriot XI may have inspired Watt's next actions. In mid-April *Aeroplane* was reporting that, although Oswald had been having 'a good time' flying his Bleriot at Heliopolis, he found that landing there was 'abominable', as 'one is always dodging big stones and washouts, like miniature editions of the Pyramids and the Nile mouths, and it is like having to alight on a chessboard.' This appeared to be the only explanation offered for the following statement that Watt would be leaving Cairo for London 'very shortly'.[103]

Oswald did leave Egypt within a matter of weeks—departing Cairo with his Bleriot sometime in May—only he was heading not for England, but to France and the Bleriot works at Buc.[104] Later accounts have described the move as 'a six months' apprenticeship'[105] which was undertaken 'in order to obtain a thorough grasp of the intricacies of aeronautics' and supposedly involved Watt taking up employment as 'a mechanic' at the Bleriot factory. [106] While Watt's technical knowledge of aviation may very well have gained from this experience, the evidence is that his focus was definitely more on the flying side.

Early in June reports appeared that showed Watt had been applying himself to developing skills at looping an aircraft. First came a report that, on 2 June at Buc, Watt along with Samuel Pierce and a Norwegian army officer, had all succeeded in looping the loop in Bleriots.[107] Hard on the heels of this came word from Paris on 7 June, that Watt had made a triple loop—using the same Bleriot machine that French flyer Adolphe Pégoud had first performed this feat in September 1913.[108] This exciting news was telegraphed around Australia and appeared in countless papers across the country.

In fact, it would subsequently be established that Pégoud's feat was not the world first it was believed to be—a Russian army pilot named Pyotr Nesterov had actually beaten him to it by 12 days—although he could probably fairly claim to be the first true "ace" (an airman who destroys at least five opponents in aerial combat) of World War I, not fellow Frenchman Roland Garros as commonly asserted. It was also sadly true that by mid-1914 the triple loop was no longer the amazing novelty it had once been, having been repeated by a lengthening list of flyers in a growing range of countries. One Australian capital city newspaper was prompted to describe Watt's achievement in distinctly unimpressed terms, as 'plucky and hair-raising, but a trifle risky, and more ornamental than useful.'[109]

Something of Watt's purpose and frame of mind in France emerges from a letter he sent to the wife of his doctor friend in Sydney, while visiting London late in June. Addressing Roslyn Jamieson as 'Dear old "Auntie"', the letter (written at Buc and dated 22 June) reads in part:

… I live on the aerodrome some 17 miles from Paris & have been there twice since I got here on May 8th. It is charming here in the real country & I'm really doing some serious flying & happier than I have been for many years … I did "looping" first for once just to show myself—& a few other people—that I wasn't altogether a dead dog, but am finished with it & all other aerial "acrobatics", & am back to real cross country flying again, the only sort that really counts for military purposes. [After attending 'my niece's (Joan Caldwell) wedding' in London] I … then return to continue my aerial training under Bleriot's guidance.[110]

Watt's presence in France in the middle months of 1914 had at least placed him close to the major events and developments then taking place in the rapidly evolving field of aviation, and even allowed him to sometimes make his own small contribution. In the second week of July he was an official for the London-Paris-London Air Race (from Hendon to Buc and back again), serving as an observer at the Buc turning point.[111] This was the last of the great air races before the outbreak of the First World War, and Watt's life was about to take another radical change of course.

Chapter Five
UNFRIENDLY SKIES

Fighting for France

For a month after a Serbian fanatic shot dead the heir to the Austro-Hungarian throne in Sarajevo on 28 June 1914, the world remained on tenterhooks as the great powers of Europe threatened each other, issued ultimatums, and mobilised their armed forces. Then came the declarations of war: Austria-Hungary against Serbia on 28 July, then Germany (Austria's ally) against Russia (Serbia's backer) on 1 August; by 3 August historical enemies France and Germany had both declared war on each other, and that night Germany began an invasion of its southern neighbour.

Although sharing a border along France's north-eastern frontier, Germany directed its attack through the territory of the neutral kingdom of Belgium, whose status had been guaranteed by Britain for 75 years. The German move unified the Liberal government led by Herbert Asquith in London, which until then had been divided over whether to become involved in the unfolding catastrophe. On 4 August Britain declared war on Germany, bringing in on its coat-tails all the dominions and colonies of Britain's worldwide empire.

From his vantage point outside Paris, Oswald Watt could hardly avoid becoming infected with the war fever sweeping France—even before Germany's actions formally brought the French into the conflict. Under the Triple Entente pact binding Russia, France and Britain since 1907, the German declaration against Russia had pointed irrevocably to France's involvement. The only question remaining was whether reluctant Britain would honour its commitments and come into the war on France's side.

Doubts about the British position were undoubtedly on Watt's mind at Buc. As he wrote ten days later to Roslyn Jamieson in Sydney, he had been fearful that 'Asquith & Co were trying to shuffle England out of her treaty obligations'. This was an attitude which he could only deplore as an Australian, 'first because I always call myself such & second because if Asquith had succeeded I would have been fairly ashamed to call myself English.'[1] As a result, as early as 2 August he had volunteered both himself and his Bleriot aircraft to France for war service.

On his offer being accepted, Watt was issued with French military pilot's brevet No 509 and formally enlisted on 3 August as an ordinary soldier in the *Aviation Militaire* section of the French Foreign Legion. His status was that of *soldat de deuxième*, a second class private,[2] or in his case a *sapeur* (sapper) because the engineer branch had taken control of aviation in the French army from 1910. This made him the equivalent of a third-class air mechanic in the British army's air service, but Oswald did not mind this lowly rank because the Bleriot works at Buc had been converted into a military aerodrome and he found himself in 'excellent company' with, as he told Roslyn Jamieson, 'every famous aviator in France' also waiting there for orders.

The wait to find out how his services would be utilised in the first fortnight of war brought with it frustrations. At one stage Oswald thought that he had been chosen to deliver to Antwerp one of three Bleriot machines that the French had gifted to the Belgians, but at the last minute the civilian pilots given this task had their place taken by army officers. Instead, he found himself under orders to fly his "Malleleu" to Dijon to join the Reserve there. He did not want to do that, he told Roslyn Jamieson, 'as Dijon is a regular backwater & I fancy all the pilots who go there will be kept there for months.' Fortunately, these instructions were superseded when he was told on 18 August to fly across to Saint-Cyr, near Versailles, to receive fresh orders.

At the Saint-Cyr aviation depot Watt found himself in a small pool of pilots also awaiting allocation to units.[3] During the first week of September this group coalesced into an informal *escadrille* (squadron) with four Bleriots and a lieutenant observer who happened to be passing through to Vincennes, east of Paris, placed in charge. On 3 September Watt was himself granted the brevet (honorary) rank of captain, in recognition of his previous service at that rank in the Australian forces—although stories also appeared in the press in Britain and Australia that the promotion was made 'on the strength of a fine flight from Mourmelon-le-Grand to Saint-Cyr in a fog without a compass'.[4] The promotion did not mean that he was now in command of the Saint-Cyr Bleriot unit, as one British aviation magazine assumed.[5]

Oswald Watt in French uniform.

While the Saint-Cyr Bleriot unit began flying reconnaissance missions in the days after its formation, moving up temporarily to Villers-Cottérêts 80 kilometres north-east of Paris (where the British Expeditionary Force (BEF) fought a rearguard action on 1 September following its retreat from Mons), it is not known whether Watt was involved in any of these. The only flying task known definitely to come his way—as evidenced by photographs appearing in *Flight* and *Aeroplane* magazines—was to take up from Saint-Cyr a British businessman named Wallace Barr in late September, during one of the latter's regular visits to France to secure supplies of cellulose acetate needed to make fabric dope at his London factory for Britain's aeroplane manufacturers.[6]

It was at the Saint-Cyr depot that Oswald also became acquainted with Georges Carpentier, the pre-war world champion boxer who had joined the French army as a motor driver.[7] It was as Watt's assistant and mechanic that the 20-year-old Carpentier worked at the airfield, before Watt departed for the front and the boxer was sent to Avord to undergo flying training, which he completed in May 1915 when he qualified as a sergeant pilot in a Maurice Farman squadron.[8]

On 17 September the Bleriot squadron at Saint-Cyr had its identity further confirmed when it became administratively independent. Two days later, with its aircraft now increased to the usual squadron complement of six, it was formally established as a numbered unit on the *Aéronautique Militaire* order of battle, becoming 'BL30'—the BL prefix denoting the aircraft type that it flew. Despite these indications that the unit was finally preparing for battle, Watt told 'Mrs Jim' (as he addressed Roslyn Jamieson) that he still fretted about being kept out of action. The only comfort to be had was the fact that the squadron was 'first on the list for the frontier'.[9]

The promise became reality on 23 September, when BL30 was ordered forward to Villers-Cottérêts once again. On the 25th the squadron joined the Sixth Army, and the very next day Oswald received his "baptism of fire".[10] A postcard he sent to Roslyn Jamieson on 27 September recorded that this had occurred as he flew across the front lines on a reconnaissance mission. The Germans had 'fired their big special guns' at him, an experience he described as: 'Exciting very but not very nice when they get close tho' barring one stray all went very wide. Tho' I was flying at 1½ mile height some of the shells burst above me.'[11]

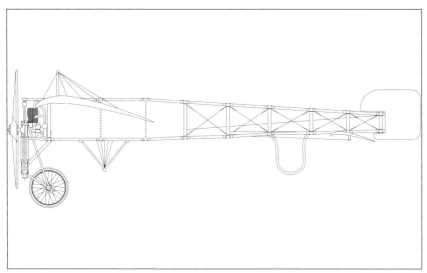

Diagram 1: Bleriot XI

A day after Watt penned his postcard home, BL30 received a new commanding officer. This was Captain Maximilien Van den Vaero, a regular officer whose aviator's certificate from the Aero Club of France dated from May 1911 and who had previously served with the French air detachment sent to Morocco in March 1912. With this experienced pilot at the helm, the squadron was moved another ten kilometres closer to the front line on 4 October, occupying an airfield on Cravancon Farm at Chaudun, nine kilometres south-west of Soissons.

For the two weeks before 27-28 September, the Aisne River which runs past Soissons had been the scene of a great counter-offensive launched by four French armies and the BEF, aimed at dislodging the Germans from a defensive position established on the tableland running east-west between the Aisne and Ailette valleys, and crossed by the road known since the eighteenth century as the "Chemin des Dames". With the First Battle of the Aisne now ended in the deadlock of trench warfare which would come to characterise the whole Western

Front for the next four years, the BEF was transferred to Flanders early in October—leaving the sector of the Allied line which it formerly occupied in the hands of the French Sixth Army.

From the time of the British departure, the Soissons sector became the particular focus of BL30's operations, aimed at detecting any signs that the enemy might be preparing to subject Sixth Army—its manpower more thinly stretched across a longer section of frontline— to surprise attack. According to the squadron's adjutant, these efforts produced plenty of 'hot' action, with Captain Watt holding the record on 30 September by being on the receiving end of 24 enemy rounds without actually being hit.[12]

In letters to family and friends in Sydney (including Roslyn Jamieson, his uncle Walter Watt, and fellow aviator W. E. Hart), Oswald related many of his experiences in the air, and on the ground during time spent in the trenches when too foggy to fly. Some of what he wrote home—about the Germans using explosive bullets, or employing an ambulance wagon bearing the Red Cross to bring quick-firing guns into the front line,[13] and spies caught in a church steeple[14]—were possibly tall tales heard in the trenches rather than strictly factual, first-hand accounts.

While based at Chaudun, Watt also apparently came to the notice of Sixth Army's aviation commander, Captain Georges Bellenger. An artillery officer before becoming involved with aviation a decade earlier, Bellenger had taken a professional and scientific interest in flying. In 1910-12 he was a member of a group of specialists brought together at the main artillery establishment at Vincennes to train as pilots, test new aircraft types and devices useful in the air, at the same time developing doctrine for operational application. While at Vincennes Bellenger had experimented with aerial photography, bombing, and the arming of aircraft, becoming a passionate and pugnacious advocate of the power of aircraft to transform the battlefield.[15]

In an account of Watt's adventures with BL30 published half a century later, Bellenger presents a view of Oswald as something of a well-intentioned amateur airman who struggled with making the transition from the sport of civilian flying to the more hazardous and demanding environment of war operations. According to Bellenger, once it was realised in the squadron that Watt had never performed full-time military service such as was required of every French male, it was conjectured that he owed his rank in the French service to having been captain of his local football team in Australia![16]

Bellenger recorded being approached by several of BL30's observers—the officers who, it was said, 'carry out practically all the work' in a reconnaissance squadron (the pilots being simply expected to chauffeur their passenger to the area nominated for attention and ensure a safe return). These told him of the great unease they felt whenever they flew with Watt. To find out what was happening in the air with the Australian pilot at the controls, Bellenger decided to take a flight with him.

The problems that Bellenger later claimed to have identified went beyond complaints from the observers that Watt always rigidly followed the course they requested him to fly—never letting himself be distracted by enemy shells fired in their direction or taking evasive action to put the enemy gunners off their aim. What at one level looked like Watt being fearless in his flying could also be construed as foolhardiness. Equally serious was Oswald's strange manner of managing his controls, which resulted in his Bleriot's flight path resembling 'a series of roller coasters'. This made the observers working with him airsick and interfered with their ability to fully perform their observation duties.

When Bellenger attempted to address these matters directly with Watt, he quickly came up against yet another problem. Unlike the other foreign volunteer in BL30 (Bellenger described the man as Greek but he was probably a Turkish-born Armenian named Jean Sismanoglou), Oswald was not fluent in the French language and communicated using a form of 'frenglish' which others in the unit found very difficult to understand. Oswald readily acknowledged—to Roslyn Jamieson, for example—that his French was 'awful', but possibly he did not appreciate the extent of the misunderstanding to which it contributed. As it was, Bellenger held that explaining to Watt what he needed to do to improve his flying was a very 'painful' experience, given that Bellenger totally lacked experience in speaking frenglish.

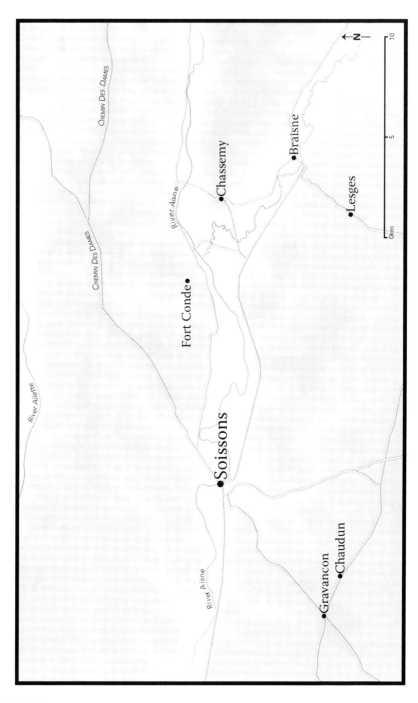

MAP 1: Soissons sector

Chapter 5

All Bellenger's doubts and concerns about Watt's effectiveness as a pilot may have seemed to be realised late in October when near-disaster came the Australian's way, but the cause of this episode was not enemy action or his mishandling of his aircraft. On 24 October Oswald was sent by Bellenger over the Chemin des Dames, accompanied by Captain Pierre Capitrel as observer, to look for signs of an impending German attack in this sector. At about 5 p.m., after two hours into the mission, Watt and Capitrel were over enemy-held ground when the engine of the Bleriot suddenly cut out. An account that appeared in the *Echo de Paris* newspaper in January 1915 (duly published in translation in the *Sydney Morning Herald*) provided grim details of the predicament which the airmen were now in, stating that they were at an altitude of only 1800 metres and a distance of five or six miles (8-9.5 kilometres) from the safety of French territory.[17]

Watt felt he had no choice but to make a forced landing in the only clear ground he could see available, which happened to be the stretch of land between the two opposing front lines in the vicinity of the Bois de Chassemy (Chassemy Wood), 13 kilometres east of Soissons. The lines here were about a kilometre apart, and after gliding noiselessly above the German trenches, the aircraft came to rest about 700 metres beyond the enemy front line—but still short of the French positions by 300 metres.[18]

The two airmen immediately jumped out of the machine and took refuge behind a hayrick 20 metres away, to conceal themselves from the rifle and machine gun fire being directed at them. Then the Germans brought 77mm and 105mm guns to bear on the aircraft sitting exposed in the open. Over the next 30 minutes an estimated 50 shells dropped around the spot, without hitting men or machine—although Watt and Capitrel found themselves smothered with dust several times, and shrapnel fell everywhere about them.[19]

Finally, after a round from a 105 burst between the Bleriot and the hayrick, digging a large hole in the ground and setting fire to the hay, the pair decided to make for the French trenches—concealed in part by smoke from the burning straw.[20] They reached their objective, safe but breathless, though the enemy rifle and artillery fire continued unabated. Neither man was touched,[21] although both were hampered in their movements by the heavy clothing and boots they wore as protection from the cold at higher altitudes.[22] As Oswald told Roslyn Jamieson, 'We both must surely have been born to be hung!' After an hour and a half of trying, the Germans finally scored a hit on Watt's 'poor old machine', flipping it up 'like a sinking ship' and reducing it to a skeleton-like frame.

Watt had miraculously survived a perilous situation with body and spirit both intact, but there was evidently a dimension to this episode of which he may never have been aware. After Oswald and Capitrel were taken to the headquarters of the French 287th Infantry Regiment at Braisne[23] and returned to the BL30 airfield later that same evening, Capitrel went to Captain Bellenger's office to report his version of what had happened.

According to Capitrel, at the moment when the Bleriot's motor stopped he was not greatly concerned because he considered that they had sufficient altitude to make it back to French territory, regardless of any enemy ground fire directed at them. They were then, he contended, over the area of Fort Condé-sur-Aisne (an abandoned French fortress—now in German hands—only about three kilometres from where the aircraft eventually came to earth). But he was horrified to see that, instead of taking the shortest route towards safety behind the French lines, Watt was circling to put the aircraft down on the nearest suitable ground he could find. Despite Capitrel's desperate attempts to persuade Watt with voice and gesture to make directly south, Watt responded in frenglish and gestures of his own that the engine was 'no longer walking' and he was forced to land. Despite Capitrel's protestations, Watt, 'impassive as always', proceeded to put the plane down in no man's land.

For his part, Bellenger was greatly annoyed that one of his aircraft remained between the lines—even if it was now fit for nothing but spare parts. It was a principle he tried to inculcate in all pilot and observer teams that they should always do everything they could to save a machine entrusted to them. The rest of his published account of the "adventures of Captain Watt" was therefore taken up with the efforts undertaken at his direction the following night to retrieve the remains of Watt's machine, dodging the beam of a powerful searchlight the Germans had erected on Fort Condé. When the wreckage was inspected in the light of next morning, an inscription was found on the fuselage left by an enemy patrol which had reached it the previous evening. By that stage Watt was already on his way to Paris to take delivery of a replacement aircraft.

Watt stands beside the tail of his Bleriot adorned with a crude British flag, taken at Lesges, February 1915.

A week after his first lucky escape Watt was back in the air and had another brush with disaster. On 30 October BL30 had moved to a new location at Lesges, 20 kilometres east of Chaudun. It was a day or so after this that Oswald was again on a reconnaissance when his new Bleriot was fired on by German anti-aircraft guns and a piece of bursting shell cracked through the vital rear spar of his left wing.[24] Refusing to be deflected from his purpose, he displayed great coolness by continuing with the mission and did not descend until the job was finished.

The tempo of operations in BL30 remained constant, even with the onset of winter as the year drew to a close. By late January 1915 Oswald was commenting to Roslyn Jamieson that it was 'terribly cold aloft' and he would 'give a lot for some sun'. By that stage he was onto his fourth aircraft since the war started, having also had his third Bleriot irreparably damaged on operations.[25]

On 11 February—Watt's 37th birthday—he received a telegram at 10 am telling him that he had been appointed a Chevalier (knight) of the Legion d'honneur [Legion of Honour] and his presence was required at a review of the Sixth Army to receive his decoration from the French commander-in-chief, General Joseph Joffre. Regardless of the view Bellenger had taken of the episode the previous October, others had obviously seen matters in a very different light. Oswald admitted that he knew he had been 'proposed' for a decoration three months earlier, but news of his award still came as a complete surprise. The published citation praised him as 'a pilot with much dash, undaunted in all circumstances, and full of go.'[26]

Describing the investiture ceremony to 'Mrs Jim' two days afterwards, Watt said that Joffre was 'very nice & seemed pleased to learn I was an Australian'—Australia was, he explained, 'very well "up"' as a consequence of the naval engagement off Cocos Islands in the Indian Ocean the previous November, in which the Australian cruiser *Sydney* had destroyed the German raider *Emden*. The review was a very big affair, although there were just seven members of the Sixth Army receiving awards, and the General made a show of embracing each recipient in turn after he pinned on their cross.[27]

Sixth Army officers presented with the Legion of Honour by General Joffre, 11 February 1915. Oswald Watt is obscured (except head) behind the general's attendant.

To his Sydney correspondent, Watt confided that he was 'looking forward to getting out [of uniform] again when this business is over', although he still hoped 'to be able to do something in the military aviation line'. It was, however, far too early to be entertaining thoughts such as these, as events would dictate that he had more than a year yet to give in the French air service, and within a matter of weeks his employment was about to take a major change of course.

In the meantime, Watt's feats at the front were widely reported back in Australia and received extraordinary attention, for the simple reason that his country's own forces had yet to make an impact in any major theatre of conflict. Although other individuals having Australian connections were also present on the Western Front, none had anything like the public image and almost romantic profile of Oswald Watt. Even a simple gesture such as his £20 donation to the benevolent fund established in London by the Royal Aero Club in January 1915—to benefit members of the Royal Flying Corps and Royal Naval Air Service incapacitated on service, and the widows and dependants of those killed—was enough to bring his name renewed prominence and popular respect.[28]

Capitaine Australien

After the first six months of the war it was clear that the military usefulness of the Bleriot XI had been greatly diminished by the better aircraft types introduced onto the battlefield by both sides in the conflict. Accordingly, during the last week of March 1915 BL30 was withdrawn to Cravancon Farm at Chaudun to begin the process of re-equipping with Caudron reconnaissance machines, before returning to the order of battle in early April with a new squadron identity as C30.

The pilots of BL30 were not kept with the old squadron during its conversion, but were dispersed to flying schools to begin retraining on a different reconnaissance type, the Maurice Farman 11. One of several designs produced by Anglo-French brothers Richard, Henry (Henri) and Maurice Farman, the MF.11 was nicknamed the "Shorthorn" to distinguish it from its predecessor, the MF.7 Longhorn. It was a biplane with wings of unequal span, a "pusher" type with its engine placed (facing backwards) behind the open-air nacelle containing the two-man crew. In early 1915 it was still unarmed, although the evolving conditions of the air war would soon change that.

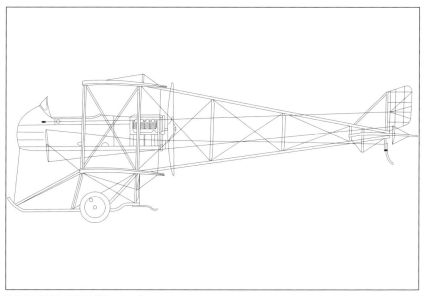

DIAGRAM 2: MF.11 "Shorthorn"

Chapter 5

Oswald Watt was among the pilots sent away at an early stage in BL30's transition, departing on 12 March. The flying school where he went to retrain four days later is not recorded on his card in the index of military aviation personnel in French archives, but by April he appeared on the RGA (Réserve Générale de l'Aéronautique) pool of pilots at Le Bourget, situated on the northeast outskirts of Paris (and after the war the location of the French capital's first airport). On 1 April he was assigned to a new MF.11-equipped squadron that was about to be formed.

On 4 April the new escadrille, called MF44, was brought into being at Fort Bron, 10 kilometres east of Lyon in the Rhône-Alpes region.[29] The next day, the mechanics and ground support staff of the squadron set off by rail to the new unit base at Toul, facing the Franco-German border 25 kilometres west of Nancy and at the southern end of the Woëvre Plain which stretches north all the way to Luxembourg. The fortifications around the city of Toul were now a vital part of French defences blocking German forces from further advances, after these captured a salient of ground at Saint-Mihiel in September 1914 and effectively surrounded the fortress of Verdun on three sides.

It was not until 14 April that the pilots of MF44—including Watt—left Le Bourget to fly into Toul with the squadron's complement of MF.11 Shorthorns. The journey was far from pleasant, as Oswald told Roslyn Jamieson that he was 'stopped several times by rain & snow', and the wind was 'just a hurricane'.[30] After landing at Châlons-sur-Marne (now Châlons-en-Champagne) for lunch, barely half-way to his destination, he was finally stopped at Bar-le-Duc by darkness[31] (still 50 kilometres short) and did not reach Toul until 15 April—the day that MF44 formally joined the French First Army. Commanded again by Captain Max Van den Vaero, the squadron now had a personnel strength of 76, including five pilots, four observers and 16 mechanics. It had arrived just in time for the First Battle of the Woëvre, aimed at retaking Saint-Mihiel.

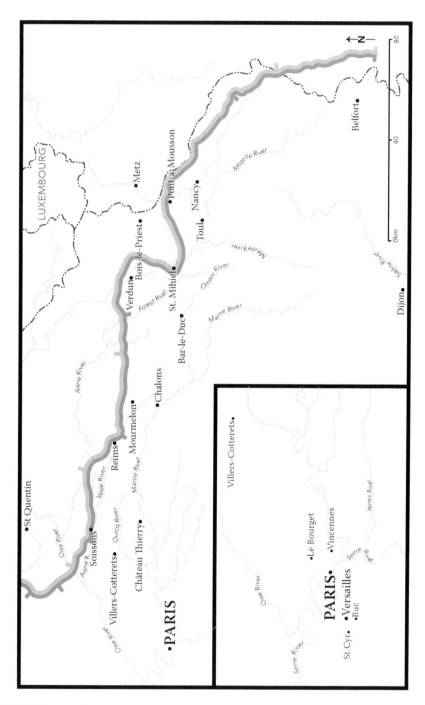

MAP 2: Northern France

Officers of MF44 pictured at Toul, May 1915. Watt is seated front left, alongside the CO, Captain Max Van den Vaero. (Service Historique de la Défense, France)

Oswald was immediately into action in the region of Bois-le-Priest, and reported that on 16 April his aircraft had received a hit from enemy fire. In a postcard to Sydney, he wrote: 'we were flying somewhat low & dodging in & out of the clouds. It was [strange] to hear the bang of the shells bursting quite close to one in the middle of a big fat cloud when we could see absolutely nothing. [Afterwards] we picked a neat little bit of shrapnel out of the tail.' He added that he was 'getting used to my Maurice Farman biplane now & like it, but it is very "dead" after the more lively Bleriot. The reliable 80 HP Renault is a joy.' He was, he said, 'very glad to be at work again & there's plenty to be done here. I'm hoping they'll let me do something with our Australian Flying Corps when the war is over. I have had & am having quite a certain amount of experience in one way or another.'[32]

Two days after his first brush with enemy fire, Oswald had a second close call. In another postcard to "Mrs Jim", he wrote that he was 'sending a piece of shell we pulled out of my bus yesterday to be made into a brooch or a charm for you as you like. The bus was hit in 18 places – too near to be pleasant – & they broke 2 wires & nearly got through a main spar as well as scarring the propeller. The big pieces of shell go right through the fabric but this little piece got left between the two layers – 2 big holes just 2 feet over my head.'[33]

By 5 May the French offensive on the Woëvre had ground to a halt, but Watt was still finding plenty of action in the air. On 24 May he wrote a long letter to his Potts Point friends, the Jamiesons, telling them that two days previously he had completed an eight-day spell of flying on the front-line—the longest continuous period he had experienced since the start of the war. The squadron's MF.11s were now being utilised as light bombers as well as for reconnaissance, and that very morning he had been out at 4 a.m. with eight bombs to drop on enemy positions: '2 on a railway line 1 on a road 1 on an isolated house with a smoking chimney & the rest amongst the more or less awake Boches so my observer assures me. In return they treated us to some 50 shells & never touched us.' Since arriving at Toul he had flown 2500 miles and had 31 hits scored on his aircraft. 'How many shells they've fired at me Heaven only knows. The machine is paid for many times over.'[34]

Watt's MF.11 viewed from above on operations near Toul. (Australian War Memorial C02797)

Chapter 5

It was in this letter Oswald also revealed that he had heard about the Allied landings at the Dardanelles the previous month, explaining that he had been hoping to go there himself:

> I had volunteered but they wouldn't have me. They explained very kindly it was meant as a compliment as they refused all the escadrille as they want all their old pilots on the western front. They took all young pilots & now (2 days ago) they are out asking for volunteers so I have applied again. I expect their young pilots have failed them & it's very difficult country to fly over … Our men have done splendidly in the Dardanelles business but it's the old old story of want of discipline. If the troops are A1 as ours are they get there alright but at terrible & quite unnecessary cost.

Within days Watt wrote again referring to news of the death at Gallipoli of Colonel Henry Maclaurin, at the head of the 1st Australian Infantry Brigade; 'We were mates years & years ago in the Scottish Rifles poor thing.' He was glad to have received the good news about Roslyn Jamieson's doctor husband Syd (who he referred to as 'old Jim') having been appointed lieutenant-colonel to head a new No 3 Australian General Hospital that was England-bound. Better still was the news Oswald had to impart that he had just qualified for award of the Croix de Guerre (War Cross):

> at least that is to say that I've the right to wear it, tho' as it is a new decoration the actual medals aren't out yet. One gets it for being cited in the orders of the Army, and I was cited three days ago in the orders of the 31st Army Corps to which we are attached … I'm especially pleased as we all 4 of us did the same thing & they've given the two NCOs Noel & Sismanoglou the Medaille Militaire [Military Medal]. Our lieutenant is promised the Legion d'honneur! The three were very overdue for the decorations & should have had them months ago.[35]

Something Roslyn Jamieson had previously seen or read had prompted her to ask Oswald whether he might also be in line to receive the Military Medal. To this suggestion, he responded: 'The Medaille Militaire my dear I can't get even if I deserved it as it is given only to NCOs & men.

No officers are eligible for it with the single exception of a general who commands an army in the field. Thus Joffre himself & General French [commander of the BEF] were given it by the President some time ago.'[36] This explanation was not sufficient to prevent Melbourne scholar Percival Serle from later stating categorically that Watt was awarded the Military Medal as a result of his war service with the French, in addition to the Legion of Honour and War Cross—a mistake sometimes repeated since.[37]

On the night of 27 May, Watt had yet another 'close go'. As he reported next day to "Mrs Jim":

> A pilot flying at 10,000 feet came in & reported something extraordinary & I was sent off to investigate with a little gunner officer. Thunder clouds were coming up & the air was rotten & we had to fly really low & got hit 8 times which makes 40 hits in all now for 2700 miles flown. We found nothing! One big shell (105m/m German gun) burst right in front of us & at our level & I heard something hit & on returning found that 5 balls (shrapnel) had hit the front of the nacelle or little box we sit in just level with my chest (I am in front) and the centre one had hit head-on & punctured the metal but not penetrated the other 4 ricocheting off.[38]

The pace of flying operations was constant, and in a letter to Mrs Jamieson in early June he again wrote:

> I left just after writing to you [last time] in my machine for Verdun. We all set off at daybreak next morning to call on "little Willie". What damage we did I don't know but they were very annoyed certainly for they pulled up a big gun next day and bombarded the hospital at Verdun … My machine was hit 3 times making a total of 44 to date some 3300 miles flown since April 13th. I was all alone in my machine – dropped 6 bombs (90m/m) on Willie & 2 on (or very close to) a long train and 2000 flechettes or little steel arrows. Waiting now for a "Boche" to be signalled & it's my turn to go & try to hunt him. They have always gone as soon as they see us but now they've imported one who stays & yesterday he wounded an observer in a very fast

machine & broke up the motor of one of ours – he was hit himself though I think & he may be wiser next time. Not much good "chasing" an 80 mile an hour machine with a 70 tho![39]

The appearance of armed Fokker monoplanes on the German side suddenly posed a serious new threat to the slower Maurice Farman machines. Ten days after Watt wrote his letter to Mrs Jamieson, MF44 suffered its first aircraft lost in action—along with its two-man crew, Warrant Officer Sismanoglou (pilot) and Lieutenant Eugène Virolet (observer). At first it was thought their aircraft had fallen victim to ground fire while spotting for a French battery in the vicinity of Flirey, near Pont-à-Mousson. Ironically Sismanoglou had taken to carrying a rifle in his cockpit, using this a month earlier to chase away an intruder who was attempting to reconnoitre French positions. He had done the same thing on 4 June, this time taking on two enemy aircraft and forcing them to turn about.[40]

While performing his spotting mission on 15 June Sismanoglou was set upon by an enemy fighter. When he was able to turn the tactical situation to his advantage and the enemy pilot broke off the attack, Sismanoglou evidently decided to take after his opponent with hopes of securing his squadron's first victory in aerial combat. It was while giving chase that his MF.11 was believed to have been hit by artillery or machine-gun fire, and was seen to explode and fall in flames into the enemy-occupied village of Essey (now Essey-et-Maizerais). Next day, however, a German fighter appeared over the airfield at Toul and dropped a letter claiming the destruction of the MF44 plane. In fact, there were grounds for doubting the truth of this second version, since the unit of the two airmen who said they had shot down Sismanoglou's aircraft declined to recommend the pair for an award for their victory; however, this conflict of evidence would not be known until nearly a century later.

For Oswald, the increased perils likely to be faced in the air became all too real within a matter of weeks. In mid-July he wrote a letter to Roslyn Jamieson relating a chilling experience he recently had while operating in roughly the same area as the lost MF44 crew. Oswald had been scheduled to fly a bombing mission in company with Warrant

Officer Louis Noel, who he described as 'my mate'. As Oswald would be carrying most of the bombs in his aircraft, he was to fly alone to save on weight, escorted by Noel in another machine accompanied by a passenger armed with a 'mitrailleuse' (machine gun) and carrying fewer bombs. The two planes took off separately, intending to meet at a pre-arranged rendezvous, but when the motor of Noel's aircraft broke down he failed to show up and Watt decided to proceed on his own.[41]

After dropping his bomb-load on the railway enclosure and sheds which were the designated target, Oswald turned for home—only to discover an armed enemy machine waiting for him:

> He cut round behind me & I couldn't see what he was doing but knew he wasn't far away as the German guns didn't fire at me. I had a … wind against me & the German was a good 10 miles an hour faster than my Farman. Anyhow here I am writing to you but it's the last time I go on such an expedition alone. Onlookers now tell me that he fired only a few shots & then cleared out for Metz & I crossed the line by Pont-a-Mousson. I think he must have seen a good friend, another Dane called Seth Jensen, who was flying some 2 miles away and taken fright – anyhow my luck was in as if he'd been brave he had me to a certainty, as I had a long way to go when he caught me.

Despite this scare, Watt went on flying missions as before. On 8 August he wrote to Mrs Jim:

> A few days ago we found a place where the Germans cook & I hope eat (war makes one into a savage!) their evening meal as the observers for the artillery on the ground used to
> see the smoke so I went & dropped 10 bombs there just at dusk as a sort of digestive. One never knows of course the result but something caught fire & we saw the smoke rising as we flew home – my mechanic & I. It was nearly dark & it was impressive when the shells they fired at us exploded in the air like rockets & very noisy ones. One rather close lit up all the instruments in front of me & another I saw burst under the glass observation window on the floor. We flew home in a beautiful red afterglow & found Toul just lighting up.[42]

Watt was taking to the skies from Toul on an average of four days a week, and at this rate the risks he ran were inevitably constant also. As he wrote:

> I've had my machine hit very very often now and have almost lost count. Last time I totted it up the total was 66 … Getting very cold here now & last night I was nearly frozen in the air as I miscalculated the temperature aloft as far as clothing was concerned. I have a reputation for hardiness born of cold water habits & open windows! Anyhow after 1½ hours of it our wireless plant struck work & saved my life as we had to come down. Under new regulations I am entitled to 6 days' clear leave in England but refuse to take it just now as things are too unsettled tho' I hope to take it before Xmas. Have been at Toul now just 5 months & flying pretty regularly & a change would do no harm. Have put in 100 hours in the air meaning between 6 & 7000 miles flying.[43]

Just two days after writing his letter to Sydney, Watt received clear confirmation that the odds were shifting against him. According to a notice appearing in the French *Journal Officiel* in late October, which constituted the formal citation for his award of the Croix de Guerre, on 10 August he was struck on the head by a piece of shrapnel from an exploding flak shell but continued the reconnaissance mission he was flying 'with the greatest coolness'.[44] An English version of the Journal reference duly appeared in *Flight* magazine which unfortunately gave the date of Oswald's wounding as 8 August[45] (a mistake subsequently repeated in Australian newspapers),[46] but the rest of the citation made for interesting reading. He was, so the Journal stated, a 'fine officer' and a 'pilot of great daring and imperturbable composure' who 'never hesitates to fly above the enemy's lines at low altitude whenever circumstances require it'. Consequently, many of the numerous reconnaissances he conducted were 'very dangerous' and resulted in his plane being frequently struck by shell-splinters—including twice more in August after he was wounded, and on three consecutive days in September.

It was perhaps as a result of his injury, or to give him the change he thought he needed, that Oswald was returned to the RGA at

Bourget for five days in September. As this period was not entered in his record as "leave", however, it was unlikely to have been intended as recreation. More likely he was sent back to Paris to bring forward one of the newer model MF.11a (or MF.11bis) machines with which his squadron was being re-equipped. These aircraft were powered by a 130 hp Renault engine, and had changed seating arrangements for the crew which put the pilot and the flight controls in the rear seat, and the observer up front where he not only had a better view but also a better field of fire for the Hotchkiss 8mm machine gun which was now carried in the nose. Once Oswald got back to Toul, he joined the other pilots in applying some personal touches to his new 'bus'. On the hinged moveable wind-mask on the aircraft's nose, he painted the words 'Advance Australia' flanked on each side by kangaroo emblems. The machine itself was dubbed "The Kangaroo".[47] As Keith Isaacs, an historian of early Australian military aviation later observed, Oswald Watt's aircraft was thus 'the first to carry kangaroo insignias into battle'.[48]

On the ground at Toul, 17 March 1916, in front of Watt's MF.11bis which he named "The Kangaroo" and decorated accordingly; Oswald in centre. (Bibliothèque de Documentation Internationale Contemporaine, University of Paris, Nanterre)

Chapter 5

In the last weeks of October or early November the period of leave which was due to Oswald finally came his way, enabling him to visit England to see both family and friends. It gave him the greatest enjoyment to turn up in French uniform to see his son ('my small Jim') at boarding school, where he found him 'well & very happy & curiously enough his head master was my house master at Bristol some 25 years ago!'[49] Afterwards he took Jim to lunch at the home of William Locke, the novelist he had met in Cairo. As the Lockes lived only a short distance away from the aerodrome at Hendon—now the home of the RAF Museum—Oswald took Jim to show him the aircraft there. Locke later wrote that, 'unsatiated by six months flying in the unhealthy neighbourhoods of Toul and St. Mihiel', Oswald felt the need to 'invest himself in airman's leathers and fly round and round on a machine entirely new to him'.[50] When Oswald told Roslyn Jamieson about his leave to England in a letter from Toul dated 4 December, he did not mention taking to the air at Hendon—only that it was delightful to be able to take his 'dear little kid' on an outing. 'This war has been a godsend for some of us, hasn't it?'[51]

Other remarks in his letter to Mrs Jamieson suggest that Watt's break from the front line had given him pause to reflect on other things. 'Time does push on,' he wrote, '& even in conscript France I'd be reckoned too old for first line service & yet somehow I manage to carry on in my job—curious really as very many men far younger than I am have given it up after only a few months at the front and applied for less jumpy work.' Perhaps this was an indication that he was beginning to think about channeling his contribution to the war effort in some different direction.

Possibly adding to Watt's shift in focus might have been a period of four days that he was on attachment away from Toul in early January 1916. It is not known where this time was spent, but a clue exists in two images contained in a photo album recording his time with the *Aéronautique Militaire*. These are views of the Nieuport 11 aircraft—a small, single-seat fighter powered by an 80 hp Le Rhone rotary engine and armed with a single Hotchkiss machine-gun—which entered French service in January 1916 and quickly helped to end the aerial "scourge" represented by the Fokker machines in use by the Germans. The caption in Watt's album, added in his own handwriting, states simply 'I flew this in Paris'.[52]

Although Keith Isaacs speculated that Watt might have flown the new type in the middle of 1915, it seems more likely that Oswald actually got the chance to test fly it in January 1916, just as the nimble scout was being introduced. Had he chosen to stay with the French flying corps, it is not hard to imagine that he might have begun thinking about applying to join a fighter unit—rather than continue trusting his luck in the rickety and increasingly vulnerable Shorthorn at MF44. In the event, another opportunity opened up a month later, and Oswald eagerly seized it.

Transfer to the AIF

On 9 February 1916 Watt proceeded on a second period of leave from his duties at the French airbase at Toul which lasted eleven days. While it is unknown where he took this further break from operational flying, there is an indication that he proceeded—as before—to Britain. The evidence for this exists in a cablegram sent to Melbourne on 15 February from the office of the Australian High Commissioner in London. The message advised that Captain Oswald Watt, now serving with the French flying corps where he had been recently decorated for distinguished work, was 'very desirous' of entering Commonwealth service. The High Commissioner went on to suggest that Watt's training and experience 'merit special consideration' for the 'Air Squadron now being formed vice Pickles who is unable to accept appointment'.[53]

The High Commissioner who originated this communication was former Australian prime minister Andrew Fisher, who had arrived in Britain with his family to take up his new role only at the end of January.[54] He had spent the first fortnight in London settling into his office at 72 Victoria Street in Westminster, and being welcomed to the duties of the appointment. On 15 February he was also sworn to the Privy Council.[55] The terms of Fisher's message strongly suggest that his representation to Melbourne was the result of a personal approach from Watt, and this could have occurred only in London—not during a tour to meet Australian troops in France or elsewhere that he (and his predecessor) would sometimes make during the war.

If Watt did not know beforehand, he must certainly have heard after arriving in Britain, of the announcement made in December 1915 that Australia intended to form a squadron of its Flying Corps within the expeditionary army, the Australian Imperial Force, that had been raised for war service in the European theatre. One of the Australian aviators who had achieved prominence in Britain before the war was Sydney Pickles from Marrickville, Sydney, who had become a Flight Lieutenant in the Royal Naval Air Service. After previously having been named to command Australia's military flying school at Point Cook in mid-1915,[56] early in January 1916 Pickles accepted appointment as a Captain in the AIF, to become a flight commander with No 1 Squadron, Australian Flying Corps.[57] Notice had even appeared in the *Commonwealth Gazette* in late January,[58] but then he had withdrawn—creating a sudden vacancy which had obviously come (or been drawn) to Watt's notice.

Despite Fisher's clear support for Watt's application to replace Pickles, when the high commissioner's cablegram was received in Army Headquarters at Melbourne's Victoria Barracks it drew a strongly negative response in one quarter. The Chief of the General Staff, Colonel Hubert Foster, was clearly sympathetic. On 21 February he drafted a minute to the Secretary of the Department of Defence proposing that a reply be sent stating that 'Oswald Watt is accepted for Australian Flying Corps', with a commission as captain from 1 March, and asking that Watt be directed to join the unit in Egypt on 12 April. But when this draft passed the desk of the Adjutant General, Colonel Thomas Dodds—the senior staff officer with special responsibility for personnel policy matters—it received an entirely different reception.[59]

Dodds spelt out his objections, and his reasons, in a forthright minute to the Secretary on 26 February:

> This gentleman appears to be rendering most valuable and gallant service to the Empire and the Allies in the capacity in which he is presently employed. Already innumerable applications for transfer of and appointment to the A.I.F.

from Australians serving in various capacities in the Imperial and other portions of the Overseas Contingents have not been approved. I do not concur with approval being granted to such applications, most of which are made in view of the higher rates of pay in the A.I.F. Unless it be determined to treat all such applications alike and grant appointments I cannot too strongly recommend that the High Commissioner be informed that the application of Captain O. Watt, R. of O. [Reserve of Officers] is not approved.

Fortunately for Oswald, a ruling in this disputed matter was requested from the Minister for Defence, who happened to be Senator George Foster Pearce—the same man who interviewed Oswald upon his return from gaining his "wings" in England five years earlier. Perhaps remembering the pioneering airman so keen to offer his services with establishing military aviation in Australian, Pearce took a very different view to Dodds and on 1 March annotated Colonel Foster's draft: 'I am prepared to approve of Minute of C.G.S.' Following this ruling, a reply went next day along the lines first proposed by Foster. Notice of Oswald Watt's transfer to the AIF appeared in the *Commonwealth Gazette* a week later.[60] A military order was also promulgated that transferred Watt from the Reserve of Officers in the 2nd Military District [NSW] to the AIF, with effect from 1 March 1916.[61]

When accounts of Watt's transfer to the Australian forces appeared in subsequent years, the explanation offered has usually been that it was because—as a foreigner in the French service—he could not be given a position of command for which he was now qualified. It was supposedly for this reason that he was somewhat reluctantly offered up by the French and 'released' by them so that he could make the transfer back to his home country's forces.[62] What the archival record really shows is that Watt himself initiated the move, and it was only because of a decision taken at government minister level that policy regarding transfers of Australians to the AIF from Allied armies was varied in his case. In confirmation of the true facts of the matter, formal Ministry of War notification that Watt's 'resignation' had been accepted by the French President was not forthcoming until 23 August 1916.[63]

That Watt was nonetheless leaving French service with his stocks still high was evidenced by a final tribute paid on his departure by Général Gaston Delétoille, commanding the 31st Army Corps, in an order issued on 20 April. This stated: 'Captain Walter Oswald Watt, pilot of Escadrille [Squadron] M.F./44, has not ceased to show the best qualities of audacity and cool resolution. Always ready to fly at low altitudes to facilitate observation or to take photographs. On 11th April when flying a French Aeroplane attacked by three Germans he put to flight the enemy's machines.'[64] Watt's feat reported in the final sentence would have been all the more remarkable because on 12 April he left Toul for the last time to return to London. He had then been flying constantly for 18 months, and was aged 38.

With No 1 Squadron

Back in London once more, Watt set about making preparations to take up his new post in the first complete Australian flying squadron due to be soon joining the Royal Flying Corps (RFC). Contrary to what he perhaps expected when he began moves to secure a transfer, the squadron would not be coming to England because the War Office had requested that it disembark in Egypt where it could do advanced training more quickly than in Britain's overcrowded schools and where it might cooperate with AIF units.[65] Nonetheless, he still needed to fit himself out with Australian officer uniforms to replace his French ones.

Suitably attired, he made an appointment at the fashionable Westminster studio of Gabell & Co. to be photographed on 21 May.[66] On both his cap and tunic he wore the "rising sun" badge of the Australian Commonwealth Military Forces (almost certainly the first time he had worn any of these items), and above his left breast pocket—immediately beneath his pilot's "wings"—appeared the unfamiliar ribbons of his two French decorations. At Devonport next day Oswald boarded the *Orsova*, an Orient passenger liner pressed into service as a troopship, bound for Egypt. By chance, the same ship had just the previous month delivered No 1 Squadron of the Australian Flying Corps to where he was now headed.[67]

Oswald Watt in AIF uniform for the first time, May 1916

Also travelling in the *Orsova* was the officer the War Office in London was sending to take command of 1 Squadron.[68] The officer who had brought the unit from Australia, Lieutenant Colonel Edgar Reynolds, was too senior and inexperienced in air operations to remain in command (he was neither a trained pilot or observer), so he had proceeded on to England to take a staff appointment with AIF units in France more appropriate to his rank. In his place the War Office had offered Captain T. F. ("Foster") Rutledge, an Australian who had been a stockbroker in Melbourne before qualifying as a pilot in July 1914. Joining the RFC as Second Lieutenant in August, Rutledge had flown in France and won two promotions before being posted to Egypt in January 1916, to one of the two RFC squadrons in that country. Illness had caused him to be invalided to England, but now recovered he was returning with the temporary rank of Major.[69] London's offer to transfer him to the AIF had been rejected by the Department of Defence—upholding the policy that had been waived in Watt's case.[70]

Both Foster Rutledge and Oswald Watt might have wondered what awaited them in Egypt, and soon after reaching Port Said on 31 May they found out.[71] The squadron that came under Rutledge's command on 1 June was in no way a functioning unit. When it became apparent to the local RFC headquarters that the 28 officers and 195 other ranks who arrived in mid-April were lacking not just aircraft and equipment (which it was always expected that Britain would provide) but training and practical experience, the decision had been made to institute drastic measures. As many of the junior pilots were short on flying hours, they were sent on to England for further training. With them went all the observers, since no courses had been available in Australia to even begin their training. The mechanics and tradesmen recruited as ground staff had little experience with aircraft, so these had been dispersed among the two flying squadrons comprising the RFC Fifth Wing along with the Aircraft Park providing depot services.[72]

With the arrival of Rutledge and Watt, the situation began to change markedly. The pair proceeded straight away to Cairo, and to the aerodrome at Heliopolis on the city's north-east outskirts. This area was transformed from how Oswald remembered it two years previously. The bare patch of ground on the edge of the desert where he had erected his private hangar and flown his first Bleriot was now covered with hangars, sheds, huts and tents housing No 17 Squadron of the RFC—less "C" Flight of four aircraft that had been detached to Suez, at the southern entrance to the Canal.[73] However, as described by Adrian Cole, an Australian trainee airman about to receive a commission, this jumble of buildings had 'been built in such a way that they blocked off and limited the area for landing from the miles of flat desert to the east, and the resultant space was made far more hazardous by the presence of elevated high tension wires, half way across it, on steel posts twenty-five feet high, bisecting at right angles to the prevailing wind.'[74] Regardless of its limitations, Heliopolis became the headquarters of '1st Australian Squadron' with Rutledge as its commanding officer and Watt as commander of "B" Flight.

Further altering local circumstances were orders that arrived in early June for 17 Squadron to prepare to move to Salonika (now Thessalonika in Greece) in support of an Anglo-French force landed there in late 1915 to aid the Serbian army. It was at this time that Watt's operational experience proved to be an enormous asset to the Australian squadron, because his B Flight was chosen as the first to be allocated aircraft and technical stores.[75] The aircraft type received was the BE2c, a two-seater biplane manufactured at the Royal Aircraft Factory and powered by a 90 hp RAF engine; intended for reconnaissance and light bombing duties, the type was the same as that used by 17 Squadron and the other flying unit in Egypt, No 14 Squadron. Once equipment was complete, Watt's flight was instructed to proceed to Suez to relieve the detachment that was stationed there, to allow 17 Squadron to consolidate ahead of its move.

With No 1 Squadron, AFC, about June 1916: Major Foster Rutledge and Captain Oswald Watt

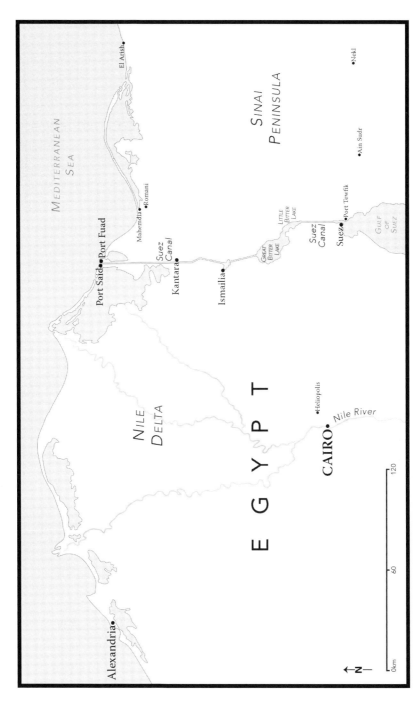

MAP 3: Egypt & Sinai

By 12 June B Flight was declared operational, and the next day Watt's flight secretary, Corporal John Morphett, reported at Suez to begin the paperwork associated with a hand-over.[76] The Suez flight happened to be commanded by Captain H. A. ("Pierre") van Ryneveld, a South African who after the war would found his country's own air force and command the Union Defence Forces for sixteen years from 1933.[77] On the 15th Watt took to the air in BE2c No 4520 (which thus became the first AFC aircraft to begin active service)—followed by the other pilots of B Flight, Lieutenants Delfosse Badgery, David Manwell and W. Ashcroft (who was not a member of the AIF and probably on loan from the RFC)—and led the way for the 160-kilometre flight from Heliopolis to Suez, actually to an aerodrome outside nearby Port Tewfik.[78]

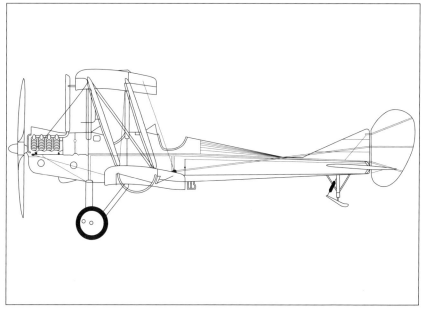

DIAGRAM 3: RAF BE2c

From the next day, 16 June, 1 Squadron was listed in Fifth Wing's daily orders, but the squadron's other two flights were not reconstituted for some weeks more. Captain William Sheldon's "A" Flight joined Watt's men at Suez on 25 June, before being transferred to Sherika in Upper Egypt about a fortnight later, while Captain Richard ("Dickie")

Williams' "C" Flight was split between Heliopolis and Kantara on the Canal (where the headquarters of 14 Squadron was based), before moving to Port Said in mid-August.[79] The Australian headquarters remained at Heliopolis, effectively controlling nothing.

The role of B Flight at its new location was to patrol eastward over the Sinai to a radius of 40-50 kilometres, looking for signs of a build-up of enemy forces. When the Turks made their first major move against the Suez Canal in January 1915, the attacking force had approached along three routes from Palestine and Syria, with the southern one being directed at Suez, and in the wake of that failed attack the Turks continued to maintain an outpost line in the desert about 100 kilometres distant, running from El Arish to Nekl. Daily reconnaissance flights sent out from airfields all along the Canal— from Port Said, Kantara, Ismailia, and Suez—were intended to provide British ground forces with early warning of any renewed attempt.

Air patrols out across the barren peninsula were tiring and dangerous work, even if they were, in the words of the official history, 'without special incident'.[80] The month of July was mid-summer in the Sinai—the worst possible time to contemplate a land crossing of the barren peninsula, or indeed undertake any military campaign. When Lieutenant Badgery wrote a letter home to his mother at Sutton Forest, New South Wales, some months later, he remarked: 'Desert work is most trying to say the best of it, always carrying two days' rations and four gallons of water in machine in case of a forced landing in the sand. Forced landings have been very rare with us, which speaks well for the air mechanics; they are a fine lot of fellows, and at their game second to none.'[81]

The prospect of an emergency landing in such terrain was to be dreaded by aircrews for more than just the fear of perishing from thirst before being rescued. Even without an enemy presence to contend with, the desert's Bedouin inhabitants were another cause for worry. Because most tribesmen were believed to be sympathetic to the Turks rather than the British cause, they were treated accordingly, and opportunity was taken to drop a few bombs whenever Arab parties were sighted simply to 'impress' them.[82] The bombing mission which

Lieutenant Ashcroft undertook on 13 July against a locality called Ain Sudr, roughly halfway to Nekl, was probably one such endeavour. According to Corporal Morphett, the flight out and back used up almost all the fuel in Ashcroft's BE2c and it 'just scraped home'—but air history had been made.[83] When Flight Sergeant Charles Harman also wrote a letter home to Hamilton, Victoria, describing a flight he made sometime in August to test new planes that had just been fitted to Captain Watt's bus, he sent with it a piece of the plane 'with an enemy bullet hole in it'.[84] It may have been a Turkish bullet that holed Watt's machine, but it could just as likely have been fired from a Bedouin rifle.

Even if a Turkish presence was absent on the ground, it was not always the case in the air. Early on the morning of 20 July two enemy aircraft, 'flying at a good height', had arrived over the Suez area and dropped bombs on the army camp at El Shatt (Esh Shat) that killed or wounded camels, horses and a few British gunners, as well as a single bomb on Port Tewfik opposite.[85] Watt and his pilots probably discovered then that their BE2c aircraft were outclassed by the superior machines used by the German airmen operating on the Turkish side, being too slow to intercept or chase their opponents and having no means to engage if they could catch them; the machine gun operated by the observer in the BE2c could not fire forward without shooting off the propeller, and had restricted arcs of fire in practically every other direction.

B Flight's location kept it far removed from the fighting that accompanied the Turks' second big thrust against the northern sector of the Suez Canal during late July, an offensive defeated mainly by Australian light horsemen of the Anzac Mounted Division at the battle of Romani (4-5 August). It was after this turn in the tide that the commander of the Egyptian Expeditionary Force (EEF), Lieutenant-General Sir Archibald Murray, decided on launching a counter-thrust aimed at pushing the Turks out of the Sinai Peninsula entirely. In support of this effort, B Flight was transferred from Suez to Mahemdia, an advanced landing ground about 40 kilometres south-east of Port Said and six kilometres north of Romani, on 18 September.[86]

Chapter 5

From Mahemdia, Watt and his pilots began flying bombing and reconnaissance sorties across northern Sinai, in conjunction with Williams' C Flight (which moved to Kantara on 27 September) and elements of 14 Squadron; these operations continued well into October. As 1 Squadron—or what the War Office unilaterally took to calling 'No 67 (Australian) Squadron, RFC', from 12 September—still lacked trained observers, officers to fill these duties were borrowed from the British. Among those who joined Watt's flight was Second Lieutenant Viscount Glentworth, the 21-year-old eldest son of the Earl of Limerick who had been commissioned in the Warwickshire Yeomanry before arriving in Palestine in May as an observer with 14 Squadron.

The post-Romani operations brought Watt and his crews, and also Williams' flight, into direct contact with the enemy airmen of *Flieger Abteilung 300* (300th Squadron), the German unit that flew in support of Turkish ground forces—covering their allies as they advanced and withdrew across the Sinai, and also working to disrupt the EEF's offensive by bombing key British facilities at Port Said and Kantara, as well as military camps in the desert. In addition to their Rumpler C.1 two-seaters, FA 300 had a small number of Fokker single-seat monoplane fighters fitted with guns synchronised to fire through the airscrew—a feature which further extended German superiority over their opponents. Watt had previously encountered Fokkers in France, and his brush with one of them over Sinai left a similar indelible impression. According to Corporal Morphett, Oswald and Lieutenant Glentworth arrived back at base with bullet holes through the fuselage of their BE2c on either side of where they sat. 'It was drinks on the House of Lords, even for the mechanics.'[87]

The operations after Romani had other consequences as well, being—according to the later autobiographical account by Captain Williams—the first occasion that many Australian light horsemen had seen aircraft close up, particularly at the landing ground at Kantara which was the main transit point for troops and supplies passing between Egypt and the Sinai. No 1 Squadron found itself inundated by inquiries from junior officers wanting to become pilots, and from men with trade qualifications wishing to transfer to the AFC. For the latter there were no vacancies, as the squadron had arrived in Egypt already accompanied by its first quota of reinforcements. There had been precious little wastage among the squadron's original personnel, and it was known that a further batch of reinforcements was its way. It was, says Williams, as a direct result of the surplus of tradesmen that a decision was taken locally to form a second squadron. This was begun at Kantara from mid-September, with the intention that once sufficient personnel had been assembled the new unit would proceed to England—minus pilots or observers—to receive further training and equipment.[88]

Arrangements for this plan were initially fairly informal, and it was not until 26 October that the new unit became an official entity when it was announced that No 68 (Australian) Squadron, RFC, had been formed at Kantara—with Captain Oswald Watt appointed next day as its acting squadron commander.[89] Of course the RFC designator meant little to AFC personnel, to whom the unit was always regarded as No 2 Squadron. When this scheme was originally hatched, nobody in Egypt then knew that a No 2 Squadron, AFC, had already been raised back in Australia, at Point Cook, on 6 July. Only when military authorities in Melbourne discovered that another user of that title already existed in Egypt was the unit at Point Cook renumbered No 3 Squadron on 25 October.[90] On arrival in England in December, this third AFC squadron also received an RFC designator, becoming 'No 69 (Australian) Squadron'.

Many accounts on the AFC's first year in Egypt—including the official history—have made the assumption that Watt's appointment to command the new 2 Squadron marked the end of his connection with 1 Squadron, and that shortly afterwards, still in October, he had 'gone away' to England to begin arrangements for the new unit's transfer.[91] In fact, Watt's AIF personal dossier makes clear that he remained in Egypt for another three months, only leaving with the rest of his new unit. Precisely when he handed over his command of B Flight at Mahemdia is not clear, but it seems certain there was no move in anticipation of the announcement that he was to act as

2 Squadron's commanding officer. When Lieutenant Badgery wrote his letter home on 25 October, he still stated categorically that 'Capt. Oswald Watt is my flight commander'.[92]

Within a short period after his appointment—certainly within a matter of weeks—Watt was focusing on building up the number of tradesmen for what would be the ground staff of his new squadron. Most of these were air mechanics transferred from 1 Squadron, but Watt evidently set his sights on recruiting men with mechanical training and skills from the multitude of mounted units stationed in and around Kantara. The methods he instituted to obtain them have been described as 'somewhat unorthodox'. One recruit from the 11th Light Horse camp later recounted that 'AFC personnel in three Leyland trucks arrived … calling out for "any trades, any mechanics, any engineers". When queried if the volunteers should be processed through the orderly room, the response was: "No, we have to snatch them".'[93] The volunteers were trade tested and those found unsuitable were returned to their units.

Among the tradesmen obtained from the existing personnel of 1 Squadron was Second Air Mechanic George Jones, who was himself a new recruit to the AFC, having just transferred from one of the Australian companies of the Imperial Camel Corps in October. He would later recount an incident at Kantara which marked his first acquaintance with Dickie Williams:

> I was helping to install an engine in a BE2e aeroplane, and sandflies kept getting in my eyes and nose. I swore, and Williams, who was standing nearby, severely reprimanded me. It was almost the end of my service with the Flying Corps. Fortunately I left for Europe a few weeks later in No. 2 Squadron …[94]

Jones—later to become the Chief of the Royal Australian Air Force from 1940 for an unbroken term of ten years—remained convinced that the sandflies incident 'led to my transfer to No 2 [Squadron]; he [Williams] didn't want my kind in his squadron'.[95]

Not all Watt's time at Kantara was apparently taken up with forming his new unit. During October 1916 a new aircraft type, the Martinsyde G100 "Elephant", began entering service in Egypt, initially just a few machines per squadron. This aircraft was a single-seat fighter-bomber with a performance considerably better than the BE2c, and it would have been natural for Watt to want to test fly it. For more than 45 years a photograph has been in published existence purporting to show a Martinsyde that Watt crashed—presumably on landing, as the machine appears lying on its back minus its starboard wheel. The caption to this image reads: 'Even an experienced pilot like Captain Oswald Watt was subject to the vagaries of the desert winds and the Martinsyde', which clearly implies that his flying skills had not been equal to dealing with such an advanced aircraft.[96]

All may not be as it first appears, however, since it is known that the first two Martinsydes received at Kantara went to 14 Squadron and to Williams' C Flight. The 14 Squadron machine was lost on its first operational flight, shot down by an enemy aircraft, and C Flight's machine was promptly pranged by Williams himself, when he struck a tent of a small Egyptian Labour Corps camp in a corner of the aerodrome which he had not seen on landing. As Williams later recorded, he found himself 'hanging on the belt of the aircraft which was upside down on the ground', the tent having wrapped itself round the undercarriage and 'softened the fall'.[97] As the number of Martinsydes delivered to the Australians by the end of 1916 was only three, and none of the other two appears to have suffered a similar mishap, it must be wondered whether a mistake has occurred and Watt was not the pilot involved in the alleged accident.

By December, 2 Squadron's establishment was starting to fill up, and thoughts were turning to getting the unit to England and completing its structure. Watt would later be quoted as saying that 2 Squadron was 'composed (except for ten of its ground personnel) entirely of men who had been on service in Egypt with the light horse or with No. 1 Squadron, or with both.'[98] It was, however, only on 23 December that Watt was formally transferred from '67 Australian Squadron RFC to 68 Australian Squadron'—that is, from 1 Squadron to 2 Squadron—and promoted to the rank of Major.[99] His appointment as commanding officer of 2 Squadron was confirmed three days later.[100]

Chapter 5

By then he would most likely have known that he—along with Flight Sergeant Harman from B Flight—had been mentioned in dispatches by General Murray (as Commander-in-Chief of the EEF) on 13 October,[101] the award being promulgated in the *London Gazette* in December.[102] These were the first of any awards made to members of the Australian Flying Corps in Egypt.

Chapter Six
THE WESTERN CRUCIBLE

Move to England

On 13 January 1917 the 180 men of 2 Squadron, with Major Watt at their head, proceeded to Egypt's main seaport of Alexandria and boarded a ship bound for France.[1] The vessel was the 6,560-ton steamer *Kingstonian*, built in 1901 and owned by F. Leyland & Co. from Liverpool, England. It had been used formerly as a cattle transport, and (as Second Air Mechanic George Jones later recounted) the men 'slept in its cattle stalls'.[2]

The voyage westward across the Mediterranean was not without its hazards, although claims that two ships in the convoy including the Kingstonian were torpedoed are almost certainly an exaggeration.[3] That there were enemy submarines loose in the Mediterranean is not doubted. One picked off the small steamer *Garfield* 110 kilometres north-east of Alexandria on 15 January, but this was not where *Kingstonian* would have been on that date and records also do not reveal a second sinking in the Mediterranean that month; it is on record, too, that Britain did not institute a convoy system for its shipping in these waters before May 1917. It was ironic then that *Kingstonian* did fall victim to German U-boats west of Sardinia in April 1918, while again plying between Alexandria and the south of France, and became a total loss.

When the ship made a stop-over at Malta, Jones recalled that he and his colleagues were allowed to go ashore at Valetta Harbour and were even taken on a tour to see something of the island's history. The story was completely different when *Kingstonian* arrived at its destination, Marseilles, on 24 January. Presumably owing to the late hour of arrival, the men were kept on board overnight and not permitted ashore until morning. This did not stop 'some of the more adventurous members of the squadron'—according to one recent account, some 80 in number[4]—from climbing down a rope over the ship's stern and going to sample the sights of the city. Included in this group was Jones, but he was unimpressed by what he saw and soon decided to return. 'I walked boldly up the gangway, and when … challenged I told the guard that I had gone down to retrieve my hat which had fallen overboard.'[5] He believed that most of the others involved also managed to get back on board without being missed, but in fact the escapade had not passed unnoticed.

Next morning Watt assembled the squadron personnel on deck and asked if any had been ashore. Those who, in Jones' words, were 'silly enough to admit it' were charged with being absent without leave (AWL) and fined 28 days' pay.[6] 'A debit entry was marked in my pay book, and we all felt that the punishment had been too severe. (When we reached England, however, … Watt relented and reduced the fine to fourteen days.)'[7] Jones' recall of events may well be correct, because although his AIF personal file only records that he was awarded 14 days' forfeiture of pay by Watt for being AWL on 25 January, this entry was dated 1 February—after the squadron had arrived in England. According to the most recent historian of the AFC, Watt also put the misbehavers at the bottom of the squadron's leave roster.[8]

Once disembarked at Marseilles, the squadron boarded a train for a three-day rail trip north, skirting Paris on the way to the channel ports along France's northwest coast. The journey was neither scenic nor enjoyable, being made in the middle of a northern winter which was rated as the most severe in living memory. The men travelled in unheated boxcars without windows, with straw on the floors to sleep on. Having come from the Egyptian desert only a fortnight earlier, the Australians were completely unprepared for such conditions. 'We had no over-coats', recalled Jones, 'and tried to keep warm in our summer issue of shorts and shirts.'[9] There was also little to eat and drink, after the food and water provided on board froze solid. The only relief from this misery came at a point when the train stopped on a viaduct. Passing on the road below was a French woman carrying a basket containing a bottle of wine and a loaf of bread, which she was persuaded to sell to the famished travellers. 'We hauled the basket up with a rope, [made from] our boot laces joined together.'[10]

Arriving at Le Havre on 27 January, the squadron was sent to a transit camp to await shipping to take it to England. Although the men received their first hot meal there since arriving in France, the tents in which they were accommodated provided little protection against the persistent freezing cold. Conditions were reportedly so bad on the night they arrived that, according to Second Air Mechanic Fergus Cox from Queensland, two British soldiers on sentry duty at the camp gate froze to death at their posts.[11]

After enduring two nights in these billets, on 30 January Watt and his men were finally put on board a ferry steamer named *Donegal* for the trip across the Channel to Southampton. Although there was no talk now about the danger posed by enemy submarines, the threat this time was actually more real than in the Mediterranean—had they only known it. Less than three months later, the *Donegal* was torpedoed and sunk while crossing from Le Havre to Southampton with more than 600 wounded soldiers. Recalled Jones: 'I lost no time in climbing down into the engine room to sleep beside the boilers, for warmth. Large blocks of ice were floating down Southampton waters.'[12]

At Southampton the squadron was put aboard a train to London. Arriving at Waterloo Station at 7.30 that evening, they gratefully accepted the mugs of tea and coffee, and sandwiches, that were pressed into their hands by English women on the platform while they waited for their next train.[13] After a short trip on the Underground to Charing Cross, they boarded another train to the market town of Grantham in Lincolnshire—a distance of 160 kilometres north of London, and a little over 50 kilometres south of the county town of Lincoln—a journey made in falling snow. Arriving the next morning, 31 January, the Australians marched to the village of Harlaxton lying three kilometres to the southwest, then another 1.5 kilometres southeast of the village to where the RFC had established an aerodrome behind the bizarre mansion combining Jacobean, Tudor and Baroque architecture known as Harlaxton Manor. The airfield was to be 2 Squadron's new home for the next eight months.

Chapter 6

The squadron's transfer from Egypt to England had been safely accomplished, but under such arduous circumstances that questions must be raised about Oswald Watt's capacity for administrative command. How could he have allowed the men who were his responsibility to be subjected to such deficient arrangements? Did he not know, and why did he not make it his business to find out whether they were being looked after? If he did know, why did he not do more to relieve the unnecessarily brutal conditions of their transport?

Unfortunately, it is not possible to find answers to these questions, since records pertaining to this episode are nowhere to be found— not even nominal rolls of the unit members making the journey from Alexandria to Harlaxton appear to have survived. A partial answer no doubt exists in the fact that once the Australian unit came under the control of British army movements staff, and the staff of the French railway system, Watt would have had very little power to change or ameliorate any arrangements. It must also be true that the state of 2 Squadron's organisation at the time the move began lacked any of the elements for unit administration that would have normally existed. Since the squadron was moving without any pilots or observers, Watt had few officers to whom he could delegate or rely upon to even check the conditions of the men. The only officers known to have accompanied 2 Squadron on its move were Temporary Captain William Guilfoyle and Lieutenant Stanley Muir, both of whom joined the unit very shortly before embarking in the *Kingstonian* with Watt.[14]

Although the debacle of the squadron move remains a low point in Oswald Watt's record, one of the most telling aspects that emerges from personal accounts of the journey is that none of the men directly held their commanding officer to blame for the discomforts they were forced to endure during their journey to England in January 1917. If Watt himself saw what happened as a black spot on his name, one which he later worked to overcome, none of his men appear to have held the episode against him. Even those who felt his disciplinary wrath at Marseilles seem not to have been left embittered against him.

Training up No.2 Squadron

At the time that 2 Squadron arrived in England, it was actually the second AFC unit located in Lincolnshire. No 3 Squadron—which the British named 69 (Australian) Squadron, RFC—had already arrived directly from Australia in the last days of December 1916, under command of Major David Blake, and had taken up residence at South Carlton, a few kilometres north of Lincoln, where it came under control of the RFC's 23rd Training Wing.[15] Whereas 2 Squadron was slated to be turned into a fighter-scout unit, 3 Squadron was being trained for the 'corps reconnaissance' role—work more aligned to army cooperation duties.

Late in March 1917 a third AFC squadron would also reach England, this being No 4 (given the RFC number 71). Raised in Australia from October 1916, it was sent on arrival to Castle Bromwich, near Birmingham, to also begin preparing for a fighter-scout role under 25th Training Wing.[16] Taking command of 4 Squadron soon after it landed was Captain William Sheldon, formerly with 1 Squadron in Egypt. By the start of the northern spring, therefore, Watt's unit was part of a large Australian air contingent—amounting in size to a wing if left grouped together—that was being prepared for combat on the Western Front.

When the 'dishevelled and unsoldierly mob of light horsemen' marched into Harlaxton after the rigours of their transfer from Egypt,[17] 2 Squadron was at the beginning of a long process to prepare it for operational duty. Having little more than half-trained personnel to begin with, the unit was fortunate to find that it shared the aerodrome with No 44 (Reserve) Squadron—like itself, part of 24th Training Wing based at Spittlegate (on the southeast fringes of Grantham)—so there were at least basic facilities to make a start. Joining it, too, were a few headquarters and ground staff members posted from Australia to help it reach establishment.[18]

Watt discovered that, to fill a vacancy in the headquarters administrative staff, the RFC had given him a young British infantry officer, Lieutenant Basil Hart, to temporarily act as adjutant. A Cambridge man (like Watt), Hart had seen action on the Western

Front until gassed at the Somme in July 1916 and was now downgraded to light duties in an office. He was to spend only two months at Harlaxton—leaving after Captain Roy Phillipps [later MC & Bar, DFC] (a former infantry officer from Western Australia, also convalescing from wounds) arrived in April to take over.

Hart went on to become adjutant of Volunteer Force units at Stroud, Gloucestershire, and from January 1918 at Cambridge. Joining the post-war Army Education Corps, he would change his surname to Liddell Hart in 1921, but was forced to retire from the army as a Captain in 1927 after suffering several mild heart attacks. He then went on to work as military correspondent for leading British newspapers, and also began publishing military histories, biographies and books on strategy and theory which gained for him an international reputation. He was appointed Knight Bachelor in 1966.

In memoirs published many years later, Hart left an account of his brief time with Watt's 2 Squadron which seemed to strive to reinforce the popular British stereotype of Australians as "wild colonials". Recalling the first parade that he inspected as 'a shock to anyone accustomed to British regimental ideas', he observed that there was 'hardly any man dressed identically or with uniform complete in all respects':

> But I found them quite willing to come reasonably into line with what seemed to them curious customs. More important, they had the fundamental discipline of doing every job well and never neglecting any detail of their work on the aircraft. The officers were brilliant pilots but rather a wild lot when off duty—I often remarked, caustically, that my main job in their regard was to put them to bed at night when they were too drunk to get there on their own.[19]

Hart's memoirs at least confirmed that the squadron very quickly got down to the business of training pilots, although here, too, his observations were not altogether complimentary:

> Some of them liked to go out rabbit-shooting "by air" before dinner in couples—one of them handling the machine, while the other took pot-shots at rabbits from the gunner's seat in its

nose while it was skimming very low over the fields and hedges. With the "pusher" biplanes then in use such "rough" shooting was possible although the bag was scarcely in proportion to the effort and expenditure of shot. While I was there one of them got married, and on return from a brief honeymoon amused himself in the early morning by waking up his bride with aerobatics round their house, and almost scraping its walls with his wing-tips.

While the aerial antics that Hart described may have happened on one or two occasions, it is difficult to imagine that this behaviour would have continued on a frequent basis once it came to the attention of the commanding officer. Watt is reputed to have quickly acquired a reputation as 'a taskmaster with an abrupt manner', although it was also acknowledged that he possessed a leadership style ideal for volunteer soldiers who appreciated a just and commonsense approach to discipline.[20] When confronted with the refusal of some air mechanics to do early morning drill in England, he addressed the squadron by saying:

> You boys have had a hard time on Gallipoli and Sinai, most of you have been through hell, now I want you to have as good a time as possible during your stay in England but I want you to remember that I am a Major and anyone up before me will find I'm no milksop.[21]

Among those who felt the uncompromising side of Watt's nature was the future fighter "ace" of 4 Squadron, Harry Cobby, who was posted to 2 Squadron 'for instruction' in mid-May. The 22-year old bank clerk from Melbourne had enlisted only in December 1916, and arrived at Harlaxton with two colleagues intending to scam a 48-hour leave pass from their new CO—only to find themselves on the receiving end of a lecture for having delayed doing anything 'to help win the war' for several years. Cobby later recalled:

> He dressed us down like a trio of pick-pockets and laid it on thick and heavy. It was rather extraordinary to be jumped on like that, without waiting or asking for an explanation. … We all had something to say, but not much as "Ossie" just silenced us

and instructed the Adjutant, Roy Phillipps, to march us out. We discovered … that he was terribly keen on beating up the enemy and that he was absolutely intolerant of everyone not in the War in some capacity or other. … We later found him to be one of the kindest and most thoughtful people we had ever met… Obviously we did not try and work the forty-eight-hour trick on him.[22]

Cobby found himself in trouble with Watt a month later, when posted to another flying school to train on Sopwith "Camel" fighters. To celebrate, he planned a night of carousing in Grantham with fellow pilots from the squadron, and to conserve their money for drinking the group decided to borrow a tractor-drawn road grader (complete with tractor) being used in construction of the aerodrome, rather than hire a more conventional form of transport. 'It was regrettable that the old man, "Ossie Watt", should be coming back by car at the same time as we were, as it cost all the other chaps leave for a couple of weeks, but I was lucky in that respect as I was posted from the next day.'[23]

An aspect of special interest in Hart's description of aerial rabbit-shooting antics around Harlaxton concerns the aircraft first in use with the squadron—a "pusher" biplane (like Watt had flown in France) with a gunner's seat in its nose—since this does not match any of the types usually associated with the unit's training program. In fact, it is George Jones' autobiography which reveals that the squadron 'started training pilots on Horace Farman biplanes', adding: 'There is no mistake in calling the aircraft a Horace rather than a Maurice; a combination of the original Henri Farman 13/14 structure and the same type of nacelle as that on the Maurice Farman, resulted in our Horaces.'[24]

Also according to Jones, only later came Avro 504 "tractor" machines fitted with Gnome engines. 'Initially', he wrote, 'I was a mechanic in charge of the engine of a Horace Farman, but later, being a reasonably good turner, I was put in charge of a workshop lorry, and given the job of making small parts for Gnome engines. I was promoted to First Class Air Mechanic.'[25] Fairly soon after that, the squadron received Sopwith "Pups" and Sopwith two-seaters known as "1½ Strutters"—also tractor types—so that the unit's A and B flights would then be equipped with two Pups and four Strutters while C Flight flew Pups and Avros. The later historian of 2 Squadron recorded that the Strutters were 'adorned under Watt's guidance with kangaroo markings, similar to that which had adorned his Maurice Farman in France, to promote the new squadron's Australian identity.'[26]

During April and May the squadron began receiving deliveries of the aircraft it would be taking into combat, including several machines which had been paid for by public subscription in Australia. This was the Airco DH5, a single-seater biplane powered by a 110 hp Le Rhone rotary engine. It was fitted with a single Vickers .303 inch (7.7 mm) machine-gun that was fixed to the engine cowl, synchronised to fire forward through the propeller—one of the first British fighter-scouts to have this arrangement—and also racks for carrying four 25-pound (10 kg) bombs under the fuselage. The aircraft's designer, Geoffrey de Havilland, had incorporated an unusual wing configuration into this machine. By positioning the upper wing further back than the lower one, towards the rear of the cockpit, the pilot was afforded excellent vision forward, above, and to the sides.

A DH5 aircraft paid for by public subscription in Australia that was received by No 2 Squadron at Harlaxton in September 1917. (Australian War Memorial C01862)

Chapter 6

Initially, the pilots were pleased with their new buses. Second Lieutenant Richard ("Dick") Howard, who joined 2 Squadron on 18 April, was delighted to be flying a 'machine which can travel at 120 mph, flying level with the engine flat out…[and] manoeuvres very quickly [which] makes up for the disadvantage of having no observer to protect the tail of the machine. … They are very strongly built and can be looped or spun easily, and can be dived at 180 mph without the wings dropping off.'[27] Oswald Watt was probably as impressed as his 20-year-old new arrival. Although the DH5's engine was comparable to the Nieuport scout he had flown in Paris, this was undoubtedly the most advanced type he had so far had the chance to fly.

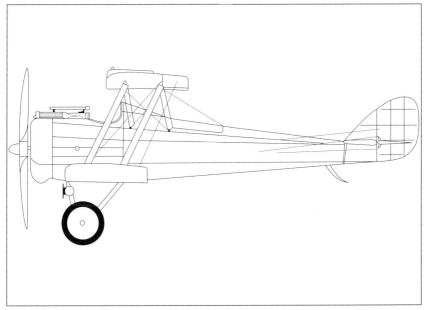

DIAGRAM 4: Airco DH5

During this preparatory phase, the pressing need for 2 Squadron— and throughout the AFC—was to obtain sufficient trained pilots to complete aircrew establishment, and also provide a pool of trained replacements once the squadron became operational and began suffering combat losses. To produce a pool of trainees from which an adequate supply of pilots could be drawn, a call went out to the men in the ground staff of the various squadrons inviting them to apply for a flying course. Among those who put their names forward was George Jones, although not before he had given the matter a great deal of thought. Jones' biographer suggests that Jones was 'shy' because he was aware that pilots were automatically commissioned as officers, and therefore mindful of the associated social and class implications. As a result, he only lodged his application on the very day that these closed.[28]

Jones' delay, however, prompted Watt to ask why he had not applied earlier, to which he responded: 'I understood one had to be recommended by at least a Colonel, in order to stand a chance'. Unimpressed with that answer, Watt replied: 'Do you know what I do with such applications?' He pointed to his wastepaper basket, 'I put them in there', he said. Jones' application was successful, and on 6 July he was in a group of 30 mechanics who marched out of 2 Squadron to commence flying training. On qualifying for his wings in November Jones was posted as a pilot to 4 Squadron, the other AFC fighter unit being prepared for operations.

Watt himself needed some additional training to prepare him for his squadron's new role. On 28 May he departed Harlaxton for a course of instruction at Turnberry, on the west coast of Scotland, where the RFC had established its School of Air Gunnery at the grand Edwardian-style Station Hotel, built ten years earlier as Britain's first planned golfing resort. The surrounding greens and dunes had been levelled to make way for landing grounds, hangars and huts for the military aviators to hone their skills over the Ayrshire countryside. Watt was away only a week, and by 4 June was back at Harlaxton.[29]

Late in July, Watt and many of his pilots were sent to France to gain operational experience on attachment to RFC squadrons. This was valuable preparation for the squadron's initiation to combat, since the first weeks of a pilot's appearance over the front lines were already recognised as the most dangerous. Most of the 2 Squadron pilots flew the DH5 during their attachments—mainly it seems with No 32 Squadron at Droglandt (an airfield close to the Belgian border, west of Poperinghe)—but several flew the Sopwith Camel and other fighter types.[30] Watt himself flew with No 41 Squadron, a DH5 unit operating from Léalvillers, 25 kilometres north-east of Amiens. He returned to Harlaxton by 18 August, as did most of the others.[31]

The claim in the official history that one of Watt's pilots on attachment was shot down and captured on 29 July is wrong; Lieutenant Victor Norvill was a member of 69 Squadron, RFC (3 Squadron, AFC) when actually lost on 29 June.[32] However, a number of 2 Squadron pilots did suffer mishaps while on attachment, including Lieutenant Henry Forrest who crashed soon after take-off on 5 August and received an injury above one eye. Another was Captain Roy Phillipps, who had forsaken his role as adjutant to undertake flying training and came back to the squadron as a senior pilot. He was shot down by ground-fire near Ypres on 6 August, but was unharmed.[33]

On 19 August Second Lieutenant Adrian Epps, who had been a member of 2 Squadron since April, was also wounded in combat while serving with No 70 Squadron (a Sopwith Camel unit) based at Ervillers, near Saint-Omer. He sustained a crippling injury to his left elbow which caused him to be returned to Australia and discharged. As Epps' commanding officer, Watt wrote to Epps' parents praising their son for effecting 'an extraordinarily fine landing on our side of the lines … [with] his machine shot to bits, … for which he was warmly commended by the general commanding the R.F.C. in the Field.'[34]

These attachments to operational squadrons very likely gave 2 Squadron pilots an awareness that the DH5 was not popular or well-regarded within the wider RFC. British pilots had quickly come to dislike the fact that the type was seriously under-armed, having a single machine-gun when most fighters already had two, and gave a disappointing lack of performance which meant that maximum speed dropped sharply above 10,000 feet. Although the engine was the same that powered the Nieuport scout, the DH5 was nearly 250 pounds (more than 15 per cent) heavier in gross weight, suffered from a greater amount of vibration, and displayed an alarming tendency to shed engine valves. Moreover, the staggered wing configuration blocked the pilot's view to the rear and created a dangerous blind spot when dogfighting. Perhaps worst of all, while overall construction seemed robust and durable, there had already been instances when the DH5's wings had collapsed while the aircraft was being stunted or tested for manoeuvrability—with tragic consequences. Despite this, the Australians retained faith in their machines and were becoming eager to enter the fray.

By the first week in September, 2 Squadron was close to being ready for deployment to the front. It was at this point that the London correspondent for the *Melbourne Herald* visited the unit and wrote an account of what he saw which was subsequently carried in newspapers in several states of Australia. 'On a wide green field in Southern Lincolnshire', began the article, was 'an Australian squadron that is just about ready to fly across the Channel and take its place on the Western Front.':

> here in the late hours of a sunny autumn day I found Major Watt, and together we watched a group of keen, laughing, young Australians going through their evening "stunts". A pilot in a Sopwith "pup" gave an aerial display, and as the airman slid down unerringly to the field again, Major Watt remarked, "That's Captain Muir, of Melbourne, one of the finest flyers I have ever seen. With any luck he is certain to make a big name. He has already done good work in the Egyptian campaign, where he won the Military Cross.[35]

The newspaper account concluded with a final demonstration that Watt was determined to maintain the highest standards in his unit, and would not tolerate risky or unnecessary showmanship:

> With a quick, nervous movement, and the remark, "Look at that young devil!" Major Watt directed my attention to a "pup" machine twisting and twirling overhead at a dangerously low level. "This training job is more nerve-wracking than fighting," he remarked. ""These fellows don't know the meaning of fear, and are always trying new 'stunts', which may smash either themselves or the machines. Wait till he comes down!" The squadron commander left me with the impression that he was going to talk to the daredevil in well-chosen words on the subject of his latest experiment.[36]

Chapter 6

There was irony in the fact that Watt objected to one of his junior pilots stunting at low altitude, because a bare three months later every pilot in the squadron would find their survival dependent on their ability to manoeuvre at this level.

Watt may have meant his disciplinary style to be strict and demanding, but by some accounts his attitude to his pilots was almost paternal when correcting their shortcomings. To illustrate Watt's methods, Horace Brinsmead (in 1917 the staff captain to the Staff Officer for Aviation at the AIF's Administrative Headquarters in London) later told the story of Watt's treatment of a 'young and enthusiastic' pilot named "Mac" who performed the "zoom" take-off despite being warned previously about the dangers involved:

> "Mac" did it again, with the result that he 'stalled' and only recovered just in time to avert a serious crash. … 'Awfully sorry, Sir, I really won't do it again.' 'No, please don't,' and after a short homily, 'and now go to your room, sit on the end of your bed and for a quarter of an hour say to yourself, 'what a bloody fool I was'.[37]

Despite what might seem like indulgence, Watt's methods nonetheless achieved results. Major-General John Salmond, commander of the RFC's Training Division, would later declare: 'Major Watt trained his squadron to such a pitch of excellence that I have no hesitation in saying that it was one of the best Squadrons that … left England for service with the Expeditionary Force'.[38]

Even as the squadron's press visitor returned to London to lodge his story on 7 September, Major Watt was also showing the more human side to his leadership style by agreeing to stand as best man at the wedding of one of his flight commanders. This was Captain Phillipps, who had just returned to the unit after his crash-landing in France. The wedding itself was a hastily-arranged affair at Kensington, London, on 8 September—rushed due to the fact that Phillipps had only obtained leave the previous day. The bride, who was the daughter of the Attorney-General for Western Australia, Robert Robinson, was working in a London hospital and the wedding was attended by a number of nurses who were 'the bride's fellow workers'.[39]

No sooner had Watt returned to Harlaxton than the unit experienced a tragedy which was a body-blow to every pilot's confidence in their DH5s. On 12 September the unit's senior flight commander, Captain Stan Muir, was test flying one of the new aircraft when its lower wing suddenly snapped and folded up at 500 feet, and the machine plunged to earth. 'When the onlookers went to the smash,' reported First Air Mechanic Vern Knuckey, they found the pilot was 'unrecognisable, every bone in his body must have been broken'.[40] Instead of finding further glory in the skies over France, Muir was buried in the churchyard of Saint Mary and Saint Peter at Harlaxton. Watt wrote to Muir's father in Melbourne, saying: 'His sad death deprives the flying service of one they can ill afford to lose. Never was an officer more truly mourned by his fellow-officers or by his men.'[41] Before the month was out, the squadron was gone from England for the front— but the portent for what lay ahead for Watt and his men could hardly have been worse.

Crisis at Cambrai

Three days after Captain Muir's funeral, 2 Squadron began its move to France. On 16 September an advance ground party left by road for Portsmouth to make the Channel crossing to Le Havre. On reaching France the ground party set off in their vehicles again, heading northeast to the Picardy region north of Paris, to a place called Baizieux (roughly midway between Amiens and Albert) where the aerodrome that was to be the squadron's new base was situated. Five days later the rest of the unit's 170 ground staff departed Harlaxton by rail for Southampton, also headed for Baizieux.[42]

The same day as the main ground party set off, 2 Squadron's fifteen DH5s took to the air. Under Major Watt's leadership, the aircraft left Harlaxton at 9.30 a.m. and flew first to Lympne, on the sea cliffs above the coastline of Kent. Then "A" Flight—with Watt at its head—took off again to make the 40-minute over-water leg across the Channel in beautiful weather. A second flight followed soon afterwards and the two groups lunched together at Saint-Omer. The third flight joined them there at 5 p.m.

No 2 Squadron aircraft about to depart from Harlaxton for France, 21 September 1917. (Australian War Memorial C01852)

The squadron's Channel crossing was not the first made by a whole unit of the Royal Flying Corps, but is believed to be a record in the British service because it was the first deployment overseas completed in a single day. Two weeks earlier, 3 Squadron actually became the first AFC unit sent to France, following the same route from Lincolnshire to Lympne and from there crossing to Saint-Omer; but in that case the unit had been delayed at Lympne for several days by bad weather.[43] Apart from its record-breaking dimension, the crossing made by 2 Squadron was reportedly noteworthy for another reason.

According to a story later put about by Captain Horace Brinsmead (still in the AIF's Administrative Headquarters in London at the time), it was while the squadron was approaching the French coast that Watt removed his goggles and inserted a monocle to consult his maps, whereupon his machine went into an involuntary half roll and 'capsized overboard not only the maps but also the eyeglass, and very nearly ... [Watt] to boot'. Oswald suffered the indignity of having to surrender the lead to Captain Wilfred McCloughry, "A" Flight's commander, and trail into their destination towards the rear of the formation.[44] Although Brinsmead's account is the first mention found of Watt's alleged use of a monocle, the veracity of the claim (and indeed Brinsmead's entire story) is strengthened by a second mention of Watt wearing an eyepiece of this kind a year later.

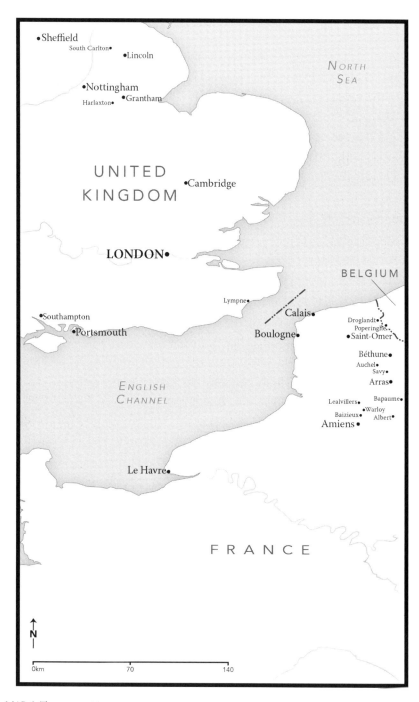

MAP 4. The move to France

Chapter 6

The day after landing at Saint-Omer, 2 Squadron's aircraft flew to an aerodrome at Warloy [Warloy-Baillon], just west of Albert and close to Baizieux. There the unit became formally attached to the 13th (Army) Wing of the RFC, operating with the British Third Army.[45] It was only the next day, 23 September, that the unit flew into its new base at Baizieux, 3 kilometres south of Warloy, to be joined by its advance ground party three days later. Once the second ground party arrived, bringing with them the unit's spare pilots, the whole of the squadron was finally together in one place again. At Baizieux, too, the squadron was issued with a further three DH5s from No 2 Aeroplane Supply Depot, bringing its aircraft strength up to 18 machines.[46] By 28 September Watt's squadron was ready to begin operations on the Western Front.

In the first half of October the squadron had several encounters with enemy aircraft, although these were fleeting affairs with outcomes which were hardly satisfactory to the Australians. On the 2nd a patrolling flight twice discovered enemy two-seaters carrying out reconnaissance and attempted to engage them, only to have their opponents dive away and make good their escape each time—demonstrating only too well the performance deficiencies of the DH5.[47] (Even so, Watt was so delighted that his pilots had 'driven down' two opponents that he laid on a tender that afternoon to take the flight's members into Doullens for shopping and sightseeing.[48]) Both that encounter and another on 13 October also saw the squadron suffer combat losses essentially because of the DH5's lack of mechanical reliability, resulting in one pilot being captured and the other shot down with wounds which would result in his death a fortnight later.[49]

By the time one of the squadron's flights found itself in a proper dogfight on 16 October, involving four DH5s against eight Albatros machines at 10,000 feet above Gouy, on the enemy's side of the front line, the Australians had it brought home to them that their aircraft were 'duds' in the fighter-scout role. Although the attackers were beaten off, it was beginning to be realised that the enemy had the faster machines and unless he chose to stay and fight there was little the Australians could do to bring him to battle. In the words of the official history: '[They] looked forward to the newer and faster scouts known to be coming to them.'[50]

The first month after his squadron arrived in France proved to be an intensely frustrating time for Watt personally. By this stage in the war RFC instructions debarred squadron commanders from participating in aerial encounter or crossing the enemy lines, so Watt was required to leave it to his flight commanders to lead patrols into action.[51] According to an account written at second-hand after the war, Watt felt this restriction 'very bitterly' but was 'too good a disciplinarian to defy it.' He accordingly compromised by accompanying his starting patrols as far as the actual line before waving 'God-speed', then flew up and down the outside edge ('like an anxious old bathing instructor watching his pupils swimming without the belt') until their particular mission was accomplished. 'Then, mustering his flock—so to speak— he would lead the formation back to the aerodrome for breakfast.'[52]

Watt may have played aerial shepherd to his patrols on one or two occasions at first, but whether this became his regular routine may be doubted. Accounts left by officers at Baizieux portray a very different pattern to his behaviour. Several spoke of his practice of insisting that his pilots turn in to sleep about 10 p.m., without them knowing whether they would be required to fly the following morning or what work might be coming their way. He himself kept working in the squadron's office until well after midnight, when orders from the Wing were received, and then wrote the squadron's orders for next day before finally turning in about 3 a.m. Only when the officers' batmen woke them at 5 a.m. were they informed whether they would be flying the dawn patrol. And those pilots required for the day's first mission could always be sure that the CO would be awake and standing punctually beside the flight line to see them take off.[53]

Towards the end of October, it became known that 2 Squadron would soon be participating in a major operation that the Third Army had in planning preparation. This was to be a full-blown offensive against a section of the German defensive system called the "Hindenburg Line" (by the Germans it was known as the "Siegfried Line"), to the southwest of the major transport and communications hub at Cambrai. This attack would be undertaken along a front of nearly ten kilometres by two infantry corps, supported by 1003 artillery pieces, 374 tanks, and 289 aircraft from fourteen squadrons—including Watt's unit.[54]

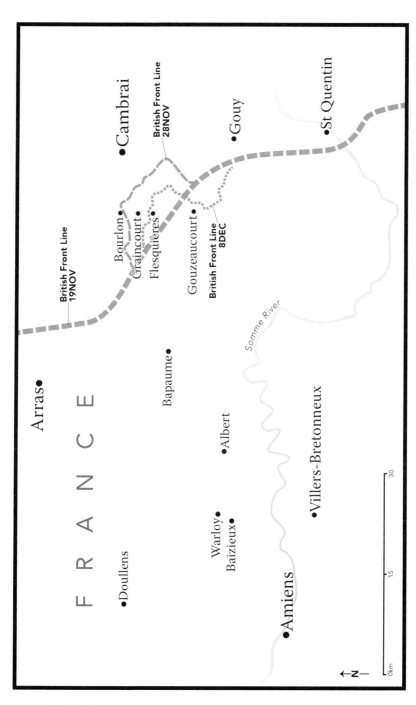

MAP 5: Battle of Cambrai

The operation had been conceived essentially as a surprise 'hit-and-run' raid, aimed at demonstrating the value of the new tank weapon in smashing through the three formidable trench barriers that formed the Hindenburg Line system. But as the plan evolved, provision was made to exploit a break-through—should this be achieved—by pouring British and French cavalry through the breach, capturing Cambrai, and rolling up the German lines on either flank. The opening day of the attack was set for 20 November.

In final and damning recognition that the DH5 had proved a failure as a frontline fighter, Watt's squadron was—along with three other RFC units (one also equipped with the DH5)—allotted to a secondary role of low-level ground attack in the upcoming operation against Cambrai. For this purpose, 2 Squadron's aircraft were fitted with their bomb-racks and for ten days leading up to the start-date the pilots were set to practising low-level bombing in a field next to their aerodrome. Flying in pairs, they also trained in machine-gunning ground targets.[55]

On 19 November an advanced landing ground was established on the northeastern outskirts of the town of Bapaume, and that evening the pilots from the designated ground attack squadrons gathered there to receive final briefings. Considering Watt's previous practice with departing patrols, it is inconceivable that he would have been absent from the Bapaume landing ground at this time—or the following morning, when the squadrons were sent off to begin their deadly work in support of the attacking force.

At 7.05 a.m. six aircraft from "C" Flight of 2 Squadron took off, despite heavy fog and mist which obscured visibility more than 30-50 feet above ground level. Conditions were recognised as so bad that "C" Flight immediately broke into pairs, rather than attempt to operate as a single formation. At 8.00 a.m. the other two flights, also each with six machines, became airborne, too, and Watt could only await their return to find out anything of the battle's progress. By midday, the weather became worse and orders were received from the wing headquarters to cease flying. In the five hours since the first aircraft were dispatched, 2 Squadron had come close to being shattered.

Four aircraft had been shot down with the loss of three pilots (two wounded—one mortally—and one captured; the pilot of the fourth machine was subsequently returned to the airfield uninjured). Another three aircraft had made it back to base so badly damaged by ground fire that they were effectively unflyable wrecks that needed to be returned to depot for rebuilding.[56]

The next day the weather over the battlefield was again judged to be so bad that flying was cancelled. On whose authority that decision was taken seems to be open to question. The operation orders issued by 13th Wing the night before made clear that the wing commander expected squadron commanders to check with him if weather appeared 'doubtful'. Yet sources within 2 Squadron are adamant that, such was the trust placed in Major Watt's judgment, 'it was left to him to say if it [flying] were possible or not'. AFC historian Michael Molkentin states that the responsibility weighed heavily on Watt, but ultimately he decided to keep his pilots on the ground at Bapaume.[57] Although the whole of 13th Wing stayed grounded on 21 November, the conditions were not so bad as first appeared: another air formation involved in the battle, the 12th (Corps) Wing, had its squadrons up and managed 24 sorties that day, and German aircraft were also airborne.[58]

By Day 3 of the operation, 13th Wing's aircraft were back in the air despite persistent low cloud and mist across the battlefield. Third Army's infantry, led by tanks, had pushed eight kilometres into the Hindenburg Line system, over-running the first two trench-lines but failing to capture the Bourlon Ridge which overlooked Cambrai itself. To help secure the hoped-for breakthrough, five pilots from 2 Squadron left the advanced landing ground at 10 a.m. to support the fight for Bourlon Ridge by low-bombing and machine-gunning enemy positions and strong-points.[59]

Enemy aircraft were also up this day, spotting for their troops but at lower altitudes (because of the cloud cover) which were where the DH5 was at its most manoeuvrable. Before lunch the Australians had shot down three German two-seaters—their first victories in the sky. These successes had come at a significant cost, however: three 2 Squadron aircraft were shot down by ground fire that day, their pilots all killed or wounded (although the fate of one of them would not be known until after the war). More aircraft were reduced to battered wrecks, their pilots limping back to Baizieux from the advanced landing ground for repairs or to collect replacement machines.

During the battle of Cambrai, a Mark IV tank passes a captured German 77mm gun as it moves forward on the Graincourt side of Flesquières Ridge in support of the British 40th Division's attack on Bourlon Wood, 23 November 1917.

Also on 22 November, Watt's squadron received a visit from Major General Hugh Trenchard, commander of the RFC in the field. Trenchard had been keenly conscious of the Australians' involvement in the battle, to the extent that on the evening of 20 November he sent a message to Watt asking him to 'Congratulate all pilots on their gallant work under impossible conditions.'[60] After talking to the pilots passing through the advanced landing ground at Bapaume, Trenchard wrote to General William Birdwood (the British officer holding administrative command of the Australian Imperial Force) upon returning to RFC Headquarters at Saint-Andre, declaring that the work of the pilots of 'Australian fighting Squadron No. 68' was 'really magnificent':

These pilots came down low and fairly strafed the Hun ... with machine-gun fire from 50 feet, flying amongst the tree tops; they apparently revelled in this work which was of great value. ... I think them really great men ... They are splendid.[61]

The next day, Watt's pilots were back in the air for another day of gruelling low-flying work in support of the fight for Bourlon Ridge, where the British ground forces were facing stiffening resistance from strong German reinforcements.[62] The squadron was now down to only nine serviceable aircraft and a dozen pilots, but still managed 14 sorties—albeit at the cost of another pilot shot down and killed, and yet another aircraft reduced to a completely wrecked state.[63] The Australians were not the only RFC squadron sustaining such losses, but after only four days of the Cambrai offensive 2 Squadron was already looking, in Molkentin's description, 'threadbare'.[64]

While fighting subsided over following days, as the exhausted British ground troops attempted to consolidate their gains against an expected German counter-offensive, the Australians found there was still considerable action to be had in the air. On 26 November a German DFW reconnaissance aircraft was shot down, and three days later a two-seater was forced down near Cambrai after its observer had been put out of action; that same morning a 2 Squadron patrol of four aircraft clashed with eight Albatros scouts over Bourlon Wood.

On the morning of 30 November the Germans' long-awaited response to the British offensive was finally delivered. Concentrating on the sector of British gains east of Bourlon, where the trenches were more-weakly held, the enemy threw in masses of fresh infantry employing new "stormtrooper" tactics to penetrate the defences deeply and isolate strong-points that were left for following forces to subdue. Supporting the ground onslaught were low-flying schlachtstaffeln (battle flights) employing fast, nimble fighters with the same close-support tactics as the RFC ten days earlier. So successful was the German assault that Gouzeaucourt, which was within British lines before 20 November, was quickly captured.

The pilots of 2 Squadron were at breakfast when the klaxon sounded the alarm at Bapaume. Although pilot numbers in the Australian outfit had been built up to 15, with the arrival of some rookie pilots to replace men lost, there were only ten aircraft available to respond to the desperate situation in which the Third Army now found itself.[65] Even with these limited resources, the unit managed to fly 37 sorties over the course of the day, with most pilots flying at least two missions while five pilots crossed the lines three times. Losses that day were, surprisingly, just one aircraft shot down (although the pilot managed to get home the next day) and another damaged with a shell splinter through the fuel tank which forced a hasty return to Bapaume.

Watt's men were again heavily committed the next day, 1 December, with eight aircraft sent up in pairs. That day four squadron machines were forced down by enemy fire, including 22-year-old Lawrence Benjamin, one of the raw replacements, who was so badly shot up while patrolling beyond Gouzeaucourt that he barely managed to make an emergency landing at the advanced landing ground. By 4 December the British had been forced to give up their gains on Bourlon Ridge and withdraw, to avoid being cut off by the German advance on their right flank.

With this, the battle of Cambrai was effectively over. The Australian squadron's role reverted to reconnaissance scouting and offensive patrols, leading to a number of final aerial encounters. On the 5th, a flight of seven 2 Squadron machines found itself pitted against an enemy formation of 12 Albatros and four two-seaters which fortunately declined to give combat beyond some preliminary skirmishing. The next day, one of two afternoon bombing patrols came across a DFW two-seater and shot it down—making this the eighth enemy machine accounted for by 2 Squadron over the course of the battle. It was also the squadron's last fight in its DH5s, because the unit was about to be rested to undergo re-equipment with newer and better SE5a aircraft. From 7 December the squadron ceased appearing in 13th Wing's orders, emphasising that its part in its first great offensive on the Western Front was finally ended.[66]

As Molkentin points out, Cambrai 'is today almost unknown to the Australian public, as none of the AIF's infantry divisions took part. But it was a defining event for the AFC. … The squadron also received the highest praise from British and Australian commands and was lauded by the press in both countries.'[67] It would have been on Watt's recommendation as squadron commander that six of his officers received the Military Cross for their flying during the battle.[68]

When these awards were announced on 12 December it prompted General Birdwood to write to Watt offering his congratulations: 'This is indeed a magnificent record for your squadron, and one of which I am sure everyone of you must rightly be extremely proud: I doubt if it has been beaten anywhere.'[69] In March 1918 the award of the Military Medal to four mechanics of the squadron was also promulgated, in recognition of their work in salvaging aircraft under fire.[70] Watt himself was mentioned in Sir Douglas Haig's dispatch of 7 April 1918, the award appearing in the London *Gazette* the following month.[71]

Following the battle of Cambrai, Major Watt stands among surviving pilots of his squadron at Baizieux, 7 December 1917. (Australian War Memorial E01434)

The outstanding performance of 2 Squadron at Cambrai had come at a heavy cost. Half its pilots became casualties and a staggering total of 27 aircraft had been wrecked during the battle's 17-day course. The human legacy of this toll was no less serious, with many survivors suffering nervous disorders—or what would now be identified as post-traumatic stress. Several were sent back to England with 'nervous debility' or 'aero-neurosis'. Some who stayed subsequently fell apart under the strain.

Watt well understood what his pilots were going through, and did his best to ameliorate the effects of the acute stress each man experienced each time they flew out over the battlefield. A case in point was Second Lieutenant Harry Cornell, a 25-year-old electrician from Tasmania who had been with the squadron only a week when the Germans mounted their counter-offensive. Sent off on his first patrol on 30 November, he was airborne in the mist when his engine suddenly stopped and he was forced to make a crash-landing in contested territory. Although he regained the British trenches and was able to return to Baizieux next day, a doctor diagnosed him as suffering shock.

In what was described by Molkentin as 'a characteristic demonstration of his care and devotion to his men', Watt provided Cornell with a five-day leave pass to Paris and arranged for his niece, who lived there, to show the rookie pilot around. Watt also recommended a good hotel offering hot baths, meals, shows and shopping, with the result that Cornell duly returned to the squadron refreshed and eager to fly. Unfortunately, all was not well with the young pilot, and five minutes into his first flight on 11 December—ironically described in the squadron record book as an 'air test'—he stalled his aircraft at 500 feet and nose-dived to his death.[72]

In the days immediately after the Cambrai battle ended, 2 Squadron received a visit from the Australian official war correspondent (later the official historian), Charles Bean. He arrived at Baizieux on 7 December to find that Watt was away 'lecturing at the Army HQ at Albert to 200 officers and NCOs on the cooperation of aircraft and infantry'. Bean was nonetheless persuaded by the recording officer (or adjutant), Lieutenant William Turner (a shellshock victim on loan from the infantry), to stay the night, which ensured that he was able to meet and interview the squadron commander on his return to the unit.[73]

Bean already knew before he arrived that 'this first Australian fighting squadron' had been 'winning themselves a magnificent name'. What he heard from the unit's officers now prompted him to record in his notebook the view that 'It is Watt who has worked them up to this remarkably high level of conduct and general tone.' Bean heard at first-hand the high opinions everyone in the squadron held of their CO, and understood that the pilots idolized him for his devotion to them. He also learnt of the punishing hours Watt kept in administering the squadron and providing his moral support for those constantly facing the perils of combat. 'I hope to God,' Lieutenant Turner told Bean, 'we don't lose him through his overwork; for believe me we shall never get another like him!'

It was Turner who also told Bean of the immense strain the CO had been under during the weeks of heavy fighting just concluded—Watt himself 'did not mention it' when Bean finally met him. The one aspect that had most troubled Watt, that he would speak of, was the decision that rested with him whether to send his young pilots out on days 'when flying was exceedingly dangerous and almost impossible':

> It was not as if they were a battalion or even a company say of 120 men. They were … boys who sat at the same table every day for 6 months and had become exceedingly well loved friends. He had to make the order for these friends to go. "You can just imagine the feelings with which I used to sit there during two hours waiting for them to come back", he said.

Bean received a glimpse of precisely what the recent experience of Cambrai had meant for Major Watt. Noting that constant days of little sleep had left Oswald looking 'very worn', Bean observed him fall asleep directly after dinner in front of the mess room fire. 'It was not a cold night, but he was shivering.' It was patently clear that, now two months short of his fortieth birthday, and with three years of war experience weighing on him, Watt himself could no longer maintain the pace.[74]

It was while Bean was visiting Baizieux that 2 Squadron began receiving the first Royal Aircraft Factory SE5a aircraft to replace its DH5s—in fact, Bean was able to photograph one of the very first machines (B55) on 7 December.[75] Even with re-equipment complete, the unit stayed out of operations during the onset of the winter season. By early January 1918 it was under orders to move to an aerodrome at Auchel/Lozinghem near Bethune, 60 kilometres north of Baizieux, where it joined the 10th Wing working with the First Army. Shortly after this, it was learnt that the British War Office had finally agreed to recognise AFC nomenclature for the Australian squadrons, instead of the RFC numbers foisted onto them. Later that same month the squadron moved again, to an aerodrome at Savy near Arras, 20 kilometres to the south.[76]

By the middle of February, it was Oswald Watt who was on the move, under orders to take up a new assignment. After he was treated to a farewell concert in his honour 'somewhere in France 1918'— featuring vocal performances, recitations and comedy by "The Kook-A-Burras"[77]—on the 16th he handed over command of 2 Squadron to Major William Sheldon and left to return to England. The unit was about to re-enter the air war on the Western Front once more, but without the commanding officer who had done so much to forge its identity and its already considerable name. There was an irony in the fact that Watt had been quoted as saying: 'At this game—those who live, learn—and those who don't, teach others by their mistakes', because he was about to become the AFC's principal trainer.[78]

AFC Training Wing

The position that awaited Oswald Watt was command of the training wing being raised as the largest component of the AFC's training establishment in Britain. Between June and October of 1917 four Australian reserve squadrons (numbered 5 to 8) had been raised on RFC aerodromes at Shawbury in Shropshire and Yatesbury in Wiltshire, each attached to British training wings, in line with advice from the War Office that this number would be sufficient to train new pilots for the AFC's three fighting squadrons in France as well as 1 Squadron in Palestine.[79]

In May 1917 Lieutenant Colonel Edgar Reynolds, the original CO of 1 Squadron who had left the AFC in Egypt to fill a succession of AIF staff jobs in France, became Staff Officer for Aviation at AIF Administrative Headquarters in London. It was largely through lobbying by him that in September British authorities agreed to bring together the Australian training squadrons in a single area, though not on a single base. Having won this concession, Reynolds then initiated a new proposal next month for a single wing to be formed comprising the four squadrons along with an aeroplane repair section. This, he argued, would make the AFC 'self-contained' and with all its administration and training in the hands of Australian officers.[80]

Once the establishment of the wing headquarters and the aeroplane repair section had been approved by General Birdwood (in his capacity as commander of the AIF), moves were begun by the AIF Administrative Headquarters to identify the personnel to staff them. By mid-January 1918 the AIF's Commandant in London, Colonel Thomas Griffiths, recommended Major Richard Williams (then commanding 1 Squadron) to head the training wing. This selection was apparently made on the basis that Williams was the senior major of the AFC, but this belief was wrong; Williams did not reach the rank of major until May 1917, six months after Oswald Watt, and David Blake (CO of 3 Squadron since September 1916) and even William Sheldon (promoted in April 1917) were also senior to him. In the event, the error did not matter. When the recommendation was referred to AIF Headquarters in France for endorsement, Birdwood—acting on advice from General Trenchard, RFC Commander in the Field—replaced Williams' name with that of Watt.[81]

Accordingly, when Oswald Watt reached Boulogne on 17 February (the day after handing over command of 2 Squadron) to cross over to Britain, he was formally transferred to 'Home Establishment' and appointed to command the Australian Training Wing with the temporary rank of lieutenant colonel.[82] This made him the first officer to become a wing commander in the Australian Flying Corps and the first promoted to lieutenant colonel during the war, beating Williams who attained the same level four months later in Palestine when he was seconded to command the 40th (Army) Wing in what had since become the Royal Air Force.

Williams' new command was, of course, an operational not a training formation, but it contained three British squadrons in addition to the one AFC unit he formerly led. This meant that, when Watt's wing was fully established with its four squadrons under his control, the thousand AFC personnel that he commanded in England was the largest single concentration of Australian military airmen anywhere in the world. It was little wonder, then, that afterwards it was Watt who emerged as the pre-eminent and best-known figure of the wartime AFC—in the estimation of one, "The Father of the Flying Corps".[83]

Watt's accession to the top command in the AFC also prompted Reynolds to propose another step to strengthen the distinctive national identity of Australia's air corps. He had already taken to referring to his small aviation section in London as 'AFC Headquarters', although his formal position as Staff Officer for Aviation conferred no command or operational authority whatever.[84] In the first months of 1918 he proposed renaming his post as 'Officer Commanding AFC in Britain', a change which would have brought Watt's wing under him—presumably with a promotion for Reynolds to colonel. The proposal was not accepted and instead Reynolds found himself on his way back to Australia in June to take up other duties, his staff captain (Brinsmead) being promoted major in his place.[85]

Reynold's replacement can be viewed as a rejection of nationalistic ambitions for the AFC, which at least raises a question of where Watt fitted into this scheme of things—given his well-known pride in identifying himself as Australian. In fact, Oswald had already shown his solid commitment to the principle of imperial solidarity in pursuit of victory. Even Charles Bean had made this discovery the previous December, during his visit to 2 Squadron in France, when he found Watt 'careful to encourage in every way good relations between the AFC and the RFC' by promoting the view that the AFC was really only 'part of the RFC'. He was insistent on this point and determined to make his men proud of it, believing that work proceeded better and smoother when 'the boys' were more generously disposed to those engaged on the same big enterprise. Bean was forced to admit that Watt's "big picture" approach made himself 'a little ashamed of having taken a narrower view'.[86]

At the time of Watt's appointment to the wing, however, his new command was far from representing a complete and functioning organisation. Preparation had begun late in 1917 to construct two airfields in Gloucestershire's gently rolling Cotswold Hills in southwest

Chapter 6

England—one taking over fields of two farms at Minchinhampton, and the other covering a large tract of land near the Duke of Beaufort's estate at Leighterton, about 16 kilometres away. Work on these facilities was still underway in the last days of February when personnel and aircraft began arriving, and much of the wing was still housed under canvas (including Bessonaux hangars) awaiting the completion of permanent brick and wooden buildings.[87]

Lieutenant Colonel Oswald Watt, commanding No 1 Australian Training Wing, 1918.

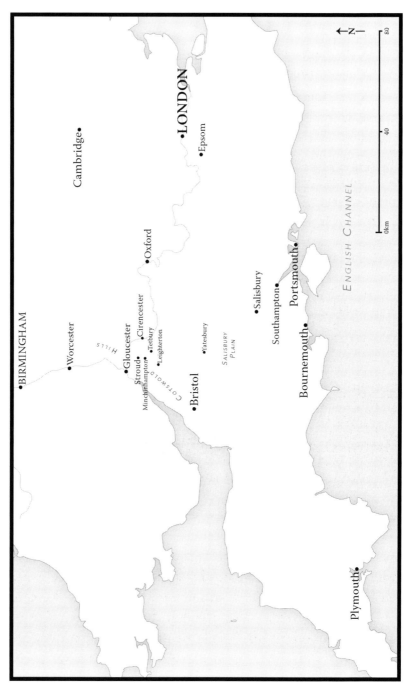

MAP 6 AFC in Britain

Watt's headquarters and other elements of the wing, including an AFC hospital, were established in the small town of Tetbury, dating from the sixteenth century and located roughly ten kilometers from both the wing's airfields. Watt's offices ended up occupying a structure known as Gordon House in Silver Street, though the nature of this accommodation was evidently a great deal less picturesque than it sounded. When Oswald's literary friend William Locke visited Tetbury for several days late in 1918, he described the headquarters as consisting of 'two horrible, empty houses, with a doorway knocked through the party-wall … furnished, as dug-outs or tents or huts were furnished, with the minimum of comfort.'[88]

Headquarters of the Australian Training Wing in Silver Street, Tetbury, with wing transport vehicles out front. (Australian War Memorial P00826.219)

Oswald arrived at Tetbury to take up command on 20 March,[89] at which time the last of the squadrons had yet to make the move to Gloucestershire; in fact, No. 5 Squadron did not arrive until 2 April.[90] This circumstance necessitated a visit to Yatesbury soon afterwards to check on arrangements for the transfer of the remaining AFC men, which gave rise to an incident which became almost legendary among the Australians who witnessed it. After Watt made a showy arrival at the airfield in his white painted Avro, he was berated for

a "swank" flying display by the British squadron major, described
as 'a bumptious individual of little ability' who tried to camouflage
'a weak personality under a screen of bullying bravado'—but only
until Oswald removed his leather flying coat, revealing his rank and
decorations. A 'smothered titter' arose from a group of Australian
officers and cadets who watched on as Watt laughingly brushed aside
the 'stammering apologies of the embarrassed and crest-fallen major',
and walked across to greet his "boys".[991]

Watt's put-down of a pompous British officer may have become
a classic moment in later AFC folklore, but it in no way fully or
truly reflected his view of the relationship between the British and
Australian flying services. Later claims that he staunchly resisted
attempts to 'absorb' the squadrons of the First Australian Wing
into the Royal Air Force, insisting that 'We are an Australian Flying
Corps, and we shall remain so'—even in the face of official threats to
withhold supplies of aircraft—are simply wide of the mark.[92] These
claims are no less fanciful than others published at the time of Watt's
death, maintaining that he became disappointed when his alleged
hopes of taking his wing across the Channel and into action in France
were 'never…realized'.[93] Since there is simply no evidence that Watt
ever misunderstood the true nature of the wing under his command,
it must be assumed that later commentators have become confused
by an entirely separate scheme dating from Reynolds' time at AIF
Administrative Headquarters, calling for the transfer of 1 Squadron to
France and the creation of an AFC combat wing on the Western Front
from the four fighting squadrons.[94]

On 9 April, barely three weeks after his arrival, Watt was sent
on what was termed a 'refresher course' lasting ten days at the RAF
School of Special Flying at Gosport, near Portsmouth in Hampshire.[95]
The purpose of this course probably had little to do with refining his
personal flying skills, rather than bringing him abreast of the dramatic
change in pilot training practice that had lately taken place within
the British service. When the Australian training squadrons were
formed, these had been organised to accord with the RFC practice
of training new pilots in squadrons providing instruction graded as

'elementary' or 'higher'. Since then, this system had been transformed into something far more scientific at Gosport by Lieutenant Colonel Robert Smith-Barry ("Smith-B", as he was known). At the start of 1918 the system was further altered so that new pilots received 'all-through' instruction at a single squadron prior to graduating, before then proceeding to specialist training.[96]

It was the new Gosport system that formed the instructional model at Watt's wing. Once all four squadrons were brought under the wing's authority—Nos 5 and 6 at Minchinhampton, 7 and 8 at Leighterton—each of these units was assigned the role of training new pilots for a specific one of the AFC's four operational squadrons in the field. Initially this included providing replacement pilots for 1 Squadron in Palestine, until it was realised that the modest needs of that theatre could be adequately met by the British flying schools operating in Egypt. Under revised arrangements that were then instituted, 5 and 8 Squadrons both trained pilots for 4 Squadron (which had the highest wastage rate of AFC units on the Western Front because its rotary-engined Sopwith Camel scouts were difficult to fly and suffered more losses from accidents and exposure to ground fire); 6 Squadron provided SE5a pilots for 2 Squadron; and 7 Squadron met 3 Squadron's needs for RE8 pilots.[97]

The role of the wing's squadrons went beyond simply producing competent pilots, but involved preparing them for conditions at the front. It was also part of the Gosport system that students were required to learn and practise manoeuvres required in aerial combat—spins, rolls and loops—along with more "dangerous" variants of these, such as climbing turns, Immelmann turns, and rolling off the top of loops.[98] Flying was accordingly conducted on standard elementary types such as the Avro 504J and K, and Sopwith Camel trainers, as well as more advanced combat types such as the SE5a, RE8, Sopwith Pup and Snipe, and the Bristol Fighter.

Predictably, accidents were frequent and resulted in a large number of casualties. During the year that the Australian training wing was in existence, the casualty rate from accidents was 20 per cent for students and 16 per cent among instructors. Although the wing was not responsible for all training provided for AFC airmen, it was striking that 50 deaths of AFC pilots during 1918 occurred in training accidents (as opposed to 44 in combat).[99] It was not surprising, therefore, that the cemetery at Leighterton would eventually contain burials of 25 members of the wing, 17 of whom—both students and instructors—were victims of aircraft crashes, while another seven fatalities were buried elsewhere.[100]

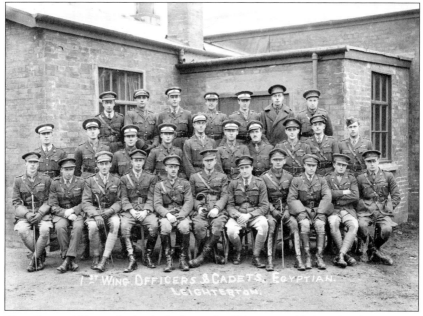

Wing officers and "Egyptian" cadets (with white cap bands) being trained for No 1 Squadron in Palestine, pictured in the early days at Leighterton, 1918. (Australian War Memorial P00048.034)

Watt was confronted very early on with this reality of his new command. On 4 April, just days before Oswald left for his course at the School of Special Flying, the wing suffered its first fatality when Lieutenant Eric Grant, an instructor with 6 Squadron, was killed while performing aerial stunts too close to the ground. Demonstrating that the headstones at Leighterton did not present a complete picture, the remains of 20-year-old Grant (a student at Melbourne's Wesley College before the war) were conveyed to London for private burial at Putney Vale.[101] Although Grant had lived in Australia from the age of 2, he had actually been born in London.

Chapter 6

Fatal accidents such as Grant's would have brought home to Oswald that the business of his new command was potentially just as lethal as his previous time at 2 Squadron in France, only the enemy to be faced was not German bullets or shell-fire but raw inexperience combined too frequently with youthful bravado—among not just students but instructors also. That many of those tasked with teaching hopeful new pilots recognised the risks and dangers of their situation was obvious from the numbers of instructors who made plain their desire to be posted elsewhere, or who resisted postings to the training wing in the first place. Watt would have realised very quickly that here was a challenge of his personal leadership abilities that was equal to anything he had faced before.

Oddly, one of the first instructors to make plain their wish for release from the wing was Major Henry Petre—the officer who had set up the Central Flying School at Point Cook (in opposition to Oswald's recommendation of Duntroon) led an AFC half-flight to Mesopotamia in 1915-16, then raised and commanded a home defence squadron of the RFC until appointed to command 5 Squadron at Minchinhampton. When Petre 'resigned' his command in April and departed on a posting to a RAF training squadron at Shotwick, however, he was most probably not expressing concern about his personal safety.[102] Just as he later complained that he had been 'done out of' the command of 1 Squadron in Egypt in 1917 by Williams, there is the strong hint that he took exception to being passed over for a command to which he probably considered himself equally entitled.[103]

A better example of the problems Watt faced with some of his instructors exists in the case of the AFC's leading "ace" on the Western Front, Captain Harry Cobby. When Cobby received a posting order in September sending him to 8 Squadron to teach Sopwith Camel fighter tactics, his first reaction was to appeal to be allowed to stay in France with 4 Squadron. Although Oswald probably realised that Cobby's posting to Home Establishment was because he was in need of a rest from frontline flying, he responded by insisting that Cobby's expertise in air combat was desperately needed at the training wing.

He could have guessed what was going through Cobby's mind long before the ace later wrote of his dread of 'being chased around the sky by enthusiastic, but partly-trained pilots'. Watt probably fully sympathised with his view that 'France was dangerous enough, but England seemed more so.'[104]

What Oswald was unprepared for were the lengths to which Cobby was prepared to go to make sure his presence was unwelcome at the training wing. Cobby himself described the 'memorable occasion' when he was airborne around Minchinhampton in his Camel painted in a distinctive black and white check pattern, in company with Captain Garnet Malley, another instructor. It was just at that moment that the 'old man' (Watt) approached the aerodrome in his personal aircraft, an Avro painted all in white with 'some gold about the place, with the pet name, "Papillon", in gold lettering along the side':

> We immediately tucked our wings in behind his and throttled back, and were so close that he would not land. We then looped round him from the side, then from the rear, and then on each side of him, just above his top plane. He finally went down and landed and, as he touched the ground, we "leap-frogged" over him and taxied in in front of him.[105]

Knowing the fury that their audacious display would have aroused, the two show-offs waited for the inevitable parading before the CO. 'The usual punishment', noted Cobby, 'for low flying, or other such foolish stunts, was overseas for instructors', and as both he and Malley had requested to be sent back to France a number of times, both were confident that this would be their fate:

> "Ossie" was in a terrible rage, and was jamming his eye-glass into his eye, then dropping it out again as we approached … We both felt a little jubilant [when] … the colonel opened up on us. He could not say 'overseas' quickly or emphatically enough …

But at that point the Wing Examining Officer, Captain George Matthews, intervened and asked to have a few words with Watt in private.

When the two miscreants were sent for again ten minutes later, they discovered that Matthews had persuaded the CO against giving them what they so patently wanted all along, and also that the 'excellent demonstration' they had delivered in the Camel actually served to prove to apprehensive trainees that this aircraft type was perfectly safe despite its fearsome reputation. Instead of being told to pack their bags for the war, Cobby was sent to attend a school of 'Special Flying' for a six-weeks instructor's course, where—he was forced to admit— he very quickly learnt how little he knew 'about the accurate flying of an aeroplane'.[106]

Cobby was certainly not Watt's only problem. Another instructor at 8 Squadron, Captain Elliot ("Tab") Pflaum from Loxton, South Australia, was also given to playing aerial pranks. Very early one morning he reputedly "buzzed" Watt's billet in Tetbury at very low level but made his escape before his Avro 504K could be properly identified. To guard against a repeat performance, Oswald insisted that Pflaum's nickname was painted in extra-large red lettering along the side of his machine.[107]

Two instructional aircraft at Leighterton—a Sopwith Camel in front (identified as belonging to No 8 Squadron by the emu marking) and an Avro 504 behind which was the personal machine of Captain E. F. ("Tab") Pflaum. Oswald Watt had Pflaum's nickname painted in red on his aircraft to facilitate identification in the event of more aerial escapades. (Australian War Memorial P10218.003)

Not all members of the wing's instructional staff were so troublesome or the cause of fraught relations. Those who accepted and respected the job that the wing had to perform found in Watt a humane and sympathetic commander. According to Captain Adrian ("King") Cole, another Camel instructor at Minchinhampton, 'He was the only man I knew in that period who called all of his officers by their Christian names or nicknames, without the slightest loss of dignity or discipline, and achieved the best results.' Having made known his desire to join 2 Squadron, without any evident impact, Cole was delighted when 'one day, early in May, I heard a shout across the aerodrome from Toby: "King, you can go out to No. 2 Squadron." That was all he said, and all I wanted to hear. Within five days I was in France.'[108]

Even non-Australians could fall under Watt's spell, an example being RAF Lieutenant Stewart Keith Jopp (his surname often shown as 'Keith-Jopp') who—despite losing a hand in a ground accident in France—still became an instructor at 6 Squadron at Minchinhampton. He later recalled: 'Colonel Watt was a most wonderful chap. I never heard anybody say a bad word against him. … He was known by everyone as the "Tiger". To me, he was most good, and when I left the Australians he gave me a beautiful propeller-tip, with a flying kangaroo in gold and white on it, with "From Lt.-Col. Watt, A.F.C., to Lt. S. Keith Jopp, R.A.F.," in gold and blue letters. … He also gave me permission to paint a baby kangaroo on my machine.'[109]

Some of Watt's biggest challenges as wing commander involved maintaining good relations with the people of the local district. From the outset he had aimed to keep the community onside, responding positively to a request from the market town of Stroud for assistance with fund-raising for the war effort—by staging an 'air raid' on the town, 'dropping leaflets instead of bombs'. And when, on 8 April, Oswald received a request from the Tetbury Council for £3 to repair a street lamp post damaged by an AFC lorry, he ensured that Wing Headquarters promptly paid up. He could hardly do otherwise in this instance, since the vehicle had been identified by its number, but he was less willing to accept liability when a second occasion arose a month later, where the town clerk stated that the lorry driver had supposedly 'cleared off' before the vehicle number could be taken.[110]

The AFC relationship with the gentry of Gloucestershire was placed under a further cloud a short time later, after three pilots from the wing joined in a fox hunt on the Duke of Beaufort's estate, in their aircraft, and sent hounds, horses and riders scattering in all directions. This was seen as a great joke within the wing—until the duke's angry protest was received in the British Air Ministry and resulted in an equally 'terrible letter' landing on Watt's desk. Determined to shield his men, Oswald did the only thing he could do and went to see the duke. At first His Grace was unbending but Watt gently persisted while acknowledging the seriousness of the complaint, and eventually the duke was 'completely won over by the charm of the Australian officer. They ended up by shaking hands and enjoying a good laugh over it.' The duke withdrew his letter and left it to Watt to discipline the 'young offenders'.[111]

Watt's position as the senior AFC officer in England was, as he quickly came to realise, a special one. When a uniformed representative was required for a ceremony in the central east midlands town of Hull on 25 May, at which Australia was to be presented with the gift of a scout aircraft by the Hull Chamber of Commerce, Watt proceeded there by rail and said thanks to the donors in support of Mr. J. C. ("Chester") Manifold, MHR, who was the Commonwealth's official representative.[112] For the first two weeks of August he also travelled across to France, for what purpose is not known but most likely entailed consultations with the Australian squadrons regarding the standard of pilots being sent to the front from the training wing.[113]

At Tetbury, Watt also held unique status for the large contingent of Australian airmen under his command, a point emphasised by a sports meeting held at Minchinhampton to mark Anzac Day on 25 April. Among the events competed for was the Tetbury Cup, which Watt himself had donated as the prize for a tug-of-war challenge, won by the Aeroplane Repair Section. On hand to present the day's prizes was Major General Mark Kerr, a former Royal Navy flag officer who had just acceded to command of the RAF's South Western Area, based at Salisbury. The meeting was followed by an entertainment put on by a concert party from London.[114]

On 21 September, Oswald was also the guest of honour at a reunion dinner held at the King's Head Hotel in Cirencester to commemorate the first anniversary of No 2 Squadron's transfer to France. The event was attended by a great many of the officers who had served under Watt at Cambrai, and during the course of the evening he was presented with a beautiful model of a DH5 sculptured in silver, a trophy of which he was afterwards reportedly 'very proud.'[115]

Wing memorial service conducted at Leighterton cemetery following the Armistice, 19 November 1918. (Australian War Memorial D00130)

During the first week of November whisperings began to be heard at the Australian Training Wing about a possible armistice. News had been received of a general retreat by the German Army in France and some form of mutiny in the German Navy, and when word came through that German plenipotentiaries had crossed the front line to commence negotiations there was a general expectation that the long-awaited development was about to break.[116] As soon as news of the signing on 11 November was official, Watt ordered the suspension of all training in the wing. Pupils who had not completed their first solo flight were 'washed out', or considered to have failed their course, while advanced students could continue their training if they wished.[117]

At 10 a.m. the following Sunday, 17 November, a parade of the entire wing was held on the aerodrome at Leighterton under Watt's command. Afterwards the men marched to the cemetery about a mile distant for a service conducted beside the graves of AFC officers and cadets killed in training who were buried there. The padre, Major Keith Dixon Norman, mounted a high stand erected in the corner of the cemetery and the troops were formed up in a hollow square around him, with the graves in the centre.[118] 'It was a cold dull day,' wrote Captain John Duigan in the war diary of 7 Squadron, which he was temporarily commanding, 'but in spite of the weather the service was most stirring and interesting.'[119] At last, the terrible years of war were at an end.

Chapter Seven
TRIUMPHANT RETURN

Farewell to England

Six months were to pass following the Armistice before arrangements were complete for the repatriation of AFC personnel back to Australia. With the wing's main purpose and core activity now reduced to irrelevance, there was ample time and opportunity to turn the focus of life at Tetbury, Minchinhampton and Leighterton to other things, and to shift the emphasis from purely wartime requirements.

For Watt, this was a process not easily or readily accomplished. Although described as a man 'deeply sympathetic to those less fortunately endowed than himself, and keenly sensible of the frailty of human nature,' he was never inclined to forgive anyone who he considered had failed to answer the clear call of wartime duty. A wing member later recounted the reception given to an officer who had spent the duration of the war in a staff position in Australia, only arriving for duty at Tetbury several weeks after the armistice:

> Meeting several old friends on the way from the railway station, he spent the ensuing hour celebrating the reunion at the local inn. On entering Colonel Watt's office, he saluted somewhat jauntily, and said: "reporting from London for duty, sir." Then, glancing at his wristlet watch, "I'm afraid I'm a little late, but—". Colonel Watt interrupted shortly: "Yes, you are a little late—four years, to be precise."[1]

While such an attitude might easily have made Watt a difficult commanding officer to work for, he actually appears to have succeeded in retaining the loyalty, regard and even affection of those under his command to a surprising degree—as William Locke discovered on visiting Tetbury for several days after the Armistice. Himself a keen observer of human behaviour, for purposes of his literary works,

Locke noticed that Watt's eyes 'saw everything' going on around him within his domain, 'from a bit of waste paper on the aerodrome to a missing button on a man's tunic'. After chiding one of his captains for preparing to go into town without wearing the cross-strap on his sword belt, Oswald afterwards turned to his guest in the mess and justified his action thus: 'That's one of the most splendid fellows … but it's time enough for him to be slack when he takes off khaki in Australia.'[2]

Locke later recorded that during the last two days of his visit he was obliged to spend time in the mess (located in Crew House in Market Place, at the top of Gumstool Hill) on his own, after Watt was ordered to stay in bed by the doctor owing to a 'slight malady'. In speaking to the officers he encountered there, the elderly writer seemed genuinely surprised that 'there was not one who, in some form or another, did not confide to me his pride in serving under a leader so distinguished and his deep personal attachment to the Colonel'. This was, Locke seemed to suggest, in part due to Oswald's determination to share the same hardships endured by everyone else, right down to his own Spartan-furnished room in the headquarters building. 'To have imported any article of luxury into that hideous chamber would have been disloyalty to his trust,' so it seemed to Locke.[3] How far had Oswald come since he showed apparent disregard of the hardships faced by the men of his squadron during a winter rail trip across France three years earlier.

A month after Locke's visit to Gloucestershire, he was able to reciprocate Watt's hospitality in his country home outside London over Christmas. Oswald's son Jimmy was staying with the Locke family for a few days of the holidays, and Watt's arrival delivered him into the thick of a children's Christmas party. Despite having visibly aged since his previous visit to the Locke household, being 'heavier in figure' with 'a suspicion of grey…at his temples', he coped admirably with being in the company of small children and 'at once took command of the entire show'.[4] Photographs dating from this same Christmas period indicate that Watt and his son also spent time with his sister Florence and her husband, Gordon Caldwell, at their home at Tangley Mere, Surrey.[5]

Oswald Watt with his son Jimmy, taken by Oswald's brother-in-law Gordon Caldwell in 1918.

With the New Year came the news that Oswald had been appointed an Officer in the Order of the British Empire in the honours list announced on 1 January 1919.[6] Whether he was back at Tetbury at the time is not known, but he had certainly returned ten days later when three commissioners from the Australian Comforts Fund arrived from London by train to distribute Christmas boxes to the officers and men of No 1 Training Wing, AFC. After carrying out their task on Sunday, 12 January, the three gift-bearers returned to London on Monday morning, prompting Watt to send a personal note of thanks the following day:

I have been in for three distributions in Egypt, France and now England and each time it fairly hits one to think of all the people 12,000 miles away who are always thinking of the fellows overseas, even though they are only serving on the "Tetbury" front. For myself, I have to thank you for an especially lovely parcel and I have been making a beast of myself ever since I saw you on Havelock tobacco. Surely the man who invented it must be in Heaven if he is dead, and if not, we should surely strike a special medal for him. Please accept my most grateful thanks and come and see us again soon and have that fly.[7]

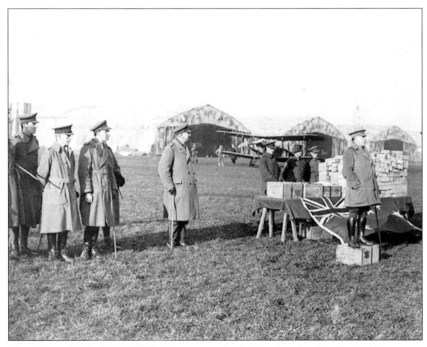

Major Thomas Henley, MLA (NSW), Commissioner for the Australian Comforts Fund, addresses officers and men at Leighterton before the presentation of gift parcels, 12 January 1919. (Australian War Memorial H02051)

In March 1919 the wing received a visit from General Birdwood in his capacity as Commander of the AIF—soon to end on the AIF's return to Australia for demobilisation. During the day-long visit the general met with cadets and members of the instructional staff of the squadrons at Minchinhampton, and toured buildings and facilities on the base, before being taken up in an Avro for a flight over the Cotswolds which delivered him to the wing's other airfield at Leighterton where he enjoyed a similar reception. Watt was at the general's side throughout the visit, along with Horace Brinsmead from the aviation section at AIF Headquarters in London (now also wearing the temporary rank of lieutenant colonel following his promotion in January). Considering the farewell nature of the visit, none of those involved with the occasion could probably have imagined that they would be renewing the association within twelve months.

General Sir William Birdwood talks to Australian pilots In the hangar at Minchinhampton during his visit in March 1919. Standing behind the general is Oswald Watt and Major Horace Brinsmead, Staff Officer for Aviation at AIF Administrative Headquarters, London. (Australian War Memorial D00427)

In the month following Birdwood's inspection, work began in earnest to pack and prepare for the wing's repatriation to Australia. According to one newspaper account, it was during this period of tidying up "loose ends" prior to departure that Watt was approached by the wing pay sergeant:

"Do you know you haven't drawn a penny of your pay since you joined the A.I.F., sir?" Knowing the extent of the Colonel's private income, this information was not surprising. "Shall I make out a cheque for the amount, sir," asked the sergeant. "Yes," replied the Colonel. Then, with a characteristic twinkle in his eyes, "and make it payable to the War Orphans' Fund."[8]

Although there had been opportunities to say formal goodbyes to members of the local community who had become special friends of the AFC presence, such as the supper hosted by the wing's officers at the Stroud Subscription Rooms in March, Watt clearly felt that something more was called for on the eve of departure.[9] On 1 May he penned a final letter to the 'Inhabitants of the town and neighbourhood of Tetbury' expressing sincere thanks from all members of the AFC in Gloucestershire for the 'never failing hospitality and courtesy' received over the previous fourteen months:

> I feel sure that the opportunities we have all had of obtaining a glimpse of that home life, on the memory of which the foundations of the most distant settlements in the Empire have been so securely based, cannot help but draw yet closer those silken threads which bind us to the Homeland. On behalf of every one of us, I thank you.[10]

Five days later Watt embarked at Southampton in the troopship *Kaisar-i-Hind* for the long anticipated voyage home to Australia. Despite its name (often misspelt as 'Kaiser'), the vessel had no Germanic connections but was actually launched for the P&O company on the eve of war for use on the mail and passenger service to India; the name derived from the Hindi and Urdu languages, meaning 'Emperor of India'. Joining the ship was the bulk of all AFC personnel still in England, including not only 1st Australian Training Wing but 2, 3 and 4 Squadrons which had been encamped on Salisbury Plain awaiting repatriation. Also in first-class were several senior AIF officers—Major-General William Glasgow, Major-General John Gellibrand and Surgeon-General Charles Ryan—along with the visiting premier of Queensland, T. J. ("Tom") Ryan. Since most of the military personnel on board were AFC, Watt was appointed Officer Commanding Troops for the duration of the voyage.[11]

The trip got off to a wet and miserable start, as it rained continuously throughout the day of departure. Captain Harry Cobby provided a memorable description of the scene:

the many distinguished visitors who came to farewell us, including Sir William Birdwood, were entitled to added decorations for turning up. In particular, the mayor and corporation, in their robes and chains of office, and the city band, put up quite a good show. They stayed on a dais, making speeches and waving hands for a couple of hours, while the troops on board tried to throw oranges down the bell-mouthed ends of the larger brass-band instruments. As we moved away from the wharf the crowd sang Australian songs and we on board joined in, and, although we were all cheered at the thought that it was all over and we were going home, there were mostly sad faces on board.[12]

The ship had only been at sea a day when Oswald was presented with the first major problem involving the men under his command. Unknown to him, members of 4 Squadron had smuggled on board a French orphan boy named Henri, aged about ten, who had attached himself to the unit while it was on occupation duty in Germany a couple of months earlier. The waif had been adopted as the squadron "mascot" and, when the time came for the unit's return to Australia, the air mechanic who was his self-appointed guardian decided to take the boy to Queensland to raise in his own home. Having been brought safely on board hidden in a 'bread bag', Henri stayed out of sight until the ship cast-off and left port—by which time it seemed that the ruse had worked.

Early the next morning the boy emerged from his place of concealment and was walking along one of the ship's decks when, according to a statement lodged with his application for naturalization in 1928, the captain of the *Kaisar-i-Hind* approached him and, discovering that he was not on the passenger roll, declared that the ship would return to port to put Henri ashore. It was, so the statement continued, then that Premier Ryan and Colonel Watt intervened. These two discussed the question of Henri's fate with the captain, 'stating that they would be responsible for my presence on the Vessel if he continued'. It was reportedly this that 'persuaded the Captain to continue the journey with me aboard.'[13] According to a later newspaper account, there may have also been a question of a 'fine' to cover the cost of the boy's passage, and this either Ryan or Watt (or both) readily paid.[14]

In another newspaper account published in Brisbane soon after the *Kaisar-i-Hind's* arrival, Henri's guardian asserted that, whenever the ship's captain subsequently passed Henri on deck, 'he used to look up at the sky as if searching for hostile aircraft'. As commanding officer of the AFC personnel for the duration of the voyage, Watt 'said nothing severe about our smuggling trick, and the premier, Mr Ryan, was good enough to send a wireless message to Queensland [from Melbourne] arranging for the lad to land.'[15] Air Mechanic Tim Tovell may well have been correct that Watt made no fuss about the entire incident, as the author who most recently documented this story notes that nowhere in the diary and associated papers that Watt kept on the voyage as OC was there any mention made of 'Henri's name or presence' on board.[16]

Oswald Watt with officers and warrant officers on board the *Kaisar-i-Hind* during the voyage home to Australia.

In anticipation of the ship's arrival at Port Phillip on 16 June, the military authorities had reportedly adopted a suggestion put forward in a newspaper for the *Kaisar-i-Hind* to be given an aerial escort from the flying school at Point Cook, as it steamed up the bay to dock at Port Melbourne.[17] Unfortunately this plan had to be curtailed because of adverse weather and the welcoming formation failed to materialise. The unwillingness of the defence department to risk its aeroplanes did not discourage one of the officers at the base—Lieutenant W. H. ("Harold") Treloar, returned from overseas service only the previous December—from approaching R. G. ("Graham") Carey, the private owner of Melbourne Air Service at Port Melbourne, seeking a loan of a Maurice Farman Shorthorn to put up a display of his own. Carey had bought four Shorthorn machines a couple of months earlier, when these had been sold off from Point Cook as obsolete and surplus to training requirements; damage from a gale on Hobson Bay had since reduced two of the aircraft to spare parts, but the remaining two were then among the very few machines in civilian ownership in the whole of Australia.[18]

Treloar was not alone in providing an aerial welcome from the resources of Carey's company since, according to the *Argus*, Carey's second flyable Shorthorn also took to the sky that day. With each carrying a female passenger, these aircraft 'swooped unexpectedly' across the bay as the *Kaisar-i-Hind* approached, circling the vessel several times before they again disappeared.[19] What Oswald might have made of this demonstration is hard to imagine, considering that the Shorthorn was an aging type that he had last flown three years earlier with the French air service and could only have been seen as an indicator of how far Australian aviation was behind the times. Perhaps it firmed any thoughts he may have entertained about making aviation a focus for employing his talents and extensive experience gained in the war.

At Melbourne the *Kaisar-i-Hind* landed 800 of its military passengers who originated from Victoria, along with other troops who were destined for Tasmania. If Oswald went ashore during this stopover, he could not fail to be impressed at the large crowds which assembled in the streets to cheer the airmen as they passed in motor cars on their way to the AIF depot for their return to be processed.[20] Early of the morning of 19 June the troopship arrived at Sydney. After clearing the Heads at 7.30 a.m., the vessel berthed at Woolloomooloo by 9.45 and the remaining 300 members of the AFC were landed.[21] In the weeks following the return, these personnel were all discharged from the AIF and the Corps disbanded. Watt's date of discharge—3 August 1919—came five years, to the day, after he had enlisted in the service of France at the start of the war.[22]

Foremost AFC veteran

Exactly a month after Watt returned to Sydney in the *Kaisar-i-Hind*, he found himself leading a contingent of returned AFC members taking part in a military parade to mark 'Peace Day'. Saturday, 19 July, was the day chosen for all parts of the British empire to celebrate the signing of the Treaty of Versailles (on 28 June) which formally ended the First World War. The highlight of a range of events planned for Sydney was a march by more than 10,000 naval and military personnel, mostly veterans. Dense crowds of onlookers watched as a procession of uniformed men stretching more than five kilometres made its way from the Domain along a route through city streets decorated with triumphal arches. First came columns of naval personnel, with members of the AIF following; first among the AIF contingents was 150 AFC veterans, and in the front rank of this group was, reported the *Sydney Morning Herald*, 'one of the most distinguished of our airmen—Lieutenant Colonel W. O. Watt'.[23]

This proved to be merely the first of a number of significant public occasions when Watt was called upon to play a leading role by virtue of his status as Australia's senior air veteran. In 1920 the British officer who commanded the AIF during the war, General Sir William Birdwood, toured Australia and New Zealand to great acclaim from the officers and men who served under him. His arrival in Sydney was marked by a welcoming banquet in the Town Hall on 10 April, organised by the Imperial Service Club and attended by more than 300 officers of the AIF who gave him a rapturous reception. The toast to the general's health, received with cheering, was proposed by Commander Richard Lambton, the naval veteran of the Australian take-over of German New Guinea who was serving as president of the club, supported by Major General Sir Charles Rosenthal and Oswald Watt as representatives of the 'army and flying forces'. When Watt rose to speak, he said that 'the one regret they of the air squadrons had had was that they were not under the direct control of General Birdwood.' In responding, Birdwood spoke warmly of Watt and added that 'probably Australia did not yet realise what she owed to the Air Force.'[24] Birdwood's stay in Sydney extended past Anzac Day, enabling him to take part in the annual parade of veterans in which Watt again led the AFC contingent.[25]

The Australian Flying Corps led the Peace Day March through Sydney on 19 July 1919; Oswald Watt is second from right in the front rank.

Even as Birdwood was wowing Australia, New Zealand was hosting a very similar visit by the eldest son of the British monarch, King George V, in the person of Edward (later King Edward VIII), Prince of Wales. The heir to the throne was on a mission to thank the dominions officially, on behalf of his father, for sacrifices and contributions made during the war. By June 1920 the prince was touring New South Wales, and on the 22nd he reviewed a parade of 10,000 returned naval and military veterans at Centennial Park before an estimated crowd of 50-60,000 onlookers. Ninety-seven units of the AIF were represented, each carrying "colours" (based on AIF colour patches) presented for the occasion by the Returned Services League. The picture of the parade carried in the *Sydney Morning Herald*, the state's leading daily, showed members of the AFC marching past the prince with Oswald Watt at the head of their column; it was the last time he appeared in public in AFC uniform.[26]

Not all the special war-related events in which Oswald was asked to participate involved Sydney, even though that city continued to be his home base. When South Australian brothers Ross and Keith Smith, with two mechanics, neared completion of the first England to Australia flight in December 1919, the Defence Department began arranging a welcome at the temporary national capital, Melbourne. An aircraft was dispatched from Point Cook, flown by Captain Henry Wrigley and Sergeant Arthur ("Spud") Murphy, to meet the Smiths on their arrival at Darwin with details of an air route south from Darwin through outback Queensland and New South Wales— bypassing Sydney to avoid unnecessary and hazardous crossings of the Dividing Range.[27] As reported in the press, these plans were expected to produce a noteworthy occasion—one intended as an AFC 'day out'. Because Captain Ross Smith had served with No. 1 Squadron in Egypt, it was thought 'only fitting that his old comrades should be first to welcome him.' A special guard of honour would be assembled from AFC veterans, and Watt was asked to come to Melbourne from Sydney to 'take command' in his capacity as the corps' senior officer at the close of the war.[28]

In the final event, a series of mishaps not only delayed the Smith brothers' southern progress for many weeks but brought about a change of plan which saw their Vickers Vimy wartime bomber routed through Sydney after all. Their arrival at Mascot on 14 February 1920 was greeted by tens of thousands of spectators, a crowd so enthusiastic that all arrangements for an orderly and dignified reception were quickly upset. Oswald Watt's presence among those waiting to welcome the 'air explorers' formally was noted in the press, although that appears to have been the extent of his official involvement.[29] Although one Melbourne paper still reported that Oswald was expected to head an AFC guard of honour when the Smith circus rolled on to the southern capital,[30] by the time the Vimy finally touched down five days later there was no mention of his name to indicate that he even made the journey to see the aviators receive the £10,000 prize awarded by the Australian government.

On 22 June 1920 the Prince of Wales reviewed a parade of veterans in Centennial Park, Sydney. Oswald Watt led the Australian Flying Corps contingent in salute.

With Watt's name so much to the fore whenever matters touching aviation arose in public discourse, it was only to be expected that he might become involved in government plans for post-war air defence. Disputes that had broken out between Army and Navy in the last year of the war, regarding separate costly schemes for air arms that each insisted were essential to their own requirements, had led to a recommendation in January 1919 that Australia should follow Britain's example and have a single air force meeting the needs of both the other Services. Despite this apparent resolution, matters now became delayed by disputes within the committee formed to implement it, and this situation would ultimately continue for two years before an independent third service called the Australian Air Force was brought into existence at the end of March 1921.

Watt's arrival home from the war had delivered him into the midst of the debate over the future air force which he joined a few short months after his return, although much of this discussion was occurring away from view by members of the general public. Watt's only involvement in matters was initially confined to membership of an informal panel, made up of former officers of the AFC, which was intended to advise defence authorities on the suitability of candidates considered for appointment to the new air force when finally established.[31] As authorisation did not occur until little more than a month before the AAF's formation, there was seemingly little for the advisory panel on staffing to actually do. The only call known to have been made on Watt's time in this regard occurred in early December 1919, when the Chief of the General Staff, Major General Gordon Legge, telegrammed him from Melbourne asking for his views on the officer proposed for appointment as first flight commander in the Australian Air Corps,[32] an interim organisation formed at Point Cook in January 1920 to take charge of a gift of surplus wartime aircraft and equipment received from the British government.

In seeking Watt's views in this instance, General Legge was perhaps influenced less by the previous advice he received about consulting with a panel of former AFC commanders than by a direct brush he had with Oswald a month earlier. On Armistice Day, 11 November, Legge had been invited to address an 'aviation luncheon' held at Farmer's in the city under the auspices of the Millions Club (later renamed the Sydney Club) and took the opportunity to urge publicly the urgent necessity for an adequate Australian air force. Afterwards the general found himself politely lambasted by Watt, who observed that the returning officers and men of the AFC should have been utilised as the nucleus of the force now outlined by Legge, but—after waiting about for months to see if their services were required—most had then been absorbed into civilian occupations. 'The loss to Australia was incalculable', he pointed out.[33]

Whether Oswald was expressing frustration that his services also had not been called upon in connection with the new air force remains unknown. Although he had said several times in earlier years that he hoped for a role in post-war military aviation, and public respect for his experience and standing in the AFC was unparalleled following his return, there is simply no evidence that indicates he was considered or asked to take charge of the Australian Air Force (or Royal Australian Air Force as it became in August 1921). Any suggestion that he was remains pure speculation. With Watt out of the equation, it was left to Lieutenant Colonel Richard Williams—Oswald's junior within the AFC—to become the dominant figure of the RAAF during its formative years.[34] Watt's personality and manner, as much as his wide personal contacts and influence, may well have made him a more popular and successful head of the air force, but the fact remained that, being privately wealthy, he had no need of paid employment and probably would have declined the post if it had been offered.

Instead, Oswald gave expression to his continued patriotic impulses by active participation in a range of veterans' organisations and defence interest groups, such as the Imperial Service Club, where he became first a director and then a vice-president.[35] He also became vice-president of the New South Wales division of the United Services Institute,[36] which he used as a platform to deliver a two-hour lecture on "The Aeroplane in Peace and War" in September 1920.[37] As a member of the management committee of the Australian National Defence League, he continued to press for the maintenance of compulsory military training.[38] Oswald was even a supporter of the Navy League, which several times led to him being invited to social occasions organised by Commodore John Dumaresq,[39] the innovative captain who in 1917 pioneered the launching of aircraft off RAN cruisers and in 1919 became the fleet commander with the battlecruiser *Australia* as his flagship.

Oswald's imperial patriotism also drew him towards the King and Empire Alliance, a loyalist organisation largely comprising ex-soldiers which came into being soon after the war in direct response to the perceived possibility of socialist revolution in Australia. When the KEA was formed at a public meeting in Sydney Town Hall on 29 July 1920, Oswald Watt was among the long list of prominent figures noted as present on the official platform.[40] Also among the Alliance's founders was Major General Charles Rosenthal, Oswald's colleague from the Imperial Service Club. At the first annual conference of the KEA, held in February 1921, Rosenthal was appointed to the post of honorary secretary.[41] Shortly afterwards, he became commander of the 2nd Division of the Australian Military Forces in New South Wales.

According to Rosenthal's own account, it was the following May that he finally persuaded Watt to resume an active role in military uniform—as CO of a militia battalion in a country district. After experiencing difficulty in finding a suitable appointee, Rosenthal later wrote he approached Watt for his assistance:

He requested a few days in which to consider the matter, and …[then] he wrote me accepting the appointment and pointing out that he felt it was his definite duty to our Commonwealth to do all in his power to assist the new defence scheme. Knowing what a busy man the Colonel was and also knowing the demands both in time and money such a command would make upon him, I all the more appreciated his promised assistance.[42]

It can only be assumed from Rosenthal's willingness to talk about the episode that he was not actually seeking to recruit Oswald to a role in the KEA's shadowy paramilitary offshoot, which became merely the first in a network of secret right-wing armies that flourished during the 1930s and even later. But for unforeseen circumstances and events which halted his appointment, Watt's time in the military service of Australia would have undoubtedly continued for at least several years past the end of the First World War.

Aviation advocate

When the *Kaisar-i-Hind* tied up at Woolloomooloo wharf with the last of its AFC passengers, on hand to meet the ship was a journalist named Edward ("Ted") Hart, then managing editor of the new magazine *Sea, Land and Air*. In the days before the ship's arrival, Hart had been exchanging wireless messages with Oswald Watt about a special 'gala performance' at Her Majesty's Theatre scheduled for 24 June, to welcome home the returning airmen formally. The event had been arranged by the AFC Comforts Fund and a new organisation known as the Australian Aero Club, which was Hart's brainchild.[43] It was he who earlier called the general meeting in Sydney, on 23 May, which led to the formal establishment of the club in New South Wales with Hart as honorary secretary. According to Hart's later account, it was while talking on board the *Kaisar-i-Hind* that he persuaded Watt to join the new organisation.[44]

Writing in 1921–by which time he had moved to Melbourne and begun a new magazine he called *Aircraft*–Ted Hart recalled the 'very frequent contact' he had with Watt in the months following the AFC's return from England, when he turned to him for 'really authoritative information' about the airmen who were constantly making news in the papers. He particularly recalled the 'scores' of personal visits that Watt paid to Hart's Sydney office—78 during 1920 alone—bringing notes and photographs of 'these "boys" of his', with the sole concern of ensuring the reading public should appreciate their records and achievements during the war. When the ship bringing Captain Wrigley and Sergeant Murphy south (after their transcontinental flight to Darwin to meet the Smith brothers) reached Sydney on 10 January 1920, it was Watt who drove them both to Hart's office to be interviewed. It was entirely understandable therefore that Hart also succeeded in persuading Watt to become president of the Aero Club.

Even if Watt did not realise immediately, he would soon have come to appreciate that by accepting Hart's invitation he had found the ideal means of achieving his often-expressed desire to play a useful role in developing aviation in Australia—especially in a period when there was so little visible progress occurring in the defence sphere. Not only was the Aero Club a body with expert and practical knowledge that made it hard to ignore on specific issues (even if politicians did not particularly want to hear its views), it represented an important platform for raising the level of airmindedness within the Australian community by keeping the public informed and interested in aviation achievements and progress generally. As the club's chief spokesman, Watt would emerge as an important figure in aviation matters.

At first Watt's role consisted mostly of hosting the numerous informal luncheons and dinners that Hart organised, as well as chairing the fortnightly meetings of the Aero Club's committee. This changed, however, as Hart began working to expand the club's structure and membership by creating sections of the club in other states. Towards the end of 1919 there were also some portents of the advocacy role that was open to the club to play. In November the Chief of the General Staff, Major General Legge, presented a briefing to the New South Wales section at the Royal Society House, with Watt in the chair, at which he gave details of the proposed arrangements for welcoming contestants in the England to Australia air race following their arrival at Darwin.[45] It was probably at this meeting, or as a result of it, that the Aero Club invited Legge back to Sydney to give a public lecture on the subject of "Commercial Aviation in Australia".

General Legge's talk, delivered in St James's Hall on 7 January 1920, turned into a major public occasion attended by several hundred prominent citizens as well as a 'full muster' of some 200 members of the Aero Club. The State premier, William Holman, was on hand to introduce the speaker, and set the tone of the evening by declaring that the principal task before all governments in Australia, and organisations such as the Aero Club, was to arouse public general recognition that the present was 'a flying age' and aviation 'is a thoroughly established and successful fact'. Echoing Holman's sentiments, Legge began by calling for immediate and generous recognition by the press and public that air supremacy was vital to the very existence of Australia. Only after giving a detailed description of the Army's plans for a military air service—down to the number of squadrons, aircraft, schools, aerodromes, personnel, and costs—did he turn his attention to 'the business side of aviation', arguing that a country like Australia could not afford what he was proposing 'unless a great portion was utilised normally in peaceful occupations'.[46]

The key to Legge's vision of Australia's aviation future was a fleet of 200 large multi-engine aircraft of the Handley-Page V/1500 type of bombers in use at the end of the war. These would be utilised for dropping high-explosive bombs in wartime, but in periods of peace they could engage in commercial activities, providing a transport service between main cities across the country. Giving detailed analysis of his scheme, the general argued that the service he envisaged could pay handsomely carrying passengers and freight, and be able to compete with many of the nation's existing transport systems. 'Air traffic', he concluded, 'is already proving its practical value in Europe and America. It carries mails at a profit, and paying passengers also, though not yet at railway costs. In Australia we have conditions so favourable that the problem is easy if handled with ordinary business ability, so the prospects are of a very encouraging character if we can only break down the prejudices of ancient habits of thought.'

Legge's presentation was later described as a 'phenomenal performance', and received with 'considerable enthusiasm'. In proposing a vote of thanks on behalf of the Aero Club, Watt observed that 'General Legge's interest in this subject, both in the military and commercial sense, has been a source of deep gratification to all concerned. His propaganda work has been absolutely priceless'. Premier Holman, speaking in reply to a second vote of thanks proposed from the audience, said the State government would cordially co-operate in the legislation necessary to make flying successful. He also announced that his government would be initiating some experimental air services with the object of popularising commercial aviation. It was, he considered, 'the duty of the Government to satisfy the general public that with ordinary care and caution travel by air was safe, reliable, and comfortable.'

Before the meeting ended, Watt called upon General Legge to launch a public appeal for funds to erect a monument to local inventor Lawrence Hargrave who was recalled as 'really the first man to start the science of aeronautics on practical lines'. Watt explained that the

Chapter 7

New South Wales section of the Australian Aero Club proposed to commemorate Captain Sir Ross Smith's great pioneer flight from England to Australia by erecting a suitable memorial, in the Domain or Botanic Gardens, to the original Australian pioneer in the conquest of the air. He also announced that the trustees of the memorial fund would be himself, as club president, and Hart as the honorary secretary. (Hart would reveal in the pages of *Sea, Land and Air* that the idea for the Hargrave monument had originally come from Watt.[47]) General Legge strongly urged the citizens of Sydney to support the appeal, adding 'I hope the monument to be erected will be worthy both of the inventor and the citizens of Sydney.'[48]

In the weeks after the launching of the Hargrave memorial appeal, Watt devoted considerable effort and energy in promoting the quest for public support. He was the author of a newspaper article which highlighted the 'prejudice, disbelief and apathy' that Hargrave faced while experimenting with kites for a quarter of a century from the 1880s to establish 'the actual principles on which modern flight is now based'. Citing the saying that 'A prophet is not without honour, save in his own country', Oswald stressed that Hargrave 'received no encouragement, financial or otherwise, from those in authority, so that all his experiments were conducted, and his models and apparatus manufactured, at his own expense. In spite of all those disabilities and the disheartening indifference of those in high places, Hargrave persisted in his work, and brought it to a successful issue.'[49] To demonstrate his own commitment to the cause, Oswald posted the first donation of 50 guineas—worth about $5000 at today's values—and Hart chipped in with five guineas from his magazine. By March the total of subscriptions stood at just over £285 (about $30,000 today).[50] A year later the fund totalled nearly £400,[51] but still insufficient for the planned monument to proceed; it was never built.[52]

In the wake of General Legge's address, on 2 March the New South Wales branch of the Aero Club heard another visiting speaker in the person of Sir Arthur Whitten Brown, an RAF officer who had been knighted after serving as navigator on the first successful non-stop transatlantic flight in June 1919 (achieved in a Vickers Vimy aircraft similar to that used by the Smith brothers). Watt was in the chair during the luncheon, at which Brown warned his listeners about the critical importance of Australia having an 'air fighting force'. But he also emphasised the need to give equal attention to commercial aviation, to contribute to the wealth and welfare of the empire, and urged the Commonwealth government to adopt uniform flying regulations for the whole country—not like in America, where there was talk of having different regulations for every State. Brown's arguments were particularly well received, and when Watt proposed a toast to the health of the club's guest it was 'enthusiastically honoured'.[53]

A week later there was a gathering in Sydney which demonstrated that the considerations mentioned by the club's recent visitor had been heard and duly heeded. Brown was actually in attendance when delegates from Australian Aero Club sections in Victoria and Queensland, in addition to New South Wales, were entertained to lunch by Watt at the Voluntary Workers' Café in Elizabeth Street. According to press reports of the conference, the secretaries of the different sections met 'for the purpose of arriving at unanimity in aerial matters, particularly with regard to control and rules for Australian aviation'.[54] It was, by all accounts, this meeting that marked the beginning of a campaign to promote the development and central control of civil aviation. Soon afterwards, Watt wrote to the Prime Minister to express the club's disapproval of the lack of flying control, pointing out that Britain had brought an Air Navigation Act into force in May 1919.

When a reply was duly received from Prime Minister William Hughes, pointing out that there was no provision in the Australian Constitution for the federal control of aviation, Watt was moved to observe from the presidential chair that the Fathers of the Commonwealth had evidently been less sanguine about the success of aviation than the Wright Brothers.[55] The club was prompted to introduce its own certificate of airworthiness in New South Wales, with a special committee to control issue, and also determined to get the States and the Commonwealth to agree to a control system to ensure public safety in air travel.

According to a version of events at this time later put about by the writer Timothy Hall, when Watt found that many politicians, particularly in the states, gave only lukewarm support for the club's proposed measures, he resorted to unorthodox measures to press the case. Supposedly one of the most bitter opponents of national control of aviation turned out to be the New South Wales Premier, William Holman, who Watt 'quickly converted … by taking him for a flight and frightening him so badly that the wretched man was willing to agree to control by anybody'.[56] The truth of this claim may well be doubted, however, since Holman's alleged stance was clearly at variance with the attitude he expressed only the previous January, and there appears to be no record of Holman ever taking a flight with Oswald Watt at the controls—or, indeed, of Watt ever piloting an aircraft after his return from the war.

In reality, the battle to persuade government of the wisdom of a national approach to aviation control was not at all protracted, and had been won before 1920 was over—in large part because a Premiers' Conference in May 1920 had already agreed to a resolution that each State should refer to the Commonwealth the control of air navigation. Accordingly, an Air Navigational Bill was passed by the Commonwealth parliament on 11 November, received assent on 2 December, gazetted on 11 February 1921 and came into effect on 28 March that year. This provided for the registration and periodic examination of aircraft, the licensing of aerodromes and also personnel engaged in flying and maintaining aircraft, along with rules of the air. A three-month period of grace applied after the legislation came into effect, meaning that the Air Navigation Act finally became law on 28 June 1921.

As soon as the Act was given assent, the government moved to appoint a Controller of Civil Aviation—the public servant charged with exercising the flying controls now prescribed by law, thereby reducing the high air accident rate due to reckless and unsafe flying which it was realised damaged the public's faith in aviation generally. According to one account, Watt was himself offered this post by the Minister for Defence (within whose portfolio the Civil Aviation Branch would reside) but declined because of his business commitments.[57] Advertisements for the position had first appeared after the Air Navigation Bill was passed in November, offering a salary of £750, rising by £50 annual increments to £1000. Watt was, of course, unlikely to be attracted by this money anyway, regardless of his business interests. Instead, he recommended Lieutenant Colonel Horace Brinsmead, the former Staff Officer for Aviation who Oswald had known from his time in command of the Training Wing at Tetbury during the war. Brinsmead had only returned to Australia on 5 July 1920, having found post-war employment in connection with the Paris Peace Conference and then the Disarmament Control Board in Germany. The appointment of Brinsmead was approved at a meeting of federal cabinet on 2 December and formally made two weeks later.[58]

With the progress of legislation for flying controls occurring throughout the latter half of 1920, apparently requiring little further pressing by the Aero Club, Watt's role seems to have mainly involved lifting the public profile of flying achievements whenever appropriate. Such was the pace of flying activity in the immediate post-war period that opportunities for this arose quite regularly, beginning when aviators Captain George Matthews and Sergeant Tom Kay, both former AFC men, arrived in Sydney on 9 June in the Java steamer *Roggeveen*. Nine months earlier they had been the first to take off on a flight from England to Australia in pursuit of the £10,000 prize offered by the Commonwealth government, but had encountered an endless series of misfortunes before a crash of their Sopwith Wallaby aircraft at Bali finally ended the attempt in April. After the ship carrying the two airmen docked in Sydney, press reports appeared stating that Matthews and Kay were 'unheralded and unmet', even by their fellow aviators.[59] This was unlikely to have been intentional on the part of the Aero Club, or Watt personally (given that Matthews had been his Wing Examining Officer at Tetbury in 1918), and steps were quickly taken to acknowledge their return publicly[60] with a dinner in their honour on 15 June at which Watt presided.

Two months later a similar opportunity arose to honour the arrival of another two contestants in the London to Australia air race, Lieutenants Ray Parer and John McIntosh, as they passed through

Sydney on their way to an official welcome at Melbourne. The Smith brothers had already claimed the prize-money before Parer and McIntosh even took off from London in their two-seater DH9 bomber, but their arrival at Darwin after another long series of mishaps had at least completed the first England-Australia flight in a single-engined aircraft. Their achievement was acknowledged at a dinner given by the Australian Aero Club at the Hotel Australia in Sydney, again with Watt in the chair.[61]

After Watt said the club felt gratified 'at being privileged to honour two men, who by their pluck and perseverance had brought such credit to Australia and Scotland,' other speakers including George Matthews and Sir Keith Smith rose to pay tribute to the two guests of honour for such a remarkable accomplishment—especially considering the machine used, which, it was pointed out, had actually been condemned by the British Air Ministry as unairworthy. According to a press account of the occasion, McIntosh's speech ended after he ingenuously observed, 'I see many faces of friends here who were above me in the Flying Corps and whom I always tried to respect'—a statement that was drowned out by laughter, led by 'Colonel Oswald Watt'.[62]

Watt was obviously not unmindful that the aircraft type in which Parer and Kay had made their flight represented a contradiction with the stated objects of the Aero Club regarding safety and airworthiness. When the question arose of their DH9 being purchased by government 'for exhibition purposes, and to preserve it for the benefit of future generations', Oswald was reported to have said that 'it would be to the point if they handed it to the theatrical company for a stage "prop" in their piece "Going Up" … [and] described it as a "Comic Opera bus".'[63] Despite deploring this aspect of the flight, he nonetheless became one of three honorary treasurers on the executive committee of the Sydney Lord Mayor's Fund who issued a special appeal to assist Parer and McIntosh, pointing out 'that these lads started from London with a few pounds, and have had no valuable prize to collect at this end, and it is felt that the patriotic and sport-loving people of New South Wales will willingly co-operate in contributing to a public testimonial to these intrepid men.'[64]

On 27 November the Aero Club organised and conducted the first Australian Aerial Derby at Sydney's Mascot aerodrome. The event was held to raise funds in aid of "Peace Loans" (to help finance the government's war debt) and attracted over 9,000 spectators who watched the start and finish of a speed/handicap race to Richmond, on Sydney's western outskirts, in which nine aircraft competed. There was also a short race of about 14 miles, and a stunting contest. Watt was on hand, as club president, to present the trophies after the derby, including a silver cup which he had himself donated to the winner of the stunting championship.[65] Such was Watt's commitment to the club's objectives in promoting the public safety of aviation that he had already made £500 available, out of his own pocket, for 'protective measures'. According to Ted Hart, this money was spent on erecting nearly 1000 metres of 'stout fencing' to keep spectators out of the aircraft enclosure at Mascot.[66]

Oswald Watt congratulates Nigel Love, the winner of the first Australian Aerial Derby, 27 November 1920. standing behind Watt is Lieutenant Colonel Horace Brinsmead, soon to become Controller of Civil Aviation.

Oswald was also to the fore when the Aero Club gave a dinner in honour of the already internationally famous Australian aviator Bert Hinkler at the Australia Hotel on 27 April 1921. Unfortunately, Hinkler had been delayed when flying from Brisbane earlier that day to attend the occasion—having encountered a torrential downpour which forced him to land on Stockton Beach at Anna Bay, north of Newcastle. Despite the missing guest of honour, the dinner for nearly 50 members of the Australian Flying Corps proceeded anyway. From the presidential chair, Watt used the occasion to press the point that Hinkler's mishap only served to demonstrate the urgent necessity for thorough organization of civil aviation in Australia. 'Were this done, an important city like Newcastle would have a properly-equipped aerodrome, and aviators landing there could have faults attended to and proceed on their journey without undue delay. It would be the duty and the responsibility of the Australian aero clubs to impress on the State and Federal Governments and municipalities the urgency of providing adequate facilities for the development of civil aviation.'[67]

Unknown to anyone present that evening, the Hinkler dinner was, in fact, the culmination of Oswald Watt's presidency of the Australian Aero Club.

Rebuilding

Watt's return to Sydney in mid-1919 brought him back to the city where he had lived much of his childhood, and nearly all his twenties and early thirties, for the first time in six years. The process of re-adapting to civilian existence was difficult enough for many AIF veterans, trying to resume a previous life in a country that had been transformed by four years of war. But the circumstances of Oswald's departure in 1913 had disconnected him from everything—family and friends, familiar places, interests and pursuits—even more abruptly and sharply than most of the men who were now trying to fit back into a society they barely recognised. The stature and standing he had acquired through his service with the flying corps were valuable assets as he set about rebuilding a future, but they had come at the price of a pervasive sense of sorrow and weariness which was shared by a great number of former Servicemen and Servicewomen who had witnessed sights they would not, could not, ever forget.

As for most returnees, restoring a livelihood seemed an early priority. Although not short of money, Oswald's investments and business interests produced nothing like the income that many people assumed or imagined he had. Along with his brother Ernest, Oswald remained a junior partner in Gilchrist Watt & Co, the once prosperous shipping firm that his father had built up, which by 1919, after the importing and exporting businesses had been hived off into separates companies in previous years, was doing little more than managing a few pastoral and financial interests. When Ernest Watt arrived back in Australia with his third wife in January 1920, having lived in England since just before the war, he reported that 'I don't suppose Oswald's and my share of the profits [from Gilchrist Watt & Co'] ever amounted to £100 in any one year'.[68]

The situation of the two brothers was about to change significantly when, over the course of 1920, the two senior partners in the firm both died—first, William Oswald Gilchrist at London in February,[69] followed by their uncle Walter Cumming Watt at his home, "Knellerpore" in Double Bay, in August[70]—creating an entitlement for them both to buy shares in the far more lucrative business of Gilchrist, Watt & Sanderson Ltd. It was not until early in 1921, however, that Ernest and Oswald were finally able to take their place on the board of this company.[71]

By then Oswald had also secured directorships of the Australian Alum Co (which had been mining alunite at Bulahdelah, NSW, since the 1880s), the Great Britain Tin Mining Co (working tin deposits in Queensland and northern NSW), the Sogeri Para Rubber Co (conducting plantation operations on the Sogeri Plateau, 50 kilometres north-east of Port Moresby in Papua), the Ulladulla Brick Co, and Art in Australia Ltd (a publishing business).[72] While the commitment of time to each of these businesses was unlikely to have been consuming, the remuneration derived from them was equally unlikely to have been large.

The last known portrait of Oswald Watt, taken in March 1920—out of uniform, now a businessman.

Most of Oswald's wealth clearly derived from his pastoral properties: "Goonal" near Moree, "Llanillo" near Walgett, both in northern NSW, and "Howlong" at Carrathool, in the state's Riverina district. His interests in the first two stations were partnership arrangements, giving him only one-sixth and a quarter share respectively, but Howlong was in his sole ownership—having been left to Oswald on the death of his brother Willie in 1908.

The affairs of Howlong did not require Oswald's constant presence, as he had a full-time manager looking after things even during his prolonged absence overseas. This was W. F. A. ("Frank") Chase, the son of Richard Chase who had managed Llanillo for Gilchrist Watt & Co for 30 years until he retired in 1910.[73] Frank Chase was manager of Howlong except from July 1917 when he enlisted—though aged 37—for active service with the 6th Light Horse, until returning to Australia three months before his employer; the management of Howlong was undertaken by William Fieldhouse, another landholder in the Hay district. Although Oswald visited the Riverina only periodically, even after his own return from the war, he took 'the greatest personal interest' in the rural community at Carrathool.[74] The part that Howlong played as a principal source of income for Oswald explains why he proudly described his occupation and address in Sands directories for 1919 and 1920 as 'grazier, of Howlong Estate, Carrathool'.

With no need to maintain a large or ostentatious residence about Sydney, Oswald took up residence at the Union Club where he had a bedroom.[75] He also probably had a work desk at the offices of Gilchrist Watt & Co at 5 O'Connell Street, which premises were shared with Gilchrist, Watt & Sanderson Ltd. It was at either address that former AFC colleagues would have sought him out, asking for help to return to civilian life through finding employment or financial assistance. According to Ted Hart, Watt 'camouflaged many an act of downright prodigality' when extending his helping hand, yet his financial aid was extended to such a generous degree that among his friends Watt became jocularly known as "Minister for Repatriation".[76] It was possibly his demonstrated concern for veteran welfare that led to a proposal that he should stand for parliament—a suggestion that he again reportedly declined.[77]

Given the kind of existence Oswald Watt was leading in Sydney, and the weary state of mind in which he arrived home from the war, it was inevitable that he found special refuge at Bilgola, the seaside property that he still owned located roughly halfway between Mona Vale and Palm Beach, on the city's northern outskirts. The simple wooden house, with its quaint tower on the roof, sat within a seven-acre grove of cabbage-tree palms, burrawangs, wattles and eucalyptus trees. Since buying the property in April 1912, Oswald had only a year to enjoy his purchase before departing overseas ahead of his divorce case; then, the peace and serenity of Bilgola had helped with restoring his health during a period of acute mental stress and turmoil, and now, six years later, it again provided a welcome form of relief during weekends spent enjoying the seclusion, sun and surf.

Throughout the war years the house at Bilgola had remained empty, unvisited except by some of Oswald's friends like Sydney lawyer Arthur Allen who during the spring and summer months of 1913 and 1914 was known to bring his family on picnics; on 23 September 1914 Allen even entertained the singer Madame Melba (not yet 'Dame Nellie') to lunch on the front porch.[78] As a recent account of this visit observed, the Allen family seemed to come and go as though they owned the place, rather than merely having access through their association with the owner—who was Oswald Watt, not his friend John Dalley, as was incorrectly surmised. But even these daytime visitors do not appear to have had access to the house's rooms within, merely enjoying the ocean views from the shade of the outside verandah. The caretaker, Stephen Jones, still lived in the cottage on the property, to ensure that the house remained secure and to cut the grass on a regular basis.

Bilgola Beach viewed from atop the headland at the northern end. (State Library of NSW a3295024h)

Allen picnic party at Bilgola, 30 November 1913. The family came and went as though they owned the place while Oswald Watt was overseas. (State Library of NSW a3292023)

Following Oswald's return from the war, he began following a routine which involved him visiting Bilgola almost every weekend. During these visits he laboured long hours in the small garden at the front of the house, when not swimming or walking the beach. He nearly always also invited friends to spend the weekend with him— not just regulars like Syd Jamieson, Syd Richardson, Harrington Palmer and his brother Ernest (with wife Bertha), but other well-known names such as the artists John Longstaff and Lionel Lindsay, and Bertram Stevens the art critic and arts promoter Ure Smith. On Sundays whole car-loads of extra visitors often came as well, staying for barbequed meals which Oswald usually cooked himself.[79] Because Oswald knew that Stephen Jones 'liked to tipple', he never kept spirits or wine in the house, so guests could expect to be provided with only fresh water to drink, or tea which they were invited to make for themselves.

Rustic simplicity was the keynote of these weekends, a feature emphasised by the sparse and basic furnishings of the house itself. The bedrooms had no carpets on the floor, no sheets (only blankets) for the small iron beds which had been left by the former owner, while wooden cases served as dressing tables. Seating in the place was provided by a small assortment of kitchen chairs variously described as old, hard and dilapidated. As visitor John Dalley was moved to observe:

> For a man of the world who had known luxury in most parts of the civilised globe he lived in greater discomfort than anyone I ever met. He loved "Bilgola" … and worked hard to beautify it—outside. But when it was suggested to him that the addition of a few elementary articles of furniture might improve the place, he said: "Good Lord, man! You'd ruin it!"[80]

The one significant indulgence that Oswald appears to have allowed himself involved going into partnership with his brother Ernest in the ownership of a thoroughbred racehorse. Despite all the interest he had previously shown in racing over the years, it was only after he had been home from the war more than a year that he finally decided, or was persuaded, to own a horse himself. In November 1920 it was reported in the Sydney press that the Watt brothers had purchased a bay thoroughbred named *King Arthur*, and placed him in the Randwick stables of noted trainer James Barden.[81] The horse was English-bred, having been sent out in February 1917 as a two-year-old by Dick Wootton, then the most successful and famous Australian involved with racing in Britain, who wanted to establish bloodstock for a breeding program ahead of his planned return to his homeland after the war.

Despite running some promising races at Newbury and Newmarket in England before arrival, King Arthur failed to find form on tracks at Melbourne, Sydney or Adelaide. After a year Wootton decided to dispose of him, with some others of his imports, and bring fresh young stock with him on his eventual return. King Arthur was sold, then quickly sold again, the third owner eventually enjoying some success when the horse won handicap races at Warwick Farm in January 1920 and Rosehill in June. His form was still erratic, however, with disappointing non-placings in between, even when racing at rural tracks like Grafton.

There was considerable surprise, therefore, when the horse won at his very first run in the colours of the Watt brothers as his new owners, taking out the Canterbury Handicap on 16 December.[82] Unfortunately, this form was not repeated at several subsequent meetings, with the best he could manage being a second place at Warwick Farm on 8 January 1921.[83] By mid-February, the word around the tracks was that King Arthur had 'eased up'.[84] His trainer decided to spell him for a while, and he was not entered for another race until 21 May.

As Oswald approached the second anniversary of his return home from the First World War he might have found time, possibly while relaxing at Bilgola, to reflect on what the future now held. With the Air Navigation Act having come into effect late in March 1921, providing a control regime for the orderly development of aviation across Australia (just as he had worked for), and the formation of the Australian Air Force at the end of the same month having settled the shape of defence aviation, the question was clearly: where to next for him?

Chapter Eight
END, AND ONGOING

Tragedy at Bilgola Beach

On the evening of Thursday, 19 May 1921, Watt left behind his room at the Union Club and drove north from Sydney in anticipation of spending another relaxing weekend at his beloved Bilgola. The next day he mostly worked in the garden around the bungalow, the 60-year-old caretaker Jones his only company, but also found time to collect driftwood on the beach and stack it for use in the house's fireplaces. Although alone on the Friday, he was expecting to be joined on Saturday morning by Syd Richardson and Syd Jamieson. He was not to know that something would turn up at the last minute to keep them both from leaving the city, so that—for the first time since returning from the war two years earlier—he would be enjoying his weekend refuge on his own.[1]

On Saturday, 21 May, Oswald was up at 7 a.m. and soon afterwards put his breakfast on the stove before going down to the beach. He was wearing a bathrobe over his bathing costume, and took with him a towel, so evidently he intended having a brief dip in the ocean. Before leaving the house Watt had asked Jones to keep an eye on the kitchen and let him know when breakfast was cooked, but the old man became wrapped up in his grass-cutting and completely forgot about his employer's request. It was between 9.30 and 10.00 when, on passing by chance through the kitchen, Jones noticed breakfast still sizzling away over the fire. Although not overly concerned by this, imagining that "the Colonel"—as Jones now always called Watt—had himself simply forgotten about eating, he decided to find out what was detaining him.[2]

There was no sign of Watt on the beach but near the northern rocks Jones came upon a towel propped on a stick, with the colonel's bathrobe lying nearby along with 8-10 pieces of driftwood piled in a heap. After calling out 'coo-ee' and receiving no answer, he climbed halfway up the headland to look around. It was then that he spotted a body in the water 50 metres or so from the beach, lying on its back and floating just beneath the surface. The old man tried to reach the body, but slippery rocks, a pounding surf and a strong under-current prevented him from getting to it. Looking about and finding no-one within sight, he realised that he would have to head by foot across the southern headland to Newport beach, a distance of several kilometres, to obtain assistance. Sometime before 11 a.m. Jones reached the Newport Hotel and raised the alarm.

While a skiff manned by a couple of fishermen and a local storekeeper was immediately launched and headed around into Bilgola Bay, Jones sent an urgent telegram to Oswald's brother at the Union Club. Ernest Watt had actually gone to his office that morning, arriving shortly before 11 a.m. He had been there only a few minutes when a young male staff member came to tell him that he had received a telephone message from his father at Newport, saying that Colonel Watt had been seen floating face upwards in Bilgola Bay and that a party was just starting off to rescue him in a boat.

Taken at face value, the phone message could have meant only that Oswald had been carried out by a current, that he was swimming on his back to keep afloat, and that assistance was on its way. Nonetheless Ernest immediately phoned Syd Richardson and another colleague named Cowell (who was probably a motor engineer named Arthur Cowell, formerly an equipment officer serving under Oswald at Leighterton during the war), and within a short time the three of them were preparing to drive to Bilgola in a motor vehicle. Before they left the city, Ernest made a dash into the Union Club to get some brandy—probably thinking the alcohol might be helpful in reviving somebody suffering from water immersion. At the club he was handed the telegram from Jones stating simply and unequivocally that Oswald had been drowned. As he later wrote:

Oh! the agony of that drive. I shall never forget it. Cowell drove, and drove fast, but it seemed ages before we got there

… even then we did not altogether lose hope. We thought it just possible there might be some mistake, that Jones had acted impulsively and all might yet be well. But when … we at last neared "Bilgola" we knew that the worst was true, for we could see the boat still searching for his body.[3]

Bilgola Beach, looking northward towards the headland off which Oswald Watt drowned.

By the time the rescue boat from Newport had reached the northern end of Bilgola Bay, the body had sunk from sight. About two hours later it was found some 150 metres from where Oswald was thought to have entered the water, lying on the bottom at a depth of about seven metres and in the process of being steadily drawn out to sea. Just at the moment that the body was dragged into the boat, Ernest Watt, with Richardson and Cowell, arrived on the beach from Sydney. The surf was too rough to allow a landing to be effected in Bilgola Bay, so the boat returned to Newport. As Ernest later recounted:

We lifted his poor body from the boat to the car and drove full speed for the cottage, and then, laying him on his own little bed, we tried for over an hour to bring back life by artificial respiration. It was, of course, hopeless from the very start, but we ourselves were like drowning men clutching at straws.[4]

A doctor named Richards who had hurried to Bilgola from Narrabeen formally pronounced life extinct.[5]

Medical examination of Watt's body that afternoon provided the first clues as to what might have happened. A large bruise was found at the back of the head, along with a cut in the middle of the forehead and some scratches on one cheek. When these injuries were considered at an inquest conducted on 30 May, the city coroner concluded that Oswald had slipped and fallen on rocks, striking his head before rolling into shallow water in which he drowned while still stunned or unconscious. A finding of 'accidental drowning' was recorded.[6]

This at least settled conjecture that appeared in the press about the 'somewhat mysterious' circumstances of the tragedy. News of Oswald's death by drowning had flashed across Australia within hours of its occurrence, appearing in Perth newspapers on the same day.[7] As a Melbourne paper observed in the days immediately after the event: 'At first it was thought to be one of the ordinary surf fatalities, of which there are so many here. The fuller particulars of Colonel Watt's end leave doubts about the cause of death, and these may never be cleared up.'[8] But the inquest found no reason to believe that it was anything more than a tragic mishap.

Over the remainder of the weekend of the drowning, Ernest Watt made arrangements for his brother's burial on Monday, 23 May. A requiem celebration would take place at St. Jude's Church, Randwick (where the brothers' parents and siblings were buried) at 8 a.m., followed by a funeral service at 4 p.m. Despite the early hour and the distance to Randwick from the city, a crowd of 150 packed the little church to capacity in the morning, while ten times that number of people turned up that afternoon.[9] Oswald's wartime friends and colleagues had insisted on giving him a military send-off, with the result that, as reported in Sydney's principal daily paper, the funeral was 'one of the largest and most representative in the history of Randwick'.[10]

Even before the service began, a low-flying aircraft appeared above the church and dropped a small parachute with a wreath and card attached. This tribute had been organised by the Australian Aero

Club, because the nation's post-war military air service, the Australian Air Force (formed at Point Cook only seven weeks earlier and not then styled 'Royal' until August), as yet had no presence in the Sydney area. In the words of one newspaper, 'As the form and expression of the sorrow of Australian airmen individually and collectively, the wreath which descended slowly from above was more eloquent in its suggestive symbolism than any words could have been.'[11]

During the service a brief address was delivered by Brigadier-General Alex Jobson, an ex-AIF commander who had served with Oswald in the Scottish Rifles before the war. Afterwards the coffin was placed on a gun-carriage sent from Victoria Barracks, drawn by six black horses, and taken in procession to the gates of the burial ground adjoining St. Jude's. It was then lifted onto the shoulders of eight pall-bearers—all ex-AFC officers—and carried to the weather-stained family vault for interment. According to a press account: 'There was a glamour rather than a gloom as the remains of the distinguished Australian airman were borne to their last resting-place.'[12]

Scene from Oswald Watt's funeral on 23 May 1921.

Reflecting Oswald's standing, not just within the military forces but the naval forces also, the procession included uniformed parties from the RAN cruisers *Melbourne* (by then the Navy's flagship) and *Brisbane* marching with reversed arms, accompanied by the band of *Melbourne*. 'Walking at either side of the gun-carriage were officers, some with decorations, who had served in the war as airmen. ... The airmen were in uniform; so were the officers and men of other services during the war who walked in khaki after the gun-carriage.'[13] After the graveside proceedings, two buglers from the flagship sounded the "Last Post" and then a naval firing party brought the service to a close.

The day after the funeral, Oswald's will was opened in the office of the Perpetual Trustee Co. where it was found to contain a request that he be cremated. As the vault at Randwick containing Oswald's coffin had not yet been resealed, Ernest Watt took immediate steps to give effect to his brother's wish. In an attempt to avoid attracting the notice of the press, he arranged to have the coffin sent to Adelaide by rail for the cremation to be carried out there, and once the ashes were returned to Sydney the following week there was a short private service at St. Jude's, held at 8.30 p.m. on 31 May in the presence of small number of relations and close friends, to place the remains back in the family vault. With them went an AFC pennant, Oswald's flying helmet and his goggles.[14]

With that, the tragedy played out at Bilgola Beach—so sudden, swift and almost pathetic in the brutal simplicity and smallness of its dimensions—had come to an end. Gone from the Australian stage was one of the nation's best-known military figures, at the relatively early age of 43. Although frequently in the public eye in the years before the war, Oswald's achievements had never been on such a big scale to cement for him a place in history. In the words of one press commentator, it was his 'wonderful career abroad' during the war with its 'touches of romance' that had brought him to prominence, followed by his role promoting the new flight industry that emerged afterwards. As was stated more than once on his death, Oswald Watt had become 'the father of Australian Aviation'.

The Watt family vault in the churchyard of St Jude's Church at Randwick, Sydney, pictured in 2012.

Memorials and legacies

When Oswald's will was opened three days after his death it was found to contain, apart from a request for cremation instead of burial, a direction that—irrespective of whether his body was cremated or buried—'no memorial of any kind should indicate where his ashes or body lay'.[15] The discovery that these were his wishes caused Ernest Watt to change the arrangements for disposal of his brother's remains at Randwick, but it did not discourage several proposals that were initiated for memorialising him in various ways. For instance, the Imperial Service Club had decided in July to erect a memorial to him in its new city premises in O'Connell Street.[16] By then another scheme was already afoot, either for building a home for boys on the Havilah Estate at Wahroonga, on Sydney's upper north shore, under the control of the Church of England Committee for Homes and Hostels for Children, or for a wing to the existing orphanage buildings.[17]

Sufficient funds for the Havilah project were forthcoming from subscriptions, with the result that on Anzac Day of 1922 the foundation stone for a new "Oswald Watt Wing" that would nearly double the capacity of the existing Havilah Home (from 32 orphans and needy children, to 62) was laid by Oswald's sister-in-law, Ernest's wife. Also on hand was the Vicar-General of Sydney, Archdeacon D'Arcy Irvine, to conduct a dedicatory service, and it was from him that those attending the ceremony were given information about Oswald Watt's 'large-heartedness' that would surprise even those who thought they really knew him.[18]

Although the great majority of Sydney's population would be unaware of Havilah's very existence, said the archdeacon, it was 'characteristic of the late Colonel Oswald Watt that he should have discovered the Home, that he should have been a frequent visitor to its tiny inmates, and a generous supporter of the work of making life worthwhile for them. … His numerous pilgrimages to this remote haven and the joy which his "surprise parties" brought to these poor little waifs, were suspected by none but the most intimate of his friends.' Following the archdeacon's remarks and speaking on behalf on his wife, Ernest Watt said that his brother had been 'always fond of children'. A year later, on 15 May 1923, the Oswald Watt Wing at Wahroonga was officially opened by the Governor-General of Australia, Lord Forster.[19]

One of the more remarkable memorials for Oswald Watt was a book, described as 'a tribute to his memory by a few of his friends'. Though this bore '1921' as its year of publication on the title page, its appearance was not reported in the press until mid-1922.[20] Edited by Sydney Ure Smith, Bertram Stevens and Ernest Watt, it was published by Art in Australia Ltd.—a firm in which Oswald had been a director, and Ernest still was. As a multi-authored effort which sometimes blurred, compounded or skated over the mysteries surrounding certain episodes in Oswald's life and career, the book was nonetheless an invaluable collection of reminiscences from people who knew him throughout his life. Its text complemented by many extraordinary photographs, reproductions of pertinent documents and letters, and extracts from newspapers, this now rare volume—only 550 copies were reportedly printed—has remained the best single biographical account for more than 90 years.

Some of the material in the tribute book offers insights into Watt's activities and aspirations that is encountered nowhere else, a case in point being the foreword provided by Alfred Consett Stephen, who was a senior partner in the long-established Sydney law firm of Stephen, Jaques and Stephen which his father had founded. Consett Stephen was not only a grandson of a former Chief Justice and Lieutenant Governor of New South Wales, but also a long-time president of the Union Club. It was most probably at the club that Stephen got to know Oswald well in the years before the war, and discovered that he was 'a man of imagination' with a fondness for big, idealistic schemes. One of these Stephen recalled as intended to rival the Rhodes Scholarship by taking young men direct from school in Australia and exposing them to 'the finest ideals and influences of English University life', preferably at Cambridge. Another was to provide a fund which would enable up to a hundred country boys a year to see the big cities of Australia and 'give them a feeling of pride in her future'. Though neither scheme came to fruition—no doubt because of the turmoil in Watt's private life at the time—Stephen held that they showed that Oswald, while still aged in his early thirties, 'had already begun to think deeply on many matters of more than passing importance'.[21]

Consett Stephen also wrote of having received a letter from Oswald in that pre-war period in which he spoke seriously of taking up politics to 'realise the ideal nearest to his heart' of helping to 'weave closer the subtle threads of Empire':

Here at last was something definite and concrete—politics, the largest and most fertile field for any man with a will of his own and with a certain amount of money. Oswald Watt had indeed already proved that he possessed plenty of will-power and determination, but so far he had seemed to me to be merely drifting, trying desperately hard to anchor himself somewhere. Then came the war. The war was his opportunity and he seized it with both hands.

The image that Stephen painted confirms the impression that, for much of his early adulthood, Oswald had indeed been a young man of independent means and privileged upbringing, blessed also with a good education, who was searching to find some worthwhile purpose in life.

In October 1921, five months after Oswald's death, the details of his will appeared in the Australian press. Describing him yet again as a 'grazier of the Howlong estate, Carrathool,' the papers showed that the fortune he left had originally been valued at £225,752 but that, after stamp duty in respect of probate and letters of administration was deducted, the estate was worth £176,845 (an amount probably the equivalent of $18-20 million in today's terms).[22] The will, which Oswald last changed on 15 January 1920, dispersed this money across a range of beneficiaries—not just family and relatives, but friends, former comrades and employees, charities, institutions and causes—on a scale rarely seen before. As a Melbourne paper was moved to comment:

> Obviously the late Colonel Oswald Watt loved his fellow-men. He had the means of assisting many, and did so in the most open-handed way. No will that can be called to mind provided for such wide distribution of money… Apart from his gifts, however, the spirit that prompted them will keep his memory green, even though he apparently desired, by the instructions to his will, that this should not be considered obligatory.[23]

In addition to making generous donations totalling £10,000 to various charitable institutions, and £1000 each to both the Sydney and Royal Prince Alfred hospitals, the will contained a number of unusual bequests. One, of £500, was made to the Commandant of the Royal Military College at Duntroon to establish an essay prize promoting interest in military aviation. In similar vein were two bequests left to the Australian Aero Club under a codicil, one of which was for £500 to be placed in a trust account to create an annual prize for aviation achievement. Spreading his legacy far and wide, Oswald even left a sum of £250 to Carrathool Public School, the interest to be available for purchasing items for the benefit of the children and their education, at the discretion of the teacher.[24]

The residue of Watt's estate was bequeathed to the University of Sydney—perhaps following the example of Oswald's father, and in final fulfilment of Oswald's own wish to do something of educational benefit to Australia. Unfortunately, the university had to wait for the money gifted to it until a dispute between Oswald's executors and the Stamp

Commissioner of New South Wales, regarding the amount of duty payable on the estate, was fought through the Supreme Court in Sydney in August 1925. It was October that year before the executors were in a position to give the university an estimate of what it might expect to receive. This, too, was held up, after the Stamp Commissioner appealed the judgment of the full bench of the Supreme Court to the High Court in April 1926. It was 2 June that year before a full bench of the High Court upheld the appeal except in regard to some British war bonds.[25]

The money eventually delivered to the university was put into an 'Oswald Watt Fund', upon trust to the University Senate, where it would become an important source of finance for many years, generating income to be applied 'for such uses for the benefit of the institution as the Senate in its absolute discretion should determine'. In 1941 the amount of capital in the fund was more than £108,000, and six years later this figure stood at £115,744.[26]

Although the value and significance of many of Oswald Watt's benefactions may have declined over time, several of his bequests still serve to commemorate his name. The £500 left in trust to the Commandant of the Royal Military College was originally intended to produce enough in interest to permit the purchase each year of a pair of field glasses to be presented to the cadet who wrote 'the best essay dealing with any aspect of military aviation or aeronautics.'[27] What had prompted this interest from Oswald in creating such a prize is not known with any certainty now, but must be assumed to have been inspired by events before January 1920 when he updated his will. Possibly it resulted from an approach received from Lieutenant Colonel Edgar Reynolds, the former Staff Officer for Aviation in London who was Director of Military Art at Duntroon from October 1918 until February 1920, and who in 1919 himself added to the college trophy and prize list by presenting the Reynolds Gymkhana Cup for annual competition.

Under the original terms of the trust fund established under Watt's name, a single set of field glasses remained the annual prize for the Oswald Watt essay competition from 1923 until September 1938, when a special ordinance of the Australian Capital Territory was promulgated to solve 'a problem which has been troubling officers of the Defence Department for a long time'. Because the annual income from the bequest had been more than was necessary for the purchase of the prize, the commandant was faced with an embarrassment of riches and had been simply adding the surplus to the fund's principal. Reported the Melbourne *Argus*: 'The proclamation to-day solves the difficulty by empowering the commandant of the college to expend excess income in any year on the purchase of a second pair of field-glasses as a prize for the cadet who writes the second best essay on military aeronautics.'[28]

Rising costs and prices after the Second World War caused the number of prizes per year to revert to one, until the duration of the course at Duntroon underwent radical change with the establishment of the Australian Defence Force Academy, also in Canberra, in 1986. With two college graduations each year the practice of making two awards annually of the Oswald Watt Essay Prize resumed. In 1993 the conditions for the prize were amended to recognize the Australian Aviation Corps graduate on each course who was highest placed in the Queen's Medal list and the award itself renamed the 'Oswald Watt Australian Army Aviation Prize'—the name under which it continues to be awarded today.[29]

With the two bequests left to the Australian Aero Club, Oswald appears to have had a similar long-term aim in mind. The first of the sums, of £500, went to the New South Wales section, and found its use in 1927 when the club purchased a DH60 Moth aircraft for flying training purposes which was the first machine of its type wholly assembled in Australia. When christened at Mascot aerodrome on 4 June, with a bottle of champagne smashed against the propeller, the aircraft proudly displayed the name "Oswald Watt" on the side of the fuselage beside the cockpit. [30] The Moth, bearing the registration letters G-AUFV, flew until after the Second World War, when it was damaged in an accident in January 1946. After this, the fuselage remained rusting in a farm hangar at Jerilderie, New South Wales, until sold to an aircraft enthusiast who restored it and reportedly had it back in the air by the end of 1994. Whether it still carried the name "Oswald Watt" is not known.

The DH60 Moth aircraft G-AUFV, purchased by the Australian Aero Club (NSW Section) in 1927 and named "Oswald Watt", is at right in this line up for an air race of unknown date. (State Library of NSW hood_04954u)

The second bequest to the club, also for £500, was specifically to be placed in a trust account, 'with the annual interest used to present a gold medal to the airman who, in the opinion of the [club's] Council, achieved the most brilliant performance in the air during the year in Australia, or to an Australian-born airman who achieved the most brilliant performance in the air outside Australia'.[31] Due to a lapse in activities of the club, the institution of a medal could not be proceeded with until March 1926 when Sir Bertram Mackennal was invited to submit a design to be known as the 'Oswald Watt Gold Medal'.[32] Even without a medal to actually present in the first few years, awards were made from 1921—although not in every year. In the first 20 years of its existence, the medal went to many of the best-known fliers in Australian aviation history, to some of them more than once. Flight Lieutenant Ivor McIntyre, the pioneer of RAAF long-distance seaplane missions, won it twice; Bert Hinkler was a recipient on four occasions, as was Charles Kingsford Smith.

Elsewhere, evidence of Oswald Watt's presence, ownership or involvement in various places and activities soon disappeared without trace. His estate at Howlong was sold and passed through the hands of various owners—including Charles Trescowthick, known as the oldest boot and shoe manufacturer in the State of Victoria,[33] and father of the AFC ace, Lieutenant Norman Trescowthick, DFC (who served with 5 Squadron at Minchinhampton in 1918-19)—before the Henwood family, the present owners, bought it in 1970.[34]

The Oswald Watt Gold Medal awarded by the Royal Federation of Aero Clubs of Australia to recognise the most notable contribution to aviation by an Australian.

Oswald's property at Bilgola was also sold at auction in December 1921, realising a price of £4500.[35] Tragedy continued to be associated with the place, however, striking again barely two months after the sale. On Monday, 6 February 1922, one of two surveyors sent to conduct work on Watt's former beach estate mysteriously went missing after he had told Oswald's former caretaker, Stephen Jones, he planned on taking a swim. Two days later the mauled remains of the 22-year-old man were found on Bilgola Beach, identifiable only from tattered portions of his swimming costume found washed up 100 metres further along the beach. It was concluded he had been taken by 'monster sharks' that had been seen swimming in the area.[36] Watt's former bungalow remained in other private ownership until 1987, when it was demolished along with all the outbuildings; the site is now occupied by five houses.[37]

A third tragedy on the same stretch of coastline concerned Oswald's journalist friend John Dalley. On or about 6 September 1935 he was swept off rocks while fishing at the base of cliffs on the headland separating Avalon Beach from Bilgola and presumed to have drowned. He was then the associate editor of the *Bulletin* magazine, and author of three published novels which satirised the social life and manners of upper-class Sydney.[38]

On the afternoon of Oswald's drowning, the race horse King Arthur that he owned with his brother Ernest had run third in the last race of a meeting at Canterbury Park, in Sydney, winning £20 in prize money. Some papers commented that it was obvious the horse's trainer had not been made aware of the tragedy in time, or King Arthur would not have started in the race. As it was, the trainer knew nothing about the drowning until he returned to town from the racecourse that evening.[39] This placing may have seemed to promise some improvement in the horse's form, but it actually marked the end of his association with the Watt brothers. At a sale of racing stock in Sydney the month after Oswald's death, the horse was sold to his trainer for 160 guineas, then resold again six months later.[40] Although still entered in races, even winning the Canterbury Handicap in August, the bay's best days were clearly behind him.[41]

By June 1922 King Arthur was no longer registered for thoroughbred races but relegated to "pony" meetings conducted by the Ascot Racing Club.[42] In October he was again offered for sale at the annual Spring sales at Randwick, where he topped a sluggish market by attracting a bid of 60 guineas from the New South Wales Land Agency Company.[43] The next month King Arthur was headed for stud duty at 'Rockwood', a cattle station 120 kilometres north of

Longreach, Queensland, that was owned by former tennis champion Norman Brookes and his brother.[44] This became the horse's home for the next decade. His legacy to Australian racing was felt during the 1930s, when his offspring began winning races at picnic meetings 'out west'. At one amateur meeting held in May 1934 at Oakley, 180 kilometres south-west of Charters Towers, no fewer than four of 14 races were won by the progeny of King Arthur—providing a final faint echo of association with the life and career of Oswald Watt.[45]

More tangible, but probably no more appreciated publicly, was the naming of a street in Watt's memory at the national capital of Canberra, when the names selected for the then new suburb of Campbell (over the hill from Duntroon) were gazetted in May 1956.[46] Few residents—then or now—would have known anything of the man in whose honour 'Watt Street' was named.

Family fortunes

At the time Oswald Watt died in May 1921, his son "Jimmy"—then aged 15—was a student at Wellington College (a boarding school in Berkshire about 55 kilometres south-west of London), reportedly 'destined for the army'.[47] Instead of embarking on a military career, however, the youth eventually studied civil engineering at Cambridge. On 27 October 1930—16 days after James Oswald Watt's 25th birthday—he stepped ashore at Station Pier, Port Melbourne, having just arrived from London on board the P&O liner *Narkunda*.[48] Packed in his luggage was a small gift box containing gold cuff-links bearing the monogram "WOW"—his father's initials; the top of the box was marked 'J.O.W. from W.O.W. 1921'. James Watt also had with him a Rolex watch inscribed 'J.O.W. from W.O.W. Xmas 1914'.[49] Travelling with him on the ship was his mother, Muriel, now known as 'Lady Lawford'.

The young James Watt's change of career path most probably had less to do with personal preference on his part than it did with events that consumed his mother's second marriage, just a few years after his father's death, which would have made the army seem an unwise choice. Muriel's wedding to Colonel Sydney Lawford in May

Chapter 8

1914 must have seemed an inspired piece of timing, coming as it did little more than two months before the outbreak of war brought the promise of greater gongs and glory for her new husband. After first commanding an infantry brigade of the 7th Division in France, Lawford was promoted major general and appointed to command the 41st Division in September 1915. If he subsequently failed to show sufficient talent at the head of his division to deserve further promotion, it was equally his good fortune not to have bungled his command to warrant dismissal, or to have his health fail under him. As a consequence, he led the 41st Division throughout the war and became the longest-serving divisional commander in the British Expeditionary Force.[50] In 1918 he was appointed Knight Commander in the Order of the Bath (KCB), thereby enabling Muriel to call herself 'Lady Lawford'.

At the end of the war, Sir Sydney Lawford—"Swanky Syd" as he was known throughout the army, on account of his liking for stylish clothes—was ordered to India in 1920 in command of the Lahore district. Lady Lawford went with her husband, but they both returned to England in 1921, after which General Lawford returned to his Indian duties alone. In 1923 he was promoted lieutenant general, but it was also then that he wrote to his wife saying that it was impossible for them to live together again.[51] What he meant by that became clear with the public revelation soon after that he had been having an affair with the wife of one of his officers, Colonel Ernest Aylen, a doctor in the Royal Army Medical Corps. This was not the first time that Mrs May Aylen had been involved with another man. Her previous affair before the war had been resolved to enable the couple to continue the marriage happily until 1922, when she refused to break off her association with the general and even stayed with him in a hotel. This time there was no prospect of retrieving either marriages, because May Aylen became pregnant by the general and in September 1923 gave birth to a son.

The result was a sensational double divorce case through the courts in London, following which General Lawford married his lover in September 1924. His son by May Aylen, initially known as Peter

Aylen, was renamed Peter Lawford and would duly become well-known as a child actor, then famous as a Hollywood film star and eventually brother-in-law to U.S. President John F. Kennedy. The scandal resulting from the divorce ended the general's army career, forcing his retirement in 1926. The couple left England to live in France for a time, before moving to America, where they settled in Palm Beach, Florida. Eventually they ended up living on Sunset Boulevard, Los Angeles, California, where the general got uncredited roles in three movie films—including one in which his son starred ("The Picture of Dorian Gray", 1945).

The second Lady Lawford also appeared in two Hollywood movies, billed as 'Mary Somerville'. After General Lawford died in February 1953, she married one-time society entertainer Beauregard ("Buddy") Galon in 1968. (Claims that May had previously married Paramount producer Monta Bell have confused her with General Lawford's niece, actress Betty Joan Lawford, the daughter of Sir Sydney's younger brother Ernest.) In 1986 Galon published, under the sensational title of *Bitch! The Autobiography of Lady Lawford* (Brandon Publishing, 1986), the tell-all account May supposedly narrated to him before she died in 1972.

Although no longer married to Sir Sydney Lawford, Muriel continued to use the title of Lady Lawford for the rest of her life. In 1924 she made her first visit back to Australia in 12 years, travelling in company with her son Jim, by then aged 18. The pair arrived in Melbourne on 17 June in the P&O liner *Mooltan* and stayed at Menzies Hotel before both going on to Sydney.[52] She was back alone in 1928, arriving at Melbourne on 6 February aboard the *Cathay* and causing a buzz in the social papers with her 'fashion novelties'. Lady Lawford caused a bigger stir with her announcement that she was bored with 'the hectic artificiality' of London night life and was thinking of returning to Australia to live. 'I expect to be very happy here in Australia,' she reportedly said, 'if I can find a place to suit me.'[53] Clearly she could not fulfil that condition during this visit, as she returned to England and it was two and a half years before she came back again, bringing son James with her.

Chapter 8

Following Jim Watt's return to the land of his birth, he did what might be expected of any young man of his background. Presumably influenced by his mother, he chose Melbourne as his home base rather than his father's choice of Sydney, and set about joining the social scene of that city. Although reportedly a bit shy by nature, he had inherited a fondness of acting and played leading parts in several charitable performances in Melbourne.[54] The stage was possibly the medium through which he met 22-year-old socialite Beverley Rand Jackson (the daughter of Mr G. R. Jackson (deceased, formerly of Albury) and Mrs Ethel Cunningham of "Egelabra",[55] Kooyong Road, Toorak), since she shared his taste for amateur theatricals. By September 1932 the pair were engaged. On 18 April 1933 they were married in a lavish wedding at St. John's Church, Toorak—where Oswald and Muriel married 31 years earlier—after which the bride's mother and step-father entertained some 250 guests at a reception at Egelabra.[56] The groom's uncle, Ernest Watt, travelled from Sydney to attend the ceremony, but his mother was unable to travel from England reportedly due to ill-health.

The wedding of James Watt and Beverley Jackson in 1933 took place at St John's Church, Toorak—the same church where the groom's parents wed in 1902. (*Australasian*, 29 Apr 1933)

After the wedding James and Beverley ("Bunty") Watt departed on a trip abroad. They were still overseas in January 1934 when William Pomeroy Greene (grazier of "Greystones", Rowsley, near Bacchus Marsh, and the husband of Muriel's sister Edith) died, leaving an estate valued at over £200,000. It was announced in March that, under the terms of Roy Greene's will, James Watt became the recipient of a legacy worth £12,000, along with a share of Greene's jewellery and personal effects.[57] This was news that would have added extra celebration to the party for 250 guests, given at Egelabra by Beverley's parents on 4 June, to celebrate the couple's return to Melbourne the previous night.[58]

Although Lady Lawford missed most of the initial milestones in her son's life in Australia, she continued her pattern of periodic visits from her home in England. In April 1934 she arrived at Melbourne in the *Orama* but stayed only a short time—probably on discovering that James and his new bride were still overseas and not due back for several months.[59] She returned in February the next year, however, when it was reported that she spent 'a few busy days' at Sydney's Hotel Australia before leaving for Melbourne, complaining that Sydney was 'too hot'. Her future plans were described as 'uncertain' but she planned to 'take a house in Melbourne for some months' to see the 'lovely home at Frankston' that her son was building.[60] A year later she was back in Melbourne again (reportedly her 31st voyage between England and Australia), complaining that 'the English winter appeared to be increasing in severity' and announcing she intended 'taking up permanent residence in Victoria in the future'.[61] This time she evidently carried through with her declared plan, because six months later the news appeared in the press that she had died on 9 August 1936 'at her home' in Domain Road, South Yarra; cause of death was heart failure brought on by cirrhosis of the liver and pneumonia.[62]

The year 1937 was memorable for James Watt in other ways as well, because on 4 November his wife gave birth to a son who they named Robert Oswald. The christening was conducted at St. John's Church, Toorak, two days before Christmas, after which the relatives and family friends had tea at James and Beverley Watt's home at Albany Road.[64] The house at this address was one of two that the Watts owned, since James had earlier built another in Tower Road in Mount Eliza, along the south-eastern shore of Port Phillip Bay, which was named "Bilgola". Having bought 200 acres (81 hectares) there, James established himself as a gentleman farmer and apparently divided his time between the two properties.

Lady Lawford, the former Mrs Muriel Watt, from a press photograph in 1934.

"Bunty" and Jim Watt at home in Mount Eliza. (Bob Watt)

In March 1937 Bilgola had been the focus of a terrible tragedy, when three male guests were killed leaving a Saturday night party given by James and Bunty Watt, their car having failed to negotiate a curve in the Nepean Highway at the top of Oliver's Hill at Frankston and striking a fence at 3.30 in the morning. Called to give evidence to an inquest in April, James averred that all three men had been sober when they left the party, and—although he did not know which one had been driving—all were 'quite fit' to have done so. The coroner recorded a finding of accidental death.[65]

In 1939 James Watt became a member of the Mornington Shire Council, an association he maintained for the next 21 years. After the Second World War he bought into the *Mornington Post* newspaper, which incorporated the *Peninsula Post*; later he launched out into other small papers. In 1958 he moved the paper into new premises in Bentons Road, on the outskirts of Mornington, and installed a modern rotary newspaper press. It was there that he got involved in the mechanical side of publishing—taking on the role of keeping the press in working order, while leaving the journalism and editorial side to others.[66]

Chapter 8

On 14 June 1961 James lost his wife Beverley in sad and unexpected circumstances, after she went into Mornington Hospital for a gall bladder operation but suffered a thrombosis. Next year, at age 56, he remarried at Malvern, taking Margery Farquharson (nee Stephens) as his second wife. About 20 years after he built his home at Mount Eliza he had built a second house, just down the road on the same property—also named "Bilgola" after the first was demolished. After his marriage to Margery, James built a third home, also named Bilgola but often referred to as the 'white house', and this is the place still standing today at 90 Tower Road. James Watt himself died on 19 November 1967 at Mornington, after suffering from carcinoma of the throat for the previous six months; he was cremated at Springvale.[67] In his memory his wife Margery commissioned a stained glass window to go into St. James the Less Anglican Church at Mount Eliza, and this was installed in 1969.[68]

With James' passing, the Watt family fortunes were not passed to his only child Robert. Bob recalls that a nursery had been built adjoining the original Bilgola and he lived there in the care of a Scottish nanny until, at age nine, he became a boarder at Geelong Grammar School. He left school shortly after turning 19. After taking some time off, in 1957 he began a cadetship with the Melbourne *Herald*, having previously evinced interest in journalism. During the three or four years he had at the paper, he also studied journalism at the University of Melbourne and received his diploma on 8 March 1961.[69]

Deciding to expand his professional horizons, 23-year-old Bob Watt set off by ship for Britain in June 1961. He had reached Perth when news was received of his mother's death; leaving the ship, he had to return back east to attend the funeral. When he finally made it to England he worked for a couple of years on a bi-weekly newspaper in Surrey. Upon returning from Britain, he worked for a while on the *Mornington Post* then—following a falling out with his father— went to Sydney to work with the *Sydney Morning Herald*. In 1967 Bob moved to Alice Springs as chief reporter with the *Centralian Advocate*. He became the author of a booklet called 'The story of the *Centralian Advocate:* Alice Springs' and Central Australia's first newspaper', based on a series of articles he published in the paper in April-May 1975. Three years later he was appointed the *Advocate's* editor, and held that post for the next decade.[70]

Oswald Watt's grandson Bob attended the Anzac Day service at Leighterton, England, in 2007. (Bob Watt)

After spending a total of 21 years in Alice Springs, in 1988 Bob Watt transferred to the *Northern Territory News* as a sub-editor. About two years later he was offered the court round, with the result that he ended up as the paper's court reporter for 15 years before retiring in August 2005. In 1997 Bob had married Alison Fraser (nee Bartlett). She had a daughter Ruth and a son Michael from her first marriage, but there was none with Bob. At age 78 Robert Oswald Watt still lives in retirement in Darwin's suburbs, proudly aware of his grandfather's part in Australian history. In 2007 he and his wife visited England and attended the Anzac Day service which still occurs annually at Leighterton. But he is also aware that, since his grandfather's brother Ernest was survived by four daughters, when he eventually passes from the scene the male line of descendants of John Brown Watt must inevitably come to an end, more than 170 years after the patriarch of the family arrived in Australia to begin the connection.

In changing times

In his tribute to Oswald Watt, Union Club president Alfred Consett Stephen wrote:

> Unfortunately, it is useless to speculate as to what the future held in store for [him]. I only know … that when I heard of his tragic and unexpected death, the shock to me was as though some bright bird of gorgeous plumage, which I had been watching in full flight, had suddenly dropped stricken at my feet.[71]

Though florid and a bit overblown, Stephen's description probably reflected the feelings of many people in 1921—not just Oswald's close friends and associates. By the time he died, Oswald's name had so frequently appeared in newspapers over nearly two decades that for many Australians it had become almost a byword for glamour and adventure. But the face and nature of Australia, and the world view focused on Britain that Oswald Watt had known and revered, was soon beginning to change.

Late in 1938, when Consett Stephen advised the Girl Guides Association to 'give the children toy soldiers this Christmas', arguing that 'we must do something to revive the splendid military spirit which has made our empire great', it was viewed against a backdrop of events in international affairs that would again see the world at war less than a year later. The *Australian Women's Weekly*, however, pilloried the now 81-year-old for spouting 'aggressive poison', with an editorial declaring that his views were 'a counsel from the bad old days of jingoism, of a boastful type of narrow patriotism which fostered national hatred'.[72] Oswald Watt would almost certainly have been dismayed to see his old friend's commitment to the British empire being challenged and dismissed in such fashion, but it was one measure of the extent to which Australia had begun to move on.

When the long-anticipated war began on 3 September 1939—11 days before Consett Stephen himself passed away—this began almost as a replay of the First World War 25 years earlier. As soon as Britain declared war on Germany, Australian Prime Minister R. G. Menzies made a national radio broadcast advising his countrymen that Australia was 'also at war'. Menzies' address still used empire-flavoured language that would have thrilled the heart of Oswald Watt and a great many others of his generation—Australia was acting in company with the other 'British Dominions', playing its part in 'a great family of nations'.[73] And for the first two years of the conflict, that is how events played out. Australian troops were committed to operations in the Middle East, North Africa and the Mediterranean littoral; Australian warships likewise went into action in waters far from home shores.

Developments in the air initially appeared to have taken a similar path—one that, if anything, strengthened and even deepened the old imperial bonds. Before the war was a month old, Australia's first Minister for Civil Aviation, James Fairbairn (appointed by Menzies in April 1939), visited Camden, New South Wales, on 30 September to open the Macquarie Grove aerodrome, on ground formerly used by the Macarthur-Onslow family, for a flying school. It was at the new Commonwealth aerodrome, within line of sight of the Wivenhoe estate which Oswald Watt once owned, that Fairbairn pronounced: 'The final decision of the war will be won in the air.'[74]

This was a prediction that Menzies himself did not dispute, although he was more circumspect when he gave another national radio address on 11 October, stating only that: 'In this war air power might turn out to be the determining factor.'[75] The Prime Minister was announcing Australia's participation in a new scheme for a vast 'Empire Air Armada' to confront the German Luftwaffe in Western Europe, and that Fairbairn would be Australia's representative at a conference in Canada to finalise details of the scheme. All these arrangements came to fruition, with the result that the Empire Air Training Scheme became the primary focus of Australia's contribution to the air war over England and Europe. While still in Ottawa, Fairbairn was sworn in on 13 November as Australia's first Minister for Air and became responsible for all matters involving the RAAF until he was killed in an aeroplane crash nine months later.

Ostensibly the realisation of EATS merely confirmed the imperial dimension of Australia's contribution to the war effort in the new global conflict underway. As the London *Daily Mail* newspaper saw it, the dominions had committed themselves to sustaining an 'Imperial Air Force' to ensure Britain ruled the skies as well as the seas.[76] But there were subtle differences in evidence behind the appearances. Menzies' announcements in October had explained that, in addition to the empire defence element, Australia was motivated to join the air training scheme because it had its 'own problem of defence' to consider. 'Our interest in this war is not founded only on our sentiment as British people,' he said, but 'upon the cold fact that our own existence is at stake.' Australia needed a strong air force to protect against the prospect of having to deal with 'transports filled with invading troops', and participation in EATS was necessary to help train the number of aircrew needed to rapidly build up home air defences.[77]

Until Menzies lost office in late August 1941, little more than three months before a new war front opened in the Pacific, his government had kept a watchful eye on the apparent intentions of its most powerful neighbour in the region. Once Japan entered the conflict, Australia was propelled towards a new relationship with the United States—forging an alliance which would endure long after the Second World War ended in 1945, inevitably at the expense of the ties that Australia traditionally enjoyed with Britain. For the generations of

Australians alive today, far removed from the Second World War and even more distant from the First World War, the deep and staunch devotion shown by Oswald Watt to the defence of the British empire and interests seems mystifying and incomprehensible—or at best anachronistic and irrelevant.

Viewed from the perspective of a century after the events which became the high point in Oswald Watt's life, it becomes difficult to find a basis for understanding what impelled him (and more than 300,000 other Australian men and women) to take part in a conflict in which Australian territory, homes and lifestyle were so little threatened in a direct sense. Yet there is no denying the impact of the First World War on the shape and direction of developments in Australia ever since, so we rightly continue to remember and commemorate the participants in that and all other conflicts in which the country has taken part.

In similar vein, the other central passion in Oswald Watt's life—aviation—has also continued to move on from the expanding but still largely undeveloped state in which he left it in 1921. Although the medal instituted in his name continues to be presented in recognition of Australian achievement in the skies, there, too, changes have occurred to give the award ongoing relevance. In 1950 the terms of the bequest contained in Watt's will were varied by the executors to allow the Oswald Watt Gold Medal to be awarded for the 'most brilliant performance in the air or most notable contribution to aviation by an Australian during the year'. Five years later the conditions of the award were further amended slightly to read; 'For the most brilliant performance in the air or the most notable contribution to aviation by an Australian or in Australia'.[78]

These were changes which moved the Oswald Watt Gold Medal beyond achievements of the simple record-breaking variety which defined awards in the early years. The medal was not awarded during any of the six years of the Second World War, and in the 70 years since its resumption there have been several periods of three or more years—in one case 11 years (2000-2010)—in which no awards were made. As a result, only 34 medals have been presented in the post 1945 era.[79]

Chapter 8

Now administered by the Royal Federation of Aero Clubs of Australia, the medal has gone to individuals who have contributed to aviation through planning air races, setting gliding records, maintaining flights in especially harsh environments like Antarctica and the North Territory, aircraft manufacture, developing transport services, and developing hang gliding. In 1983 it went to Sydney businessman Dick Smith for making a solo around-the-world flight in a helicopter. In 1992 it recognised Chris Dewhirst's achievement in becoming the first person to fly a balloon over Mount Everest. In 1998 Dr Andrew Thomas was recognised as the first Australian-born NASA astronaut.

Sir Angus Houston, recipient of the 2015 Oswald Watt Gold Medal, speaking at the national memorial service for victims of the MH17 disaster held at Parliament House, Canberra, on 17 July 2015. The medal was presented at Parliament House two months later, after Sir Angus delivered the Sir Reginald Ansett memorial lecture; Ansett was himself a recipient of the Oswald Watt Gold Medal in 1975. (Department of Defence)

From the beginning, the Oswald Watt Gold Medal has often been awarded to members of the Royal Australian Air Force, so that it was no great surprise when the award for 2011 went to RAAF fighter combat instructor Squadron Leader Paul Simmons.[80] In 2015 retired Air Chief Marshal Sir Angus Houston received the medal for his leadership in directing the search for a missing Malaysian Airlines flight MH370, as well as leading the effort to recover the remains of Australian passengers killed in the shooting-down of another Malaysian airliner MH17 over Ukraine in July 2014.[81]

For as long as the Oswald Watt Gold Medal continues to awarded, the man for whom it was named will continued to be remembered by Australians—though hopefully now with a clearer and more accurate understanding of who Oswald Watt was, and what he did in his lifetime.

REFERENCES

CHAPTER ONE – Privileged background

Mr Watt goes home

1 *Sydney Morning Herald*, 7 Dec 1842, p. 2.
2 *A Few Records of the Life of John Brown Watt collected by his son*, Sydney: Art in Australia,c.1922, pp. 3, 87
3 G. P. Walsh, 'Gilchrist, John (1803-1866)', *Australian Dictionary of Biography*, vol. 1, Carlton, Vic: Melbourne University Press, 1966.
4 *A Few Records of the Life of John Brown Watt*, p. 54
5 *A Few Records of the Life of John Brown Watt*, p. 30.
6 Walsh, 'Gilchrist, John', *ADB*.
7 *Sydney Morning Herald*, 30 Jan 1854, p. 5.
8 G. P. Walsh, 'Watt, John Brown (1826-1897)', *Australian Dictionary of Biography*, vol. 6, Carlton, Vic: Melbourne University Press, 1976.
9 Sydney Ure Smith, Bertram Stevens & Ernest Watt (eds.), *Oswald Watt: A tribute to his memory by a few of his friends*, Sydney: Art in Australia, 1921, p. 9; Charles F. Maxwell, *Australian Men of Mark*, vol. 1, Sydney: 1889, pp. 78-79.
10 Maxwell, *Australian Men of Mark*, vol.1, p. 78.
11 Maxwell, *Australian Men of Mark*, vol.1, p. 77.
12 Maxwell, *Australian Men of Mark*, vol.1, p. 77.
13 *Sydney Morning Herald*, 15 May 1852, p. 4.
14 *Sydney Morning Herald*, 21 Mar 1866, p. 9.
15 *Sydney Morning Herald*, 10 Jan 1866, p. 1.
16 *Sydney Morning Herald*, 23 Aug 1866, p. 6.
17 Walsh, 'Watt, John Brown', *ADB*.
18 T. H. Irving, 'Holden, George Kenyon (1808-1874)', *Australian Dictionary of Biography*, vol. 4, Carlton, Vic: Melbourne University Press, 1972.
19 NSW Birth Deaths and Marriages, birth reg.no.1630/1863.
20 Bernard Burke, *Genealogical and heraldic history of the colonial gentry*, vol. 2, London: Harrison & Sons, 1895, pp. 719-720.
21 *Sydney Morning Herald*, 19 May 1868, p. 1.
22 *Sydney Morning Herald*, 19 Dec 1868, p. 6.
23 Maxwell, *Australian Men of Mark*, vol.1, p. 78.
24 NSW Birth Deaths and Marriages, birth reg.no.4421/1870.
25 NSW Birth Deaths and Marriages, death reg.no.847/1873.
26 Martha Rutledge, 'Watt, Ernest Alexander (1874-1954)', *Australian Dictionary ofBiography*, vol. 12, Carlton, Vic: Melbourne University Press, 1990.
27 *A Few Records of the Life of John Brown Watt*, pp. 94-95.

28   *Sydney Morning Herald*, 2 May 1876, p. 5, 5 May 1876, p. 10.
29   *Sydney Morning Herald*, 6 May 1876, p. 4, 8 May 1876, p. 4; *Australian Town and Country Journal* (Sydney), 6 May 1876, p. 751.

Two years abroad

30   *A Few Records of the Life of John Brown Watt*, p. 8.
31   *New Zealand Herald* (Auckland), 8 Apr 1879, p. 6.
32   Walsh, 'Watt, John Brown', *ADB*.
33   *Sydney Morning Herald*, 5 May 1877, p. 1.
34   Susan Johnston, 'Watt, Oswald Watt (Toby) (1878-1921)', *Australian Dictionary of Biography*, vol. 12, Carlton, Vic: Melbourne University Press, 1990.
35   *A Few Records of the Life of John Brown Watt*, p. 96.
36   *A Few Records of the Life of John Brown Watt*, p. 96.
37   *A Few Records of the Life of John Brown Watt*, p. 8.
38   *Sydney Morning Herald*, 11 Dec 1878, p. 5, 18 Dec 1878, p. 4.

Growing up in Sydney

39   *A Few Records of the Life of John Brown Watt*, p. 9.
40   Susie Rankine & Ernest Watt, *Being Ernest: the life of Ernest Watt 1874-1954*, Double Bay, NSW: SGR Press, 1998, p. 14.
41   *Being Ernest*, p. 20.
42   *Being Ernest*, p. 24.
43   Sydney Ure Smith, Bertram Stevens & Ernest Watt (eds.), *Oswald Watt: A tribute to his memory by a few of his friends*, Sydney: Art in Australia, 1921, pp. 10-14.
44   *Being Ernest*, pp. 24-25.
45   *Oswald Watt: A tribute to his memory*, p. 12.
46   *Oswald Watt: A tribute to his memory*, p. 14.
47   *Oswald Watt: A tribute to his memory*, p. 11
48   *Sydney Morning Herald*, 29 Jan 1887, p. 8, 18 Feb 1888, p. 10.
49   University of Sydney Travelling Scholarships—Information for 2012, p. v (from website http://sydney.edu.au/scholarships/docs/research/travelinfo_12.pdf).
50   *Sydney Morning Herald*, 10 Oct 1887, p. 5.
51   *Illustrated Sydney News*, 12 Jun 1880, p. 7.
52   *Sydney Mail*, 11 Jun 1881, p. 948, 23 Jul 1881, p. 17; *Sydney Morning Herald*, 16 Jun 1883, p. 2, 19 Oct 1885, p. 8, 18 Oct 1886, p. 5.
53   *Sydney Morning Herald*, 14 Sep 1882, p. 8
54   *Sydney Morning Herald*, 12 Oct 1891, p. 3.
55   *Sydney Morning Herald*, 5 May 1883, p. 2.
56   *Australian Town and Country Journal*, 26 May 1883, p. 26.
57   *Sydney Morning Herald*, 23 Nov 1883, p. 7, 21 Feb 1884, p. 11.
58   *South Australian Register* (Adelaide), 5 Apr 1884, p. 5.
59   *Being Ernest*, p. 20.
60   *Being Ernest*, p. 25.
61   *Brisbane Courier*, 2 Jan 1885, p. 6
62   *Brisbane Courier*, 24 Dec 1884, p. 6.

63 *South Australian Register* (Adelaide), 9 May 1885, p. 4; *Argus* (Melbourne), 11 May 1885, p. 4.

64 *Being Ernest*, p. 23.

65 *Sydney Morning Herald*, 15 May 1885, p. 6.

66 Powerhouse Museum (Sydney), collection database, reg. no. B1499.

67 *Oswald Watt: A tribute to his memory*, p. 11.

68 *A Few Records of the Life of John Brown Watt*, pp. 10-11; *Being Ernest*, p. 48.

69 *Sydney Morning Herald*, 13 Oct 1887, p. 10.

70 *Sydney Mail*, 22 Oct 1887, p. 12.

The monotremes man

71 *Sydney Morning Herald*, 18 Sep 1883, p. 7, 24 Sep 1883, p. 4.

72 Nicholas Drayson, *Love and the Platypus*, Melbourne: Scribe, 2007, see bio note at end.

73 W. H. Caldwell, 'The Embryology of Monotremata and Marsupialia—Part I' *PhilosophicalTransactions of the Royal Society (B)*, vol. 78, 1887, pp. 463-485.

74 Caldwell, 'The Embryology of Monotremata and Marsupialia', p.463; *Sydney Morning Herald*, 13 Sep 1884, p. 11.

75 *Being Ernest*, p. 28.

76 Peter Macinnis, *Curious Minds: the discoveries of Australian naturalists*, Canberra: National Library of Australia, 2012, p. 181; *Sydney Morning Herald*, 8 Sep 1884, p. 5.

77 *Sydney Morning Herald*, 18 Dec 1884, p. 5.

78 *The Queenslander* (Brisbane), 1 Aug 1885, p. 200.

79 *Science*, vol. VII, issue 176, 18 Jun 1886, pp. 544-546.

80 *Argus* (Melbourne), 20 Sep 1884, p. 8.

81 Alan G. Cock and Donald R. Forsdyke, *Treasure your exceptions: the science and life of William Bateson*, New York: Springer, 2008, pp. 33-34.

82 *Treasure your exceptions*, p. 33.

83 *Being Ernest*, p. 26.

84 *Sydney Morning Herald*, 21 Jan 1887, p. 6.

85 *Sydney Morning Herald*, 28 Jan 1887, p. 1.

86 *Sydney Morning Herald*, 5 Mar 1887, p. 10; *Colonies and India* (Britain), 22 Apr 1887, p. 27.

87 Caldwell, 'The Embryology of Monotremata and Marsupialia', p.463-485.

Chapter 2 – Inherited wealth

1 Being Ernest, p. 24, and information from Archivist, Hutchins School, 2015.

2 Sydney Morning Herald, 14 Mar 1888, p. 8.

3 Being Ernest, pp. 29-30.

4 Being Ernest, p. 29.

5 Oswald Watt: A tribute to his memory, p. 14.

6 Mercury (Hobart), 14 Feb 1888, p.2, records that H. F. Caldwell and 'R. Bloxom' travelled from Launceston to Melbourne in the steamship *Flinders* on 13 Feb 1888.

7 *Being Ernest*, p. 29.

8 *Being Ernest*, p. 31.

9   *Being Ernest*, pp. 29-30.

10   *Sydney Morning Herald*, 14 Dec 1887, p. 1.

11   *Being Ernest*, p. 28, recalled the address as being in 'Grove Road' but records of the Marine Biological Association clearly state Caldwell lived at Harvey Road, Cambridge.

12   *Journal of the Marine Biological Association of the United Kingdom*, no. II, Aug 1888, p. 107.

13   J. A. Venn, *Alumni cantabrigiensis: a biographical list of all known students, graduates and holders of office at the University of Cambridge, from the earliest times to 1900*, part II, vol. 1, London: University of Cambridge, 1940, p. 490; *Being Ernest*, p. 29.

14   *Being Ernest*, p. 29.

15   *Sydney Morning Herald*, 27 Mar 1890, p. 1.

16   *Illustrated Sydney News*, 17 Apr 1890, p. 9.

17   Walsh, 'Watt, John Brown', *ADB*.

Toby's English education

18   *Oswald Watt: A tribute to his memory*, p. 14.

19   *Being Ernest*, p. 32, recorded Oswald's 'terrible accident' as having occurred 'in the summer of 1889' but other family events in this period which can be dated indicates that it must have been the following year.

20   *Being Ernest*, p. 32.

21   *Being Ernest*, p. 32.

22   *Being Ernest*, p. 33.

23   *Oswald Watt: A tribute to his memory*, pp. 14-15.

24   Australian War Memorial 2DRL/0101 Personal record of W. O. Watt.

25   *Being Ernest*, p. 33.

26   *Oswald Watt: A tribute to his memory*, p. 15

27   F. Borwick (ed.), *Clifton College annals and register, 1862-1925*, Bristol: J. W. Arrowsmith, 1912, p. 285; *Being Ernest*, p. 33.

28   *Being Ernest*, p. 31.

29   *Being Ernest*, pp. 30-31.

30   *Being Ernest*, p. 33.

31   *Oswald Watt: A tribute to his memory*, p. 15; *Being Ernest*, pp. 33-34.

32   *Being Ernest*, p. 34.

33   *Being Ernest*, p. 37.

34   J. A. Venn, *Alumni Cantabrigienses*, part II, vol. 6, Cambridge: University Press, 1954, p. 377.

35   *Being Ernest*, pp. 40-41, 43.

36   *Oswald Watt: A tribute to his memory*, p. 15.

John Watt's will

37   *Sydney Morning Herald*, 21 Feb 1891, p. 1, 15 May 1893, p. 1; headstone on grave of Henry Gordon Caldwell in Dean 2h cemetery at Edinburgh, Scotland.

38   *Sydney Morning Herald*, 11 Jun 1892, p. 1, 18 Jun 1892, p. 35; *Australian Town & Country Journal* (Sydney), 18 Jun 1892, p. 35.

39   Jane de Falbe, *My dear Miss Macarthur: the recollections of Emmaline Maria Macarthur (1828-1911)*, Kenthurst, NSW: Kangaroo Press, 1988, pp. 9, 11.

40   *Being Ernest*, p. 32.

41   *The Times* (London), 26 Nov 1901, p. 14.

42   *Natural Science* (London), vol. 3, no. 17, July 1893, p. 8.

43   *Being Ernest*, p. 36.

44   A. Dykes Spicer, *The Paper Trade: a descriptive and historical survey of the paper trade from the commencement of the nineteenth century*, London: Methuen & Co., 1907, p. 221.

45   *London Gazette*, 24 Jul 1894, p. 4273.

46   *Edinburgh Gazette*, 5 Jan 1900, p. 18, 5 Jul 1901, p. 766.

47   *Being Ernest*, p. 36.

48   *London Gazette*, 8 Jan 1897, p. 152.

49   *Edinburgh Gazette*, 27 Dec 1898, p. 1408.

50   *Being Ernest*, p. 36.

51   *A Few Records of the Life of John Brown Watt*, pp. 9-10; *Being Ernest*, p. 35.

52   *Sydney Morning Herald*, 18 Dec 1890, p. 3.

53   *Being Ernest*, p. 35.

54   *Being Ernest*, p. 31.

55   Walsh, 'Watt, John Brown', *ADB*.

56   *Being Ernest*, p. 48.

57   *Being Ernest*, p. 48.

58   Walsh, 'Watt, John Brown', *ADB*.

59   *Sydney Morning Herald*, 3 Aug 1898, p. 7.

After Cambridge

60   *Being Ernest*, p. 49; *Sydney Morning Herald*, 16 Dec 1897, p. 4.

61   *Oswald Watt: A tribute to his memory*, p. 16.

62   *Being Ernest*, p. 52.

63   *Sydney Morning Herald*, 5 Sep 1898, p. 4.

64   J. A. Venn, *Alumni Cantabrigienses*, part II, vol. 6, Cambridge: University press, 1954, p. 377.

65   *Oswald Watt: A tribute to his memory*, p. 16.

66   *Being Ernest*, p. 57.

67   www.gaestbuecher-schloss-neubeuern.de-biografien/Watt_Walter_Oswald.pdf, accessed 12 Feb 2015.

68   *Oswald Watt: A tribute to his memory*, p. 16.

69   Christopher Dyment, *Toscanini in Britain*, Woodbridge, Suffolk: Boydell Press, 2012, p. 5.

70   *Being Ernest*, p. 57.

71   *The Era*, 16 Apr 1898, p. 13.

72   *Being Ernest*, p. 57.

73   *Being Ernest*, p. 57.

74   *Argus* (Melbourne), 24 Jan 1900, p. 4.

75   *Being Ernest*, p. 58.

CHAPTER THREE – Life in Australia

Return to Sydney

1   *Sydney Morning Herald*, 27 Jan 1900, pp. 8, 12.

2   *Being Ernest*, pp. 52-53.

3   *Oswald Watt: A tribute to his memory*, p. 16.

4   *Being Ernest*, p. 59; *Sydney Morning Herald*, 7 Apr 1900, p. 7.

5   *Narrandera Argus and Riverina Advertiser* (NSW), 16 Nov 1900, p. 2.

6   Harold M. Mackenzie (compiled by Caroline Merrylees), *Mackenzie's Riverina: a tour of the Hay District Pastoral Holdings in the 1890s*, 2nd edition, Hay, NSW: Hay Historical Society, 2008, p. 30.

7   *Sydney Morning Herald*, 14 Nov 1900, p. 5.

8   *Australian Town and Country Journal* (Sydney), 10 Nov 1900, p. 53.

9   Roy H. Goddard, *The Union Club 1857-1957*, Sydney: Halstead Press, 1957, p. 139.

10   *Sydney Morning Herald*, 2 Feb 1900, p. 5.

11   NSW *Army List*, 1903, p. 102; *Sydney Morning Herald*, 8 May 1900, p. 3.

12   T. F. Wade-Ferrell, *In All Things Faithful: a history and album of the 30th Battalion and New South Wales Scottish Regiment, 1885-1985*, Sydney: Fine Arts Press, 1985, p. 3.

13   *Australian Town and Country Journal* (Sydney), 10 Nov 1900, p. 44.

14   *Sydney Morning Herald*, 3 Nov 1900, p. 9.

15   Commonwealth Military Forces, *Military Orders*, Nos 53 and 67 of 1905.

16   Commonwealth Military Forces, *Military Orders*, No 27 of 1908.

17   *Sydney Morning Herald*, 1 Nov 1900, p. 8.

18   *Australian Town and Country Journal* (Sydney), 1 Dec 1900, p. 44.

19   *Sydney Morning Herald*, 1 Dec 1900, p. 10.

20   *Sydney Morning Herald*, 23 Jul 1901, p. 4.

21   *Sydney Morning Herald*, 27 Mar 1901, p. 5, 30 Mar 1901, p. 7.

22   *Sydney Morning Herald*, 13 Apr 1901, p. 10.

23   *Australian Town and Country Journal* (Sydney), 25 Jul 1901, p. 45.

24   *Australian Town and Country Journal* (Sydney), 23 Nov 1901, p. 16.

25   *Maitland Daily Mercury* (NSW), 6 Dec 1901, p. 4.

26   *Australian Town and Country Journal* (Sydney), 7 Dec 1901, p. 44.

The Judge's daughter

27   *West Australia Sunday Times* (Perth), 29 Dec 1901, p. 1

28   *Clarence and Richmond Examiner* (Grafton, NSW), 10 Sep 1901, p. 4.

29   *Evening News* (Sydney), 29 Mar 1902, p. 6.

30   NSW *Army List*, 1903, pp. 4, 26.

31   *Australian Town & Country Journal* (Sydney), 17 May 1902, p. 44.

32   *Sydney Morning Herald*, 31 Mar 1902, p. 4.

33   *Australian Town & Country Journal* (Sydney), 5 Apr 1902, p. 44.

34   *Australian Town & Country Journal* (Sydney), 12 Apr 1902, p. 44.

35   *Bendigo Advertiser* (Vic), 19 May 1902, p. 5; *Gippsland Times* (Vic), 19 May 1902, p. 3.

36   Robert Miller, 'Williams, Sir Hartley (1843 - 1929)', *Australian Dictionary of Biography*, vol.6, Carlton, Vic: Melbourne University Press, 1976.

37   *Advertiser* (Adelaide), 21 Oct 1902, p. 4.

38   *Argus* (Melbourne), 11 Sep 1902, p. 6.

39   *Sydney Morning Herald*, 15 Sep 1902, p. 4.

40   *Sydney Morning Herald*, 4 Oct 1902, p. 7; *Australasian* (Melbourne), 4 Oct 1902, pp. 821-822; *Australian Town & Country Journal* (Sydney), 8 Oct 1902, p. 43

41   *Bendigo Advertiser* (Vic), 6 Oct 1902, p. 6.

42   *Australian Town & Country Journal* (Sydney), 8 Oct 1902, p. 43.

43   *Australasian* (Melbourne), 4 Oct 1902, pp. 821-822; *Australian Town & Country Journal* (Sydney), 8 Oct 1902, p. 43.

44   *Sydney Morning Herald*, 4 Oct 1902, p. 7.

45   *Australian Town & Country Journal* (Sydney), 8 Oct 1902, p. 43.

46   *Australasian* (Melbourne), 4 Oct 1902, pp. 821-822.

47   *Sydney Morning Herald*, 13 Oct 1902, p. 7; *Freeman's Journal* (Sydney), 18 Oct 1902, p. 30.

48   *Sydney Morning Herald*, 18 Oct 1902, p. 7; *Argus* (Melbourne), 14 Oct 1902, p. 5.

49   *Evening News* (Sydney), 18 Oct 1902, p. 6; *Australian Town & Country Journal* (Sydney), 22 Oct 1902, p. 44.

50   *Freeman's Journal* (Sydney), 1 Nov 1902, p. 30.

51   *Freeman's Journal* (Sydney), 1 Nov 1902, p. 30.

52   *Australian Town & Country Journal* (Sydney), 12 Nov 1902, pp. 44-45.

53   *Argus* (Melbourne), 6 Nov 1902, p. 5; *Freeman's Journal* (Sydney), 15 Nov 1902, p. 30.

54   *Evening News* (Sydney), 15 Nov 1902, p. 5; *Sunday Times* (Sydney), 16 Nov 1902, p. 7.

55   *Sydney Morning Herald*, 13 Sep 1902, p. 7; *Australian Town & Country Journal* (Sydney), 8 Oct 1902, p. 43; *Evening News* (Sydney), 22 Nov 1902, p. 3S.

Among the social elite

56   Algernon Graves, *The Royal Academy of Arts: a complete dictionary of Contributors and their work from its foundation in 1769 to 1904*, vol. 3, London: Henry Graves & Co. and George Bell & Sons, 1905, p. 10.

57   *Sydney Morning Herald*, 15 Apr 1904, p. 6.

58   *Being Ernest*, p. 75.

59   *Sydney Morning Herald*, 18 Jul 1914, p. 8.

60   *Sydney Morning Herald*, 23 Oct 1937, p. 12.

61   *Sydney Morning Herald*, 7 May 1904, p. 12.

62   *Bendigo Advertiser* (Vic), 1 Jun 1904, p. 3.

63   *Sydney Morning Herald*, 4 Jun 1904, p. 9.

64   *Morning Bulletin* (Rockhampton, Qld), 15 Oct 1904, p. 7.

65   *Sydney Morning Herald*, 19 Sep 1904, p. 5.

66   *Evening News* (Sydney), 12 Nov 1904, p. 10.

67   *Sydney Morning Herald*, 21 Jan 1905, p. 9, 28 Jan 1905, p. 9.

68   *Queenslander* (Brisbane), 11 Mar 1905, p. 9; *Northern Miner* (Charters Towers, Qld), 4 Apr 1905, p. 2.

69   *Australian Town & Country Journal*, 15 Mar 1905, p. 40.

70   NSW Birth Deaths and Marriages, birth reg. no. 39464/1905; *Sydney Morning Herald*, 17 Oct 1905, p. 6.

71   *Evening News* (Sydney), 29 May 1905, p. 8; *Camden News* (NSW), 1 Jun 1905, p. 4.

72   *Sydney Morning Herald*, 12 Jan 1903, p. 6.

73   "Wivenhoe Historic House" booklet, 2006, pp. 10, 13; *Construction and Local Government Journal* (Sydney), 22 Jun 1927, p. 13.

74   *Evening News* (Sydney), 18 Nov 1905, p. 10.

75   *Sydney Morning Herald*, 27 Nov 1905, p. 5; *Australian Town & Country Journal*, 29 Nov 1905, p. 43; *Evening News* (Sydney), 2 Dec 1905, p. 10.

76   *Sydney Morning Herald*, 6 Jan 1906, p. 9, 20 Jan 1906, p. 9.

77   *Evening News* (Sydney), 14 Apr 1906, p. 10.

78   *Sydney Morning Herald*, 16 Apr 1906, p. 3; *Evening News* (Sydney), 16 Apr 1906, p. 4.

79   *Sydney Morning Herald*, 7 Apr 1906, p. 14.

80   *Evening News* (Sydney), 19 Apr 1906, p. 6.

81   *Sydney Morning Herald*, 23 Apr 1906, p. 4.

82   *Sydney Morning Herald*, 28 Apr 1906, p. 8; *Australian Town & Country Journal*, 2 May 1906, p. 43.

83   *Maitland Daily Mercury* (NSW), 30 May 1906, p. 3.

84   *Sydney Morning Herald*, 2 Jun 1906, p. 9; *The Newsletter* (Sydney), 9 Jun 1906, p. 10; *Clarence & Richmond Examiner* (Grafton, NSW), 9 Jun 1906, p. 2.

85   *Australian Town & Country Journal*, 6 Jun 1906, p. 43; *Sydney Morning Herald*, 9 Jun 1906, p. 6.

86   *Sydney Morning Herald*, 9 Jun 1906, pp. 6, 10.

87   *Evening News* (Sydney), 28 Jul 1906, p. 10.

88   *Australian Town & Country Journal*, 15 Aug 1906, p. 43.

Squire of Wivenhoe

89   Alan Powell, *Patrician Democrat: the political life of Charles Cowper 1843-1870*, Carlton: Melbourne University Press, 1977, p. 8.

90   *Being Ernest*, p. 75; *Catholic Press*, 23 Jul 1931, p. 5.

91   *Evening News* (Sydney), 31 Oct 1906, p. 6.

92   *Evening News* (Sydney), 1 Dec 1906, p. 10.

93   *Australian Town & Country Journal*, 20 Feb 1907, p. 43; *Evening News* (Sydney), 23 Feb 1907, p. 10.

94   *Australian Town & Country Journal*, 13 Mar 1907, p. 43.

95   *Australian Town & Country Journal*, 3 Apr 1907, p. 43.

96   *Australian Town & Country Journal*, 17 Apr 1907, p. 43; *Sydney Mail*, 10 Apr 1907, pp. 950-951.

97   *Evening News* (Sydney), 1 Jun 1907, p. 12.

98   *Evening News* (Sydney), 1 Aug 1907, p. 3, 3 Aug 1907, p. 14.

99   *Sydney Morning Herald*, 27 Jul 1907, p. 14; *Sunday Times* (Sydney), 28 Jul 1907, p. 3.

100   *Sydney Morning Herald*, 3 Aug 1907, p. 10.

101   *Sunday Times* (Sydney), 21 Jul 1907, p. 3.

102   *Australian Town & Country Journal*, 7 Aug 1907, p. 40.

103   *Clarence and Richmond Examiner* (Grafton, NSW), 10 Aug 1907, p. 2.

104   *Sydney Mail*, 7 Aug 1907, p. 374.

105   *Australian Town & Country Journal*, 21 Aug 1907, p. 43.

106   *Sydney Morning Herald*, 7 Sep 1907, p. 10; *Australian Town & Country Journal*, 11 Sep 1907, pp. 40-41.

107   *Evening News* (Sydney), 7 Sep 1907, p. 14.

108   Allen family photographs, Mitchell Library (Sydney), PX*D 581, album 40, digital items a2883025 – a2883029.

109   *Australian Town & Country Journal*, 18 Sep 1907, p. 43; *Sunday Times* (Sydney), 22 Sep

1907, p. 11S.

110   *Evening News* (Sydney), 21 Sep 1907, p. 14; *Australian Town & Country Journal*, 25 Sep 1907, p. 40.

111   *Sydney Morning Herald*, 12 Oct 1907, p. 10; *Evening News* (Sydney), 12 Oct 1907, p. 14.

112   *Australian Town & Country Journal*, 16 Oct 1907, p. 42.

113   *Sydney Morning Herald*, 11 Oct 1907, p. 5; *Sydney Mail*, 16 Oct 1907, p. 1025; *Australian Town & Country Journal*, 16 Oct 1907, p. 39.

114   *Australian Town & Country Journal*, 16 Oct 1907, p. 39.

115   Allen family photographs, Mitchell Library (Sydney), PX*D 581, album 40, digital items a2883035 – a2883041.

116   *Sydney Morning Herald*, 26 Oct 1907, p. 10.

117   H. S. Broadhead, 'Kellow, Henry Brown (Charles) (1871-1943)', *Australian Dictionary of Biography*, vol. 9, Carlton, Vic: Melbourne University Press, 1983.

118   Pedr Davis, *Wheels across Australia: motoring from the 1890s to the 1980s*, Hurstville, NSW: Marque Publishing, 1987, p. 123.

119   *Evening News* (Sydney), 29 Oct 1907, p. 5.

120   *Evening News* (Sydney), 2 Nov 1907, p. 14.

121   *Sydney Morning Herald*, 4 Nov 1907, p. 7.

122   *Sydney Morning Herald*, 7 Nov 1907, p. 7.

123   *Australian Town & Country Journal*, 20 Nov 1907, p. 40.

124   *Evening News* (Sydney), 14 Dec 1907, p. 14; *Australian Town & Country Journal*, 18 Dec 1907, p. 42.

125   *Australian Town & Country Journal*, 4 Dec 1907, p. 43.

The fizz fades

126   Military Order No 27 of 1908.

127   *Evening News* (Sydney), 14 Mar 1908, p. 14.

128   *Argus* (Melbourne), 14 Mar 1908, p. 18.

129   *Sydney Morning Herald*, 9 May 1908, p. 1.

130   *Being Ernest*, p. 72.

131   *Sydney Morning Herald*, 3 Jul 1908, p. 8.

132   *Sydney Morning Herald*, 8 Oct 1908, p. 7.

133   *Sydney Morning Herald*, 1 Aug 1908, p. 12.

134   *Evening News* (Sydney), 31 Jul 1908, p. 5.

135   *Being Ernest*, p. 99.

136   *Sydney Morning Herald*, 11 Jul 1908, p. 22.

137   *Sydney Morning Herald*, 16 Sep 1908, p. 11.

138   *Being Ernest*, p. 75.

139   *Evening News* (Sydney), 30 Jan 1909, p. 5.

140   *Sydney Morning Herald*, 24 Feb 1909, p. 15.

141   *Maitland Daily Mercury* (NSW), 17 Mar 1909, p. 3.

142   *Sydney Morning Herald*, 10 Mar 1909, p. 10.

143   *Being Ernest*, p. 74.

144   *Argus* (Melbourne), 17 Mar 1909, p. 6.

145   *Being Ernest*, pp. 74-75.

146 *Being Ernest*, p. 75.

147 *Sydney Morning Herald*, 17 Feb 1909, p. 13.

148 *Maitland Weekly Mercury* (NSW), 6 Mar 1909, p. 7.

149 *Sydney Morning Herald*, 11 Mar 1909, p. 3.

150 *Evening News* (Sydney), 17 Jul 1909, p. 14.

151 *Sydney Morning Herald*, 18 Sep 1909, p. 21.

152 *Evening News* (Sydney), 1 Jan 1910, p. 14.

153 *Wollondilly Press*, (Bowral, NSW), 22 Jan 1910, p. 3; *Sydney Morning Herald*, 27 Jan 1910, p. 9; *Evening News* (Sydney), 29 Jan 1910, p. 14.

154 *Clarence and Richmond Examiner* (Grafton, NSW), 3 Feb 1910, p. 3.

155 *Being Ernest*, p. 78.

156 *Argus* (Melbourne), 17 Jun 1913, p. 6.

157 *Sunday Times* (Sydney), 22 May 1910, p. 4; *Northern Miner* (Charters Towers, QLD), 9 Jun 1910, p. 7.

158 "Wivenhoe Historic House" booklet, 2006, p. 10.

CHAPTER FOUR – Learning to fly

Australia's first military pilot

1 *Sydney Morning Herald*, 13 Dec 1910, p. 12.

2 Peter Cahill, 'Wilson, Sir Leslie Orme (1876-1955)', *Australian Dictionary of Biography*, vol. 12, Carlton, Vic: Melbourne University Press, 1990.

3 *Argus* (Melbourne), 17 Jun 1913, p. 6.

4 *Being Ernest*, p. 75.

5 *Being Ernest*, p. 81.

6 *Commonwealth Military Journal*, May 1912, p. 426.

7 *West Australian* (Perth), 3 Nov 1914, p. 9; *Referee* (Sydney), 4 Nov 1914 (16).

8 *Flight*, 3 Jun 1911, p. 483.

9 John Connor, *Anzac and Empire: George Foster Pearce and the foundations of Australiandefence*, Melbourne: Cambridge University Press, 2011, p. 42.

10 G. F. Pearce, *Carpenter to Cabinet*, London: Hutchinson, 1951, pp. 82-83.

11 *Being Ernest*, p. 81.

12 *Flight*, 15 Jul 1911, p. 611.

13 *Flight*, 29 Jul 1911, p. 663.

14 *Flight*, 5 Aug 1911, p. 682, 2 Sep 1911, p. 759; *Sydney Morning Herald*, 18 Oct 1911, p. 5.

15 *Flight*, 5 Aug 1911, p. 679.

16 *Flight*, 16 Sep 1911, pp. 805, 807.

17 John McCarthy, 'Harrison, Eric (1886-1945)', *Australian Dictionary of Biography*, vol. 9, Carlton, Vic: Melbourne University Press, 1983.

18 *Argus* (Melbourne), 17 Jun 1913, p. 6.

19 *Argus* (Melbourne), 30 Jun 1913, p. 14.

20 *Freeman's Journal* (Sydney), 2 Nov 1911, p. 31.

21 *Evening News* (Sydney), 11 Nov 1911, p. 14.

22 *Argus* (Melbourne), 9 Nov 1911, p. 14.

23   *Argus* (Melbourne), 14 Nov 1911, p. 8, 16 Nov 1911, p. 8.

24   *Argus* (Melbourne), 17 Nov 1911, p. 7.

25   *Sydney Morning Herald*, 17 Nov 1911, p. 10, 18 Nov 1911, p. 16.

Aviation adviser to Defence

26   *Evening News* (Sydney), 2 Dec 1911, p. 14.

27   *Being Ernest*, p. 74.

28   *Being Ernest*, p. 78

29   *Being Ernest*, p. 63; Clement Semmler, 'Dalley, John Bede (1876-1935)', *Australian Dictionary of Biography*, vol. 8, Carlton, Vic: Melbourne University Press, 1981.

30   *Oswald Watt: A tribute to his memory*, p. 41.

31   National Archives of Australia (Canberra), A289 1849/8/409 "Proposed sites for CentralFlying School".

32   *Commonwealth Military Journal*, May 1912, pp. 424-429.

33   National Archives of Australia (Canberra), A289 1849/8/192 "Captain O. Watt Reserve of Officers, Visit to England 1912".

34   *Sydney Mail*, 5 Jun 1912, p. 8; *Register* (Adelaide), 8 Jun 1912, p. 17.

35   *Argus* (Melbourne), 4 Apr 1912, p. 5.

36   *Argus* (Melbourne), 13 Mar 1912, p. 10.

37   *Argus* (Melbourne), 11 Apr 1912, p. 8.

38   *Sydney Morning Herald*, 20 Apr 1912, p. 18.

39   *Argus* (Melbourne), 17 Jun 1913, p. 6.

Bilgola retreat

40   *Advertiser* (Adelaide), 16 May 1912, p. 8; *Sydney Morning Herald*, 22 May 1912, p. 22.

41   National Archives of Australia (Victoria), MP84/1 1954/23/144 "Article by Capt Oswald Watt on Training of Aviation Corps".

42   National Archives of Australia (Canberra), A289 1849/8/192 "Captain O. Watt Reserve of Officers, Visit to England 1912".

43   *Argus* (Melbourne), 10 Jul 1912, p. 14.

44   *Argus* (Melbourne), 6 Aug 1912, p. 9, 10 Aug 1912, p. 16.

45   National Archives of Australia (Canberra), A2653 Military Board Minutes 1912.

46   *Sydney Morning Herald*, 20 Sep 1912, p. 10.

47   C. D. (Coulthard-)Clark, *No Australian Need Apply, the troubled career of Lieutenant-General Gordon Legge*, Sydney: Allen & Unwin, 1988 (79).

48   National Archives of Australia (Victoria), MP84/1 1954/23/144 "Article by Capt Oswald Watt on Training of Aviation Corps".

49   *Being Ernest*, p. 33.

50   *Argus* (Melbourne), 17 Jun 1913, p. 6.

51   *Sunday Times* (Perth), 22 Sep 1912, p. 13S.

52   Military Order No 690 of 1912.

53   *Oswald Watt: A tribute to his memory*, pp. 39-40.

54   Website www.normanlindsay.com.au/gallery/gallery.php.

55   *Oswald Watt: A tribute to his memory*, p. 47.

56   *Commonwealth Military Journal*, Jan 1913, pp. 62-65.

57   Alan Fitzgerald (ed.), *Canberra's Engineering Heritage*, Canberra: Institution of Engineers–
      Canberra Division, 1983, p. 177.
58   National Archives of Australia (Canberra), A289 1849/8/409 "Proposed sites for Central
      Flying School".
59   National Archives of Australia (Victoria), MP84/1 1954/23/189 "Capt Watt and Aircraft".
60   *Sydney Morning Herald*, 28 Jun 1913, p. 16.
61   *Evening News* (Sydney), 8 Mar 1913, p. 14; *Sunday Times*, (Sydney), 16 Mar 1913, p. 25;
      Sydney Morning Herald, 21 Mar 1913, p. 8. Society divorce scandal
62   *Argus* (Melbourne), 17 Jun 1913, p. 6.
63   *Sydney Morning Herald*, 17 Jun 1913, p. 5.
64   *Argus* (Melbourne), 17 Jun 1913, p. 6.
65   *NZ Truth* (Wellington), 28 Jun 1913, p. 5.
66   *Mercury* (Hobart), 17 Jun 1913, p. 5.
67   *NZ Truth* (Wellington), 28 Jun 1913, p. 5.
68   *Sydney Morning Herald*, 17 Jun 1913, p. 5.
69   *Barrier Miner* (Broken Hill, NSW), 18 Jun 1913, p. 4.
70   *Advertiser* (Adelaide), 27 Jun 1913, p. 10.
71   *Sydney Morning Herald*, 27 Jun 1913, p. 5.
72   *Argus* (Melbourne), 27 Jun 1913, p. 14.
73   *Advertiser* (Adelaide), 30 Jun 1913, p. 14; *Maitland Daily Mercury* (NSW), 30 Jun 1913, p. 4.
74   *Argus* (Melbourne), 2 Jul 1913, p. 14.
75   University of California, Berkeley, U.S.A., Gertrude Jekyll collection, 1877-1931,
      collection no.1955-1, drawings box/folder FF/113, drawing for Mrs Oswald Watt,
      FulmerCourt, Buckinghamshire, 1913.
76   *Argus* (Melbourne), 16 Sep 1913, p. 12; *Advertiser* (Adelaide), 16 Sep 1913, p. 14.
77   *NZ Truth* (Wellington), 4 Oct 1913, p. 5.
78   *Mercury* (Hobart), 18 Sep 1913, p. 5.
79   *Sydney Morning Herald*, 23 Oct 1937, p. 12.
80   *Advertiser* (Adelaide), 27 Apr 1914, p. 17.
81   *Slough, Eton and Windsor Observer* (England), 16 May 1914, p. 5.
82   *Mail* (Adelaide), 30 Sep 1914, p. 1.
83   *Being Ernest*, pp. 78, 80.

Marking time in Egypt

84   *Oswald Watt: A tribute to his memory*, p. 17.
85   *Flight*, 11 Apr 1914, p. 402.
86   James Aldridge, *Cairo*, London: Macmillan & Co., 1969, p. 218.
87   *Aeroplane*, 1 Jan 1914, p. 16.
88   *Aeroplane*, 1 Jan 1914, p. 16, 22 Jan 1914, p. 88.
89   *Aeroplane*, 29 Jan 1914, p. 110.
90   *Aeroplane*, 5 Mar 1914, p. 232.
91   *Daily Telegraph* (Sydney), 9 Jun 1914, p. 7.
92   *Oamaru Mail* (New Zealand), 13 Nov 1914, p. 8.
93   *Daily Telegraph* (Sydney), 9 Jun 1914, p. 7.
94   *Aeroplane*, 5 Mar 1914, p. 232.

95   *Mail* (Adelaide), 13 Jun 1914, p. 8.

96   *Aeroplane*, 8 Jan 1914, p. 39, 15 Jan 1914, p. 64.

97   *Aeroplane*, 22 Jan 1914, p. 88.

98   *Flight*, 7 Mar 1914, p. 245.

99   *Flight*, 28 Feb 1914, p. 226.

100   *Flight*, 7 Mar 1914, p. 252.

101   *Aeroplane*, 5 Mar 1914, pp. 232-233.

102   Australian War Memorial (Canberra), image A05282.

103   *Aeroplane*, 16 Apr 1914, p. 459.

104   *Aeroplane*, 4 Jun 1914, p. 638.

105   *Sydney Morning Herald*, 23 May 1921, p. 8.

106   *Pastoral Review* (Melbourne), 16 Jul 1921, p. 534.

107   *Flight*, 12 Jun 1914, p. 636; *Aeroplane*, 11 Jun 1914, p. 666.

108   *Daily Telegraph* (Sydney), 9 Jun 1914, p. 7.

109   *Daily News* (Perth), 8 Jun 1914, p. 8.

110   Oswald Watt to Roslyn Jamieson, 22 Jun 1914, Australian War Memorial (Canberra),AWM 3DRL 5108, item 1 (letters & postcards to Mrs Roslyn Jamieson

111   *Flight*, 17 Jul 1914, p. 755.

CHAPTER FIVE – Unfriendly skies

Fighting for France

1   Oswald Watt to Roslyn Jamieson, 18 Aug 1914, AWM 3DRL 5108, item 1.

2   F. M. Cutlack, *The Australian Flying Corps in the Western and Eastern Theatres of War1914-1918*, Sydney: Angus & Robertson, 1945, p. 41n.

3   *Aircraft* (Melbourne), 20 Jun 1921, pp. 222-223.

4   *Sydney Morning Herald*, 18 Sep 1914, p. 7; *Leader* (Melbourne), 7 Nov 1914, p. 53.

5   *Aeroplane*, 9 Sep 1914, p. 241.

6   *Aeroplane*, 30 Sep 1914, p. 289; *Flight*, 2 Oct 1914, p. 996.

7   *Burrowa News* (NSW), 17 Sep 1915, p. 1.

8   *Aeroplane*, 11 Aug 1915, p. 166.

9   Oswald Watt to Roslyn Jamieson, 20 Sep 1914, AWM 3DRL 5108, item 1.

10   *Aeroplane*, 7 Oct 1914, p. 321.

11   Oswald Watt to Roslyn Jamieson, 27 Sep 1914, AWM 3DRL 5108, item 1; *Sydney Morning Herald*, 10 Dec 1914, p. 8.

12   *Aeroplane*, 14 Oct 1914, p. 342.

13   *Sydney Morning Herald*, 10 Dec 1914, p. 8.

14   *Sydney Morning Herald*, 20 Feb 1915, p. 15.

15   Ian Sumner, *Kings of the Air: French aces and airmen of the Great War*, Barnsley, UK: Pen & Sword Aviation, 2015, pp. 3, 7, 10-11, 21, 36, 42-43.

16   Lieutenant Colonel [Georges] Bellenger, "Les aventures du capitaine Watt" (The adventures of Captain Watt), *Icare*, no. 38, 1 July 1966, pp. 69-72.

17   *Sydney Morning Herald*, 18 Jan 1915, p. 10, 20 Feb 1915, p. 11.

18   *Argus* (Melbourne), 3 Nov 1914, p. 7.

19   Oswald Watt to Roslyn Jamieson, 26 Oct 1914, AWM 3DRL 5108, item 1.

20   *Sydney Morning Herald*, 18 Jan 1915, p. 10.

21   Contrary to claims later made in *Aircraft*, 20 Jun 1921, p. 223, that Watt's observer had been wounded and needed assistance.

22   *Sydney Morning Herald*, 20 Feb 1915, p. 15.

23   War diary of 287th Infantry Regiment, 24 Oct 1914, 25 Oct 1914, Service Historique de la Défense (Vincennes, France), 26 N 739/3.

24   *Flight*, 13 Nov 1914, p. 1116, 26 Mar 1915, p. 213; *Argus* (Melbourne), 22 Apr 1915, p. 9.

25   Oswald Watt to Roslyn Jamieson, 27 Jan 1915, AWM 3DRL 5108, item 1.

26   *Journal Officiel de la République Française*, 45th year, no. 54, 24 Feb 1915, pp. 968-969; *Sydney Morning Herald*, 22 Apr 1915, p. 8.

27   Oswald Watt to Roslyn Jamieson, 13 Feb 1915, AWM 3DRL 5108, item 1.

28   *Flight*, 22 Jan 1915, p. 58, 29 Jan 1915, p. 77.

Capitaine Australien

29   Website http://albindenis.free.fr/Site_escadrille/escadrille044.htm (history of MF44), accessed 12 Jul 2015.

30   Oswald Watt to Roslyn Jamieson, 15 Apr 1915, AWM 3DRL 5108, item 1.

31   Oswald Watt to Roslyn Jamieson, 24 May 1915, AWM 3DRL 5108, item 1.

32   Oswald Watt to Roslyn Jamieson, 17 Apr 1915, AWM 3DRL 5108, item 1.

33   Oswald Watt to Roslyn Jamieson, 19 Apr 1915, AWM 3DRL 5108, item 1.

34   Oswald Watt to Roslyn Jamieson, 24 May 1915, AWM 3DRL 5108, item 1.

35   Oswald Watt to Roslyn Jamieson, 28 May 1915, AWM 3DRL 5108, item 1.

36   Oswald Watt to Roslyn Jamieson, 24 May 1915, AWM 3DRL 5108, item 1.

37   Percival Serle, *Dictionary of Australian Biography*, vol.2, Sydney: Angus & Robertson: 1949, p. 468.

38   Oswald Watt to Roslyn Jamieson, 28 May 1915, AWM 3DRL 5108, item 1.

39   Oswald Watt to Roslyn Jamieson, 5 Jun 1915, AWM 3DRL 5108, item 1.

40   Website http://www.etudes-touloises.fr/archives/148/148%20art5.pdf (deaths of Sismanoglou and Virolet), accessed 7 Mar 2015.

41   Oswald Watt to Roslyn Jamieson, 14 Jul 1915, AWM 3DRL 5108, item 1

42   Oswald Watt to Roslyn Jamieson, 8 Aug 1915, AWM 3DRL 5108, item 1.

43   Oswald Watt to Roslyn Jamieson, 8 Aug 1915, AWM 3DRL 5108, item 1.

44   *Journal Officiel de la République Française*, 47th year, no. 288, 23 Oct 1915, p. 7621.

45   *Flight*, 29 Oct 1915, p. 828.

46   *Sydney Morning Herald*, 16 May 1916, p. 5.

47   *Sydney Morning Herald*, 16 May 1916, p. 5.

48   Keith Isaacs, *Military Aircraft of Australia, 1909-1918*, Canberra: Australian War Memorial, 1971, pp. 36, 123.

49   Oswald Watt to Roslyn Jamieson, 4 Dec 1915, AWM 3DRL 5108, item 1.

50   *Oswald Watt: A tribute to his memory*, pp. 18-19.

51   Oswald Watt to Roslyn Jamieson, 4 Dec 1915, AWM 3DRL 5108, item 1.

52   Keith Isaacs, *Military Aircraft of Australia, 1909-1918*, pp. 106-107.

References

Transfer to the AIF

53 National Archives of Australia (Canberra), CRS A2023, item A38/8/542 "No.1 Squadron, A.F.C. – Formation and Organisation, 1915-1916".

54 *Adelaide Advertiser*, 1 Feb 1916, p. 7.

55 *Barrier Miner* (Broken Hill, NSW), 16 Feb 1916, p. 2.

56 *Farmer and Settle*r (Sydney), 15 Jun 1915, p. 3.

57 NAA, MT1487/1, Pickles S.

58 Commonwealth of Australia Gazette, No 9, 20 Jan 1916, p. 137.

59 NAA, CRS A2023, item A38/8/542.

60 Commonwealth of Australia Gazette, No 34, 9 Mar 1916, p. 583.

61 Military Order No 126 of 1916.

62 Cutlack, *The Australian Flying Corps*, p. 41n; NAA, B2455 Watt, Walter Oswald.

63 Australian War Memorial (Canberra), 2DRL/0101, "Watt, Walter O. – certificate of transfer from French Foreign Legion to AFC, 1916".

64 Military Order No 363 of 1916.

With No 1 Squadron

65 Michael Molkentin, *Fire in the sky: the Australian Flying Corps in the First World War*, Crows Nest, NSW: Allen & Unwin, 2010, p. 24; Michael Molkentin, *Australia and the War in the Air*, vol 1 of *Centenary History of Australia and the Great War*, South Melbourne: Oxford University Press, 2014, p. 97.

66 *Oswald Watt: A tribute to his memory*, photograph 106.

67 Cutlack, *The Australian Flying Corps*, p. 32.

68 Cutlack, *The Australian Flying Corps*, p. 35.

69 *The Corian* (Geelong Grammar School magazine), vol XL, no 1, May 1916, p. 60.

70 Molkentin, *Australia and the War in the Air*, p. 22.

71 National Archives of Australia (Canberra), B2455 Watt, Walter Oswald.

72 H. A. Jones, *The War in the Air*, vol 5, London: Oxford University Press, 1935, p. 187n; Cutlack, *The Australian Flying Corps*, pp. 33, 35.

73 Jones, *The War in the Air*, vol 5, p. 178.

74 Australian War Memorial (Canberra), PR88/154 Records of Air Vice-Marshal A. T. ("King") Cole, folder 7, autobiographical manuscript "Merry Old Souls", start of chap. 2.

75 Cutlack, *The Australian Flying Corps*, p. 36.

76 Website https://rslvirtualwarmemorial.org.au/explore/people/361601 (John James Morphett diary), accessed 12 Jul 2015.

77 Article by J. Morphett in *Mail* (Adelaide), 16 Feb 1935, p. 8.

78 Molkentin, *Australia and the War in the Air*, p. 98.

79 Cutlack, *The Australian Flying Corps*, p. 36.

80 Cutlack, *The Australian Flying Corps*, p. 36.

81 *Scrutineer & Berrima District Press* (NSW), 10 Jan 1917, p. 3.

82 Cutlack, *The Australian Flying Corps*, p. 36.

83 Morphett diary, https://rslvirtualwarmemorial.org.au/explore/people/361601, accessed 12 Jul 2015.

84 *Hamilton Spectator* (Vic), 14 Sep 1916, p. 4.

85 *Flight*, 27 Jul 1916, p. 635; Michael J. Mortlock, *The Egyptian Expeditionary Force in World*

War I, Jefferson, N. Carolina: McFarland & Co., 2010, p. 46.

86   Cutlack, *The Australian Flying Corps*, p. 42.

87   Morphett diary, https://rslvirtualwarmemorial.org.au/explore/people/361601, accessed 12 Jul 2015.

88   Richard Williams, *These are facts*, Canberra: Australian War Memorial & Australian Government Publishing Service, 1977, pp. 53-54.

89   NAA, B2455 Watt, Walter Oswald.

90   Norman Barnes, *The RAAF and the flying squadrons*, St. Leonards, NSW: Allen & Unwin, 2000, p. 14.

91   Cutlack, *The Australian Flying Corps*, p. 69.

92   *Scrutineer & Berrima District Press* (NSW), 10 Jan 1917, p. 3.

93   John Bennett, *Highest Traditions: history of No 2 Squadron, RAAF*, Canberra: Australian Government Publishing Service, 1995, p. 14.

94   George Jones, *From Private to Air Marshal*, Richmond, Vic: Greenhouse Publications, 1988, p. 12.

95   Peter Helson, *The Private Air Marshal: a biography of George Jones*, Canberra: Air Power Development Centre, 2010, p. 28.

96   Charles Schaedel, *Men & Machines of the Australian Flying Corps 1914-19*, Dandenong, Vic: Kookaburra Technical Publications, 1972, p. 14.

97   Williams, *These are facts*, p. 55.

98   Cutlack, *The Australian Flying Corps*, p. 176n.

99   NAA, B2455 Watt, Walter Oswald.

100 NAA, B2455 Watt, Walter Oswald.

101 Military Order No 180 of 1917.

102 *London Gazette*, 1 Dec 1916, p. 11803.

CHAPTER SIX – The western crucible

Transfer to England

1   NAA, B2455 Watt, Walter Oswald.

2   George Jones, From Private to Air Marshal, p. 12.

3   John Bennett, Highest Traditions: history of No 2 Squadron, RAAF, Canberra: AustralianGovernment Publishing Service, 1995, p. 16.

4   Molkentin, Fire in the sky, p. 205.

5   George Jones, From Private to Air Marshal, p. 13.

6   Helson, The Private Air Marshal, p. 28.

7   George Jones, From Private to Air Marshal, p. 13.

8   Molkentin, Fire in the sky, p. 205.

9   George Jones, From Private to Air Marshal, p. 13.

10   Helson, The Private Air Marshal, p. 28; Bennett, Highest Traditions, p. 16.

11   George Jones, From Private to Air Marshal, p. 13; Bennett, Highest Traditions, p. 16.

12   George Jones, From Private to Air Marshal, p. 13.

13   Molkentin, Fire in the sky, pp. 178-179.

14   NAA, B2455 Guilfoyle, William James Yule, and Muir, Stanley Keith.

Training up No.2 Squadron

15   Cutlack, The Australian Flying Corps, p. 175.

16   Cutlack, The Australian Flying Corps, p. 175.

17   Molkentin, Fire in the sky, p. 204.

18   Barnes, The RAAF and the flying squadrons, p. 14.

19   The Memoirs of Captain Liddell Hart, vol.1, London: Cassell, 1965, pp. 27-28.

20   Molkentin, Fire in the sky, p. 61.

21   Molkentin, Fire in the sky, p. 205.

22   A. H. Cobby, High adventure, Melbourne: Robertson & Mullens, 1942, pp. 25-27.

23   Cobby, High adventure, p. 29.

24   George Jones, From Private to Air Marshal, pp. 13-14.

25   George Jones, From Private to Air Marshal, p. 13.

26   Bennett, Highest Traditions, pp. 20-21.

27   Molkentin, Fire in the sky, p. 204.

28   George Jones, From Private to Air Marshal, p. 13; Helson, The Private Air Marshal, pp. 31-32.

29   NAA, B2455 Watt, Walter Oswald.

30   Bennett, Highest Traditions, p. 27.

31   NAA, B2455 Watt, Walter Oswald.

32   Cutlack, The Australian Flying Corps, p. 177; NAA, B2455 Norvill, Victor Athelstan.

33   Bennett, Highest Traditions, p. 28.

34   Sydney Morning Herald, 12 Nov 1917, p. 8

35   Euroa Advertiser (Vic), 16 Nov 1917 p. 3.

36   Warwick Examiner and Times (Qld), 3 Dec 1917, p. 3.

37   Oswald Watt: A tribute to his memory, pp. 25-26.

38   Oswald Watt: A tribute to his memory, p. 57.

39   Daily News (Perth), 30 Nov 1917, p. 3.

40   Molkentin, Fire in the sky, p. 204.

41   Euroa Advertiser (Vic), 30 Nov 1917, p. 4.

Crisis at Cambrai

42   Bennett, Highest Traditions, pp. 29-30.

43   Cutlack, The Australian Flying Corps, pp. 177-178.

44   Oswald Watt: A tribute to his memory, p. 25.

45   Cutlack, The Australian Flying Corps, p. 178.

46   Bennett, Highest Traditions, p. 30.

47   Cutlack, The Australian Flying Corps, p. 178.

48   Molkentin, Fire in the sky, p. 207.

49   Cutlack, The Australian Flying Corps, p. 180.

50   Cutlack, The Australian Flying Corps, p. 180.

51   Bennett, Highest Traditions, p. 29.

52   Aircraft (Melbourne), 20 Jun 1921, pp. 224-225.

53   Oswald Watt: A tribute to his memory, pp. 43-44.; Bennett, Highest Traditions, p. 46.

54   H. A. Jones, The War in the Air, vol 4, London: Oxford University Press, 1934, pp. 230-231.

55   Bennett, Highest Traditions, pp. 34-35; Molkentin, Fire in the sky, p. 209.

56   Cutlack, The Australian Flying Corps, p. 188; H. A. Jones, The War in the Air, vol 4, p.239; Molkentin, Australia and the War in the Air, p. 131.

57   Molkentin, Fire in the sky, pp. 212-213.

58   Molkentin, Australia and the War in the Air, p. 130.

59   H. A. Jones, The War in the Air, vol 4, p. 243.

60   Bennett, Highest Traditions, p. 37.

61   Cutlack, The Australian Flying Corps, p. 188; Oswald Watt: A tribute to his memory, p. 56.

62   H. A. Jones, The War in the Air, vol 4, pp. 245-246.

63   Molkentin, Australia and the War in the Air, p. 132.

64   Molkentin, Fire in the sky, p. 220.

65   H. A. Jones, The War in the Air, vol 4, pp. 251, 253.

66   Molkentin, Australia and the War in the Air, p. 134.

67   Molkentin, Fire in the sky, p. 219.

68   London Gazette, 4 Feb 1918, p. 1606.

69   Oswald Watt: A tribute to his memory, p. 57.

70   London Gazette, 13 Mar 1918, p. 3249; Molkentin, Australia and the War in the Air, p. 135.

71   London Gazette, 28 May 1918, p. 6200; Military Order No 519 of 1918.

72   Molkentin, Fire in the sky, pp. 220-221.

73   Bennett, Highest Traditions, pp. 45-46, citing AWM38 3DRL 606/94/2, C. E. W. Bean, diary Nov-Dec 1917.

74   Molkentin, Fire in the sky, p. 231.

75   Bennett, Highest Traditions, p. 47.

76   Bennett, Highest Traditions, p. 51.

77   AWM souvenirs collection 2 4/1/8/6, item 6, PUBS002/004/001/008/006.

78   Bennett, Highest Traditions, p. 50.

AFC Training Wing

79   Barnes, The RAAF and the flying squadrons, pp. 33, 45, 51, 56; Molkentin, Australia and the War in the Air, p. 55.

80   Molkentin, Australia and the War in the Air, p. 33.

81   Molkentin, Australia and the War in the Air, p. 34.

82   Military Order No 353 of 1918, No 230 of 1919.

83   Oswald Watt: A tribute to his memory, p. 25.

84   Molkentin, Australia and the War in the Air, p. 32.

85   Molkentin, Australia and the War in the Air, p. 34

86   AWM38 3DRL 606/94/2, C. E. W. Bean, diary Nov-Dec 1917; Molkentin, Australia and the War in the Air, p. 31.

87   David Goodland & Alan Vaughan, Anzacs over England: the Australian Flying Corps in Gloucestershire 1918-1919, Dover, N.H.: Alan Sutton, 1993, pp. 6-7.

88   Oswald Watt: A tribute to his memory, p. 20.

89   NAA, B2455 Watt, Walter Oswald.

90   AWM4 8/2/5, War diary of 1st Wing Headquarters, AFC, Apr 1918.

91   Queenslander (Brisbane), 9 Feb 1928, p. 45.

92   Queenslander (Brisbane), 9 Feb 1928, p. 45.

93   Sydney Morning Herald, 23 May 1921, p. 8; Pastoral Review (Melbourne),16 Jul 1921, pp. 533-534.

94   Molkentin, Australia and the War in the Air, p. 35.

95   NAA, B2455 Watt, Walter Oswald; AWM4 8/2/5, 1st Wing HQ, AFC, war diary, Apr 1918.

96   David Wilson, Brotherhood of Airmen: the men and women of the RAAF in action, 1914-today, Crows Nest (NSW): Allen & Unwin, 2005, p.30; Molkentin, Australia and the War in the Air, p. 56.

97   Molkentin, Australia and the War in the Air, pp. 56-57.

98   Cobby, High adventure, p. 183; Molkentin, Australia and the War in the Air, p. 54.

99   Molkentin, Australia and the War in the Air, p. 54.

100   Goodland & Vaughan, Anzacs over England, p. 74.

101   AWM4 8/2/5, 1st Wing HQ, AFC, war diary, 7-8 Apr 1918.

102   AWM4 8/2/5, 1st Wing HQ, AFC, war diary, 23 Apr, 27 Apr 1918.

103   Williams, These are facts, p. 69.

104   Cobby, High adventure, pp. 171-172; Molkentin, Fire in the sky, p. 314.

105   Cobby, High adventure, pp. 179-181.

106   Cobby, High adventure, p. 181.

107   Goodland & Vaughan, Anzacs over England, p. 88.

108   AWM PR88/154, records of Air Vice-Marshal A. T. Cole, folder 7, ms autobiog "MerryOld Souls".

109   Reveille, 30 May 1931, p. 37.

110   Goodland & Vaughan, Anzacs over England, pp. 25, 95-96.

111   Norman Ellison, Daredevils of the Skies, Sydney: Angus & Robertson, 1941, pp. 15-18.

112   NAA, B2455 Watt, Walter Oswald; West Australian (Perth), 27 May 1918, p. 5.

113   NAA, B2455 Watt, Walter Oswald.

114   AWM4 8/2/5, 1st Wing HQ, AFC, war diary, 25 Apr 1918.

115   Oswald Watt: A tribute to his memory, photograph 104; Sydney Morning Herald, 23 May 1921, p. 8; Aircraft (Melbourne), 20 Jun 1921, pp. 224-225.

116   Cobby, High adventure, p. 187.

117   David Crotty, A Flying Life: John Duigan and the first Australian aeroplane, Melbourne: Museum Victoria, 2010, p. 143.

118   Goodland & Vaughan, Anzacs over England, pp. 103-106.

119   Crotty, A Flying Life, p. 143.

CHAPTER SEVEN – Triumphant return

Farewell to England

1   *Queenslander* (Brisbane), 9 Feb 1928, p. 45.

2   *Oswald Watt: A tribute to his memory*, p. 19.

3   *Oswald Watt: A tribute to his memory*, p. 20.

4   *Oswald Watt: A tribute to his memory*, pp. 17-18.

5   *Oswald Watt: A tribute to his memory*, frontispiece, and photograph 97

6   *London Gazette*, 1 Jan 1919, p. 86; Military Order No 262 of 1919.

7   Australian War Memorial (Canberra), 1DRL/0071, Australian Comforts Fund

8   *Queenslander* (Brisbane), 9 Feb 1928, p. 45.

9   Goodland & Vaughan, *Anzacs over England*, p. 137.

10   Goodland & Vaughan, *Anzacs over England*, p. 114.

11   NAA, B2455 Watt, Walter Oswald.

12   Cobby, *High adventure*, p. 191.

13   Anthony Hill, *Young Digger*, Camberwell, Vic: Penguin Book Australia, 2002, p. 239.

14   *Argus* (Melbourne), 25 May 1928, p. 15.

15   *Daily Mail* (Brisbane), 21 Jun 1919, p. 7.

16   Hill, *Young Digger*, p. 278.

17   *Argus* (Melbourne), 16 Jun 1919, p. 4.

18   Desmond Martin and Bertha Carey, *A message from the clouds: a biography of Robert Graham Carey: Australian pioneer aviator*, Croydon, Vic.: Edith Francis Martin, 2004, pp. 38-40.

19   *Argus* (Melbourne), 17 Jun 1919, p. 6.

20   *Argus* (Melbourne), 16 Jun 1919, p. 4, 17 Jun 1919, p. 6.

21   *Sydney Morning Herald*, 20 Jun 1919, p. 9.

22   NAA, B2455 Watt, Walter Oswald.

Foremost AFC veteran

23   *Sydney Morning Herald*, 21 Jul 1919, p. 9; *Oswald Watt: A tribute to his memory*, photograph 108.

24   *Sydney Morning Herald*, 12 Apr 1920, p. 6

25   *Sydney Morning Herald*, 23 Apr 1920, p. 6, 26 Apr 1920, p. 8.

26   *Sydney Morning Herald*, 23 Jun 1920, p. 11; *Oswald Watt: A tribute to his memory*, photograph 109.

27   *Sydney Morning Herald*, 12 Nov 1919, p. 11.

28   *Argus* (Melbourne), 18 Dec 1919, p. 7; *Sydney Morning Herald*, 18 Dec 1919, p. 7.

29   *Sydney Morning Herald*, 16 Feb 1920, p. 7.

30   *Argus* (Melbourne), 20 Feb 1920, p. 7.

31   Brogden, *History of Australian Aviation*, p. 64; *Sea, Land and Air* (Sydney), Aug 1919, p. 328.

32   National Archives of Australia (Canberra), CRS A1952, item 559/28/679 Australian Air Corps – Appointment of officers.

33   *Sydney Morning Herald*, 12 Nov 1919, p. 10.

34   Alan Stephens and Jeff Isaacs, *High Fliers: Leaders of the Royal Australian Air Force*, Canberra: Australian Government Publishing Service, 1996, p.19; Alan Stephens, *Royal Australian Air Force*, vol.2 of *Australian Centenary History of Defence*, South Melbourne: Oxford University Press, 2001, p. 8.

35   *Oswald Watt: A tribute to his memory*, p. 22; *Sydney Morning Herald*, 12 Mar 1920, p. 16.

36   *Sydney Morning Herald*, 23 May 1921, p. 8.

37   *Sydney Morning Herald*, 27 Sep 1920, p. 8; *Aircraft* (Melbourne), 20 Jun 1921, pp. 221-228.

38   *Sydney Morning Herald*, 15 Sep 1921, p. 7.

39   *Sydney Morning Herald*, 1 May 1920, p. 9; *Evening News* (Sydney), 15 May 1920, p. 2.

40   *Sydney Morning Herald*, 20 Jul 1920, p. 7.

41   *Sydney Morning Herald*, 26 Feb 1921, p. 14.

42   *Oswald Watt: A tribute to his memory*, pp. 21-22.

Aviation advocate

43   *Sydney Morning Herald*, 19 Jun 1919, p. 6.

44   *Aircraft* (Melbourne), 20 Jun 1921, pp. 221-228.

45   *Sydney Morning Herald*, 12 Nov 1919, p. 11.

46   *Sydney Morning Herald*, 8 Jan 1920, p. 7.

47   *Sea, Land and Air* (Sydney), Jan 1920, p. 664.

48   *Sydney Morning Herald*, 9 Jan 1920, p. 6.

49   *Sydney Morning Herald*, 21 Feb 1920, p. 12.

50   *Sea, Land and Air*, Mar 1920, p. 815.

51   *Aircraft* (Melbourne), 20 Jun 1921, pp. 221-228.

52   Tim Sherratt, 'Remembering Lawrence Hargrave', in Graeme Davison and Kimberley Webber (eds.) *Yesterday's Tomorrows: The Powerhouse Museum and its precursors, 1880-2005*, Sydney: UNSW Press, 2005, pp. 174-185.

53   *Sydney Morning Herald*, 3 Mar 1920, p. 11; *Examiner* (Launceston), 8 Mar 1920, p. 5.

54   *Evening News*, (Sydney), 9 Mar 1920, p. 4; *Sydney Morning Herald*, 10 Mar 1920, p. 10.

55   Brogden, *History of Australian Aviation*, p. 65.

56   Timothy Hall, *Flying High: the story of Hudson Fysh and the trail-blazing days of early aviation*, Sydney: Methuen of Australia, 1979, p. 47.

57   Brogden, *History of Australian Aviation*, p. 74; *Sydney Morning Herald*, 23 May 1921, p. 8.

58   *Argus* (Melbourne), 3 Dec 1920, p. 6; www.airwaysmuseum.com/Directors%General.htm, accessed 21 Oct 2015.

59   *Sydney Morning Herald*, 10 Jun 1920, p. 6; *Barrier Miner* (Broken Hill, NSW), 9 Jun 1920, p. 1.

60   *Sydney Morning Herald*, 16 Jun 1920, p. 8.

61   *Sydney Morning Herald*, 26 Aug 1920, p. 7.

62   *Sunday Times* (Perth), 5 Sep 1920, p. 1.

63   *Northern Standard* (Darwin), 25 May 1923, p. 1.

64   *Sydney Morning Herald*, 25 Aug 1920, p. 12, 28 Aug 1920, p. 13.

65   *Sydney Morning Herald*, 29 Nov 1920, pp. 9-10; *Register* (Adelaide), 29 Nov 1920, p. 8.

66   *Oswald Watt: A tribute to his memory*, p. 51, photograph 111.

67   *Sydney Morning Herald*, 28 Apr 1921, p. 7.

Rebuilding

68   *Being Ernest*, p. 99.

69   *Sydney Morning Herald*, 21 Feb 1920, p. 12.

70   *Sydney Morning Herald*, 23 Aug 1920, p. 8.

71   *Oswald Watt: A tribute to his memory*, photograph 107.

72   *Sydney Morning Herald*, 23 May 1921, p. 8; Johnston, 'Watt, Oswald Watt', *ADB*.

73   *Sydney Morning Herald*, 16 Feb 1922, p. 10; *Pastoral Review* (Melbourne), 16 Mar 1922, p. 191.

74   *Oswald Watt: A tribute to his memory*, p. 63.

75   *Aircraft* (Melbourne), 20 Jun 1921, pp. 226-227.

76   *Aircraft* (Melbourne), 20 Jun 1921, pp. 226-227.

77   *Sydney Morning Herald*, 23 May 1921, p. 8.

78   Website http://www.pittwateronlinenews.com/dame-nellie-melba-at-bilgola.php (Pittwater Online News, issue 18, 7-13 Aug 2011).

79   *Oswald Watt: A tribute to his memory*, pp. 38, 48; *Being Ernest*, p. 101.

80   *Oswald Watt: A tribute to his memory*, p. 38.

81   *Sydney Morning Herald*, 26 Nov 1920, p. 10.

82   *Referee* (Sydney), 22 Dec 1920, p. 4.

83   *Sydney Mail*, 12 Jan 1921, p. 31.

84   *Referee* (Sydney), 16 Feb 1921, p. 4.

CHAPTER EIGHT – End, and ongoing

Tragedy at Bilgola Beach

1   *Being Ernest*, p. 95.

2   *Oswald Watt: A tribute to his memory*, pp. 54-55, 64-69.

3   *Being Ernest*, p. 96; *Oswald Watt: A tribute to his memory*, p. 54.

4   *Oswald Watt: A tribute to his memory*, p. 55.

5   *Sunday Times* (Sydney), 22 May 1921, p. 2.

6   *Sydney Morning Herald*, 23 May 1921, p. 8; *Mercury* (Hobart), 31 May 1921, p. 8.

7   *Daily News* (Perth, WA), 21 May 1921, p. 2.

8   *Argus* (Melbourne), 24 May 1921, p. 6.

9   *Oswald Watt: A tribute to his memory*, pp. 38, 48; *Being Ernest*, p. 101.

10   *Sydney Morning Herald*, 24 May 1921, p. 8.

11   *Sydney Morning Herald*, 24 May 1921, p. 8.

12   *Sydney Morning Herald*, 24 May 1921, p. 8.

13   *Sydney Morning Herald*, 24 May 1921, p. 8.

14   *Sydney Morning Herald*, 1 Jun 1921, p. 12.

Memorials and legacies

15   *Argus* (Melbourne), 12 Oct 1921, p. 11.

16   *Sydney Morning Herald*, 1 Jul 1921, p. 9.

17   *Sydney Morning Herald*, 22 Jun 1921, p. 10.

18   *Aircraft* (Melbourne), 30 Apr 1922, pp. 47-48.

19   *Sydney Morning Herald*, 16 May 1923, p. 12.

20   Clipping from *British-Australasian* (London), 13 Jul 1922, p. 13, in Australian War Memorial (Canberra), 3DRL/5018, volume of newspaper clippings presented to AWM by Mrs Margery Watt, 27 September 1973, 'on behalf of the family'.

21   *Oswald Watt: A tribute to his memory*, pp. 5-6.

22   *Argus* (Melbourne), 12 Oct 1921, p. 11; *Cairns Post* (Qld), 9 Nov 1922, p. 6.

23   *Argus* (Melbourne), 13 Oct 1921, p. 6.

24   *Wodonga & Towong Sentinel* (Vic), 14 Oct 1921, p. 2; Caroline Merrylees, *Brave beginnings: a history of the Carrathool District*, Hay, NSW: Carrathool Centenary Committee, 1983, p. 19.

25   *Advertiser* (Adelaide), 14 Aug 1925, p. 16; *Sydney Morning Herald*, 15 Oct 1925, p. 8, 13 Apr 1926, p. 4, 3 Jun 1926, p. 10; *Argus* (Melbourne), 3 Jun 1926, p. 9.

26 Percival Serle, *Dictionary of Australian Biography*, vol.2, Sydney: Angus & Robertson: 1949, p. 469; *Official Year Book of the Commonwealth of Australia*, no. 37 – 1946 and 1947, p. 238.

27 J. E. Lee, *Duntroon: the Royal Military College of Australia 1911-1946*, Canberra: Australian War Memorial, 1952, pp. 63, 166.

28 *Argus* (Melbourne), 9 Sep 1938, p. 2.

29 RMC of Australia Association Inc., Objects and Constitution, 11 Oct 2011.

30 *Advertiser* (Adelaide), 6 Jun 1927, p. 9; *Sydney Morning Herald*, 6 Jun 1927, p. 12.

31 Neville Parnell & Trevor Boughton, *Flypast: a record of aviation in Australia*, Canberra: Australian Government Publishing Service, 1988, p. 47.

32 Website rfaca.com.au/wp-content/uploads/2013/09/Oswald_Watt_History.pdf, accessed 21 Oct 2015.

33 *Argus* (Melbourne), 17 Nov 1928, p. 27, 11 Nov 1946, p. 17.

34 Harold M. Mackenzie (compiled by Caroline Merrylees), *Mackenzie's Riverina: a tour of the Hay pastoral holdings in the 1890s*, 2nd edition, Hay, NSW: Hay Historical Society, 2008, p. 31.

35 *Sydney Morning Herald*, 10 Dec 1921, p. 11.

36 *Sydney Morning Herald*, 2 Feb 1922, p. 9, 10 Feb 1922, p. 9; *Chronicle* (Adelaide), 11 Feb 1922, p. 40.

37 Website www.pittwateronlinenews.com/bilgola-cottage-and-house-history.php, accessed 21 Sep 2015.

38 Semmler, 'Dalley, John Bede', *ADB*; *Newcastle Sun* (NSW), 10 Sep 1935, p. 7.

39 *Sydney Stock and Station Journal*, 24 May 1921, p. 9; *Western Champion* (Parkes, NSW), 26 May 1921, p. 14.

40 *Northern Star* (Lismore, NSW), 15 Jun 1921, p. 2; *Referee* (Sydney), 11 Jan 1922, p. 4.

41 *Argus* (Melbourne), 22 Aug 1921, p. 5; *Townsville Daily Bulletin* (Qld), 23 Jan 1922, p. 5.

42 *Arrow* (Sydney), 2 Jun 1922, p. 3; *Evening News* (Sydney), 12 Jul 1922, p. 4.

43 *Referee* (Sydney), 11 Oct 1922, p. 7.

44 *Townsville Daily Bulletin* (Qld), 25 Oct 1922, p. 4; *Referee* (Sydney), 17 Feb 1932, p. 15.

45 *Townsville Daily Bulletin* (Qld), 30 May 1934, p. 8.

46 Website www.planning.act.gov.au/tools_resources/place_search, accessed 22 Sep 2015.

Family fortunes

47 *Sydney Morning Herald*, 23 May 1921, p. 8; *Sea, Land and Air* (Sydney), 1 Jun 1921, p. 205.

48 National Archives of Australia (Perth), K269, 21 OCT 1930 Narkunda.

49 Personal information from Mr R. O. Watt, Darwin, 13 Jun 2014.

50 J. M. Bourne, *Who's Who in World War One*, London: Routledge, 2001, pp. 166-167.

51 *Richmond River Herald & Northern Districts Advertiser* (NSW), 29 Feb 1924, p. 8.

52 *Sydney Morning Herald*, 11 Jun 1924, p. 6; *Australasian* (Melbourne), 21 Jun 1924, p. 1353.

53 *Barrier Miner* (Broken Hill, NSW), 8 Feb 1928, p. 1; *Northern Star* (Lismore, NSW), 25 Feb 1928, p. 8

54 *Advertiser* (Adelaide), 5 Sep 1932, p. 11.

55 *Who's Who in the World of Women, Victoria, Australia*, vol.2, Melbourne: Reference Press Association, 1934 (Mrs C. S. Cunningham).

56 *Argus* (Melbourne), 19 Apr 1933, p. 5; *Sydney Morning Herald*, 19 Apr 1933, p. 6; *Australasian* (Melbourne), 29 Apr 1933 (pictorial section, p. lv).

57   *Argus* (Melbourne), 7 Mar 1934, p. 6.

58   *Argus* (Melbourne), 5 Jun 1934, p. 12.

59   *Argus* (Melbourne), 7 Apr 1934, p. 10.

60   *Australian Women's Weekly* (Sydney), 2 Mar 1935, p. 27.

61   *Sunday Times* (Perth), 16 Feb 1936, p. 1; *Argus* (Melbourne), 18 Feb 1936, p. 10.

62   *Argus* (Melbourne), 11 Aug 1936, p. 10; Vic Birth Deaths and Marriages, death reg. no.7016/1936.

63   *Sydney Morning Herald*, 23 Oct 1937, p. 12.

64   *Argus*, 24 Dec 1937, p. 6.

65   *Argus*, 9 Apr 1937, p. 13.

66   Personal information from Mr R. O. Watt, Darwin, 13 Jun 2014.

67   Vic Birth Deaths and Marriages, death reg.no. 26245/1967.

68   Website www.orvalstainedglass.com/About-Us.html, accessed 12 Mar 2016.

69   *Age* (Melbourne), 9 Mar 1961, p. 7.

70   Personal information from Mr R. O. Watt, Darwin, 13 Jun 2014.

In changing times

71   *Oswald Watt: A tribute to his memory*, p. 7.

72   *Australian Women's Weekly* (Sydney), 29 Oct 1938, pp. 3, 12

73   Website www.awm.gov.au/encyclopedia/prime_ministers/menzies, accessed 12 Mar 2016.

74   *Mail* (Adelaide), 30 Sep 1939, p. 2.

75   *Argus* (Melbourne), 12 Oct 1939, p. 1.

76   *Courier-Mail* (Brisbane), 12 Oct 1939, p. 3.

77   *Argus* (Melbourne), 12 Oct 1939, p. 2; *Courier-Mail* (Brisbane), 12 Oct 1939, p. 1.

78   Neville Parnell & Trevor Boughton, *Flypast: a record of aviation in Australia*, Canberra: Australian Government Publishing Service, 1988, p. 47.

79   Parnell & Boughton, *Flypast*, pp. 419-420.

80   Website http://australianaviation.com.au/2012/06/simmo-awarded-oswald-watt-gold-medal, accessed 20 Aug 2014.

81   Website http://australianaviation.com.au/2015/09/sir-angus-houston-awarded-oswald-watt-gold-medal, accessed 10 Jan 2016.

BIBLIOGRAPHY

Official sources

Manuscript records

National Archives of Australia (Canberra):

    A289 1849/8/409 "Proposed sites for Central Flying School"

    A289 1849/8/192 "Captain O. Watt Reserve of Officers, Visit to England 1912"

    A1952 559/28/679 Australian Air Corps – Appointment of officers

    A2023 A38/8/542 "No.1 Squadron, AFC – Formation and Organisation, 1915-1916"

    A2653 Military Board Minutes 1912

    B2455 Watt, Walter Oswald (AIF personal record)

National Archives of Australia (Victoria):

    MP84/1 1954/23/144 "Article by Capt Oswald Watt on Training of Aviation Corps".

    MP84/1 1954/23/189 "Capt Watt and Aircraft"

National Archives of Australia (Perth):

    K269, 21 OCT 1930 Narkunda

Australian War Memorial (Canberra):

    1DRL/0071, Australian Comforts Fund

    2DRL/0101 Personal record of W. O. Watt.

    2DRL/0101, "Watt, Walter O. – certificate of transfer from French Foreign Legion to AFC, 1916"

    3DRL/5108, item 1 (letters & postcards to Mrs Roslyn Jamieson)

    3DRL/5018, volume of newspaper clippings presented by Margery Watt, 1973

    AWM souvenirs collection 2 4/1/8/6, item 6, PUBS002/004/001/008/006

    AWM4 8/2/5, War diary of 1st Wing Headquarters, AFC, Apr 1918

    AWM38 3DRL 606/94/2, C. E. W. Bean diary 1917

    AWM PR88/154, records of Air Vice-Marshal A. T. Cole, folder 7, ms autobiog "Merry Old Souls"

Mitchell Library (Sydney):

    Allen family photographs, PX*D 581, album 40

    Service Historique de la Défense (Vincennes, France), 26 N 739/3, war diary of 287th Infantry Regiment, 1914

Printed records

Commonwealth of Australia Gazette, 1916

(Commonwealth Military Forces) *Military Orders*, for 1905, 1908, 1912, 1916, 1917, 1918, 1919

(New South Wales) *Army List*, for 1903

London Gazette, 1916, 1918, 1919

Journal Officiel de la République Française (Official Journal of the French Republic), 45th year (1915), no. 54

THE HIGH LIFE OF OSWALD WATT

Books

Barnes, Norman, *The RAAF and the flying squadrons* (St. Leonards, NSW: Allen & Unwin, 2000)

Bennett, John, *Highest Traditions: The History of No 2 Squadron, RAAF* (Canberra: Australian Government Publishing Service, 1995)

Borwick, F. (ed.), *Clifton College annals and register, 1862-1925* (Bristol: J. W. Arrowsmith, 1912)

Brogden, Stanley, *The History of Australian Aviation* (Melbourne: Hawthorn Press, 1960)

Cobby, A. H., *High Adventure* (Melbourne: Robertson & Mullens, 1942)

Cock, Alan G., and Donald R. Forsdyke, *Treasure your exceptions: the science and life of William Bateson* (New York: Springer, 2008)

Coulthard-Clark, C. D., *No Australian Need Apply: The Troubled Career of Lieutenant-General Gordon Legge* (Sydney: Allen & Unwin, 1988)

-----, *The Third Brother: The Royal Australian Air Force 1921-39* (North Sydney: Allen & Unwin in association with the RAAF, 1991)

Crotty, David, *A Flying Life: John Duigan and the first Australian aeroplane* (Melbourne: Museum Victoria, 2010)

Cutlack, F. M., *The Australian Flying Corps in the Western and Eastern Theatres of War 1914-1918*, Volume 7, *The official History of Australia in the War of 1914-1918* (Sydney: Angus & Robertson, 1923)

Davis, Pedr, *Wheels across Australia: motoring from the 1890s to the 1980s* (Hurstville, NSW: Marque Publishing, 1987)

Ellison, Norman, *Daredevils of the Skies* (Sydney: Angus & Robertson, 1941)

Fitzgerald, Alan (ed.), *Canberra's Engineering Heritage* (Canberra: Institution of Engineers–Canberra Division, 1983)

Goddard, Roy H., *The Union Club 1857-1957* (Sydney: Halstead Press, 1957)

Goodland, David, and Alan Vaughan, *Anzacs over England: The Australian Flying Corps in Gloucestershire, 1918-1919* (Stroud: Alan Sutton Publishing, 1992)

Hall, Timothy, *Flying High: the story of Hudson Fysh and the trail-blazing days of early aviation* (Sydney: Methuen of Australia, 1979)

Helson, Peter, *The Private Air Marshal: A Biography of Air Marshal Sir George Jones, KBE, CB, DFC* (Canberra: Air Power Development Centre, 2010)

Hill, Anthony, *Young Digger* (Camberwell, Vic: Penguin Book Australia, 2002)

Isaacs, Keith, *Military Aircraft of Australia, 1909-1918* (Canberra: Australian War Memorial, 1971)

Jones, George, *From Private to Air Marshal: The Autobiography of Air Marshal Sir George Jones, KBE, CB, DFC* (Richmond, Vic: Greenhouse Publications, 1988)

Jones, H. A., *The War in the Air*, vol 4 (London: Oxford University Press, 1934)

Jones, H. A., *The War in the Air*, vol 5 (London: Oxford University Press, 1935)

Lee, J. E., *Duntroon: The Royal Military College of Australia, 1911-1946* (Canberra: Australian War Memorial, 1952)

Liddell Hart, B., *The Memoirs of Captain Liddell Hart*, vol.1 (London: Cassell, 1965)

Macinnis, Peter, *Curious Minds: the discoveries of Australian naturalists* (Canberra: National Library of Australia, 2012)

Mackenzie, Harold M. (compiled by Caroline Merrylees), *Mackenzie's Riverina: a tour of the Hay District Pastoral Holdings in the 1890s*, 2nd edition (Hay, NSW: Hay Historical Society, 2008)

Merrylees, Caroline, *Brave beginnings: a history of the Carrathool District* (Hay, NSW: Carrathool Centenary Committee, 1983)

Molkentin, Michael, *Fire in the Sky: The Australian Flying Corps in the First World War* (Crows Nest, NSW: Allen & Unwin, 2010)

-----, *Australia and the War in the Air*, vol 1 of *Centenary History of Australia and the Great War* (South Melbourne: Oxford University Press, 2014)

Parnell, Neville, and Trevor Boughton, *Flypast: A Record of Aviation in Australia* (Canberra: Australian Government Publishing Service, 1988)

Rankine, Susie, and Ernest Watt, *Being Ernest: the life of Ernest Watt 1874-1954* (Double Bay, NSW: SGR Press, 1998)

Stephens, Alan, and Jeff Isaacs, *High Fliers: Leaders of the Royal Australian Air Force* (Canberra: Australian Government Publishing Service, 1996)

Stephens, Alan, *Royal Australian Air Force*, vol.2 of *Australian Centenary History of Defence* (South Melbourne: Oxford University Press, 2001)

Ure Smith, Sydney, Bertram Stevens and Ernest Watt (eds.), *Oswald Watt: a tribute to his memory by a few of his friends* (Sydney: Art in Australia Ltd, 1921)

Venn, J. A., *Alumni cantabrigiensis: a biographical list of all known students, graduates and holders of office at the University of Cambridge, from the earliest times to 1900*, part II, vol. 1 (London: University of Cambridge, 1940)

-----, *Alumni Cantabrigienses*, part II, vol. 6 (Cambridge: University Press, 1954)

Wade-Ferrell, T. F., *In All Things Faithful: a history and album of the 30th Battalion and New South Wales Scottish Regiment, 1885-1985* (Sydney: Fine Arts Press, 1985)

Watt, Ernest, *A Few Records of the Life of John Brown Watt collected by his son* (Sydney: Art in Australia, c.1922)

Williams, Richard, *These are facts* (Canberra: Australian War Memorial & Australian Government Publishing Service, 1977)

Articles

Bellenger, Lieutenant Colonel [Georges], "Les aventures du capitaine Watt" (The adventures of Captain Watt), *Icare* (*Icarus*, a French quarterly aviation magazine), no. 38, 1 July 1966

Burke, Bernard, 'Hon. John Brown Watt', *Genealogical and heraldic history of the colonial gentry*, vol. 2 (London: Harrison & Sons, 1895)

Johnston, Susan, 'Watt, Walter Oswald (1878-1921)', *Australian Dictionary of Biography*, vol. 12 (Carlton: Melbourne University Press, 1990)

Maxwell, Charles F., 'The Honourable John Brown Watt, M.L.C.', *Australian Men of Mark*, vol. 1 (Sydney: author, 1889)

Rutledge, Martha, 'Watt, Ernest Alexander (1874-1954)', *Australian Dictionary of Biography*, vol. 12 (Carlton: Melbourne University Press, 1990)

Serle, Percival, 'Watt, Walter Oswald', *Dictionary of Australian Biography*, vol. 2 (Sydney: Angus & Robertson, 1949)

Walsh, G. P., 'Watt, John Brown (1826-1897)', *Australian Dictionary of Biography*, vol. 6, (Carlton: Melbourne University Press, 1976)

Watt, Captain W. Oswald, 'Australia and the Fourth Arm', *Commonwealth Military Journal*, May 1912

Watt, Captain Oswald, 'Recent Aviation Developments and Australian Aerial Organisation', *Commonwealth Military Journal*, January 1913

Newspapers and magazines
Australia

Adelaide Advertiser

Advertiser (Adelaide)

Age (Melbourne)
Aircraft (Melbourne)
Argus (Melbourne)
Australasian (Melbourne)
Australian Town and Country Journal (Sydney)
Australian Women's Weekly (Sydney)
Barrier Miner (Broken Hill, NSW)
Bendigo Advertiser (Vic)
Brisbane Courier
Bulletin (Sydney)
Burrowa News (NSW)
Cairns Post (Qld)
Camden News (NSW)
Clarence and Richmond Examiner (Grafton, NSW)
Courier-Mail (Brisbane)
Daily News (Perth)
Daily Telegraph (Sydney)
Euroa Advertiser (Vic)
Evening News (Sydney)
Examiner (Launceston, Tas)
Farmer and Settler (Sydney)
Freeman's Journal (Sydney)
Gippsland Times (Vic)
Hamilton Spectator (Vic)
Illustrated Sydney News
Leader (Melbourne)
Mail (Adelaide)
Maitland Daily Mercury (NSW)
Maitland Weekly Mercury (NSW)
Mercury (Hobart)
Morning Bulletin (Rockhampton, Qld)
Narrandera Argus and Riverina Advertiser (NSW)
Newcastle Sun (NSW)
Northern Miner (Charters Towers, Qld)
Pastoral Review (Melbourne)
Queenslander (Brisbane)
Referee (Sydney)
Register (Adelaide)
Reveille (Sydney)
Richmond River Herald & Northern Districts Advertiser (NSW)
Scrutineer & Berrima District Press (NSW)
Sea, Land and Air (Sydney)
South Australian Register (Adelaide)
Sunday Times (Sydney)

Bibliography

Sunday Times (Perth)
Sydney Mail
Sydney Morning Herald
Sydney Stock and Station Journal
Townsville Daily Bulletin (Qld)
Warwick Examiner and Times (Qld)
West Australia Sunday Times (Perth)
West Australian (Perth)
Western Champion (Parkes, NSW)
Wodonga & Towong Sentinel (Vic)
Wollondilly Press, (Bowral, NSW)
Overseas
Aeroplane (London)
Flight (London)
New Zealand Herald (Auckland)
NZ Truth (Wellington)
Oamaru Mail (New Zealand)
Slough, Eton and Windsor Observer (England)
The Times (London)

Websites

http://en.wikipedia.org/wiki/Oswald_Watt
http://sydney.edu.au/scholarships/docs/research/travelinfo_12.pdf
www. gaestbuecher-schloss-neubeuern.de-biografien/Watt_Walter_Oswald.pdf
http://albindenis.free.fr/Site_escadrille/escadrille044.htm (history of MF44)
http://www.etudes-touloises.fr/archives/148/148%20art5.pdf
https://rslvirtualwarmemorial.org.au/explore/people/361601
http://www.pittwateronlinenews.com/dame-nellie-melba-at-bilgola.php
rfaca.com.au/wp-content/uploads/2013/09/Oswald_Watt_History.pdf
www.pittwateronlinenews.com/bilgola-cottage-and-house-history.php
www.planning.act.gov.au/tools_resources/place_search
www.orvalstainedglass.com/About-Us.html
www.awm.gov.au/encyclopedia/prime_ministers/menzies
http://australianaviation.com.au/2012/06/simmo-awarded-oswald-watt-gold-medal
http://australianaviation.com.au/2015/09/sir-angus-houston-awarded-oswald-watt-gold-medal

INDEX

Index

Index

Index

Index